Hip Hop Underground

Anthony Kwame Harrison

Hip Hop Underground

The Integrity and Ethics of
Racial Identification

TEMPLE UNIVERSITY PRESS
Philadelphia

In memory of Jolie Rickman (1970–2005) and Anthony Marin (1972–2008), both great musicians and friends.

Temple University Press
1601 North Broad Street
Philadelphia PA 19122
www.temple.edu/tempress

Published 2009
Printed in the United States of America
♾ The paper used in this publication meets the requirements of the American
National Standard for Information Sciences—Permanence of Paper for Printed Library
Materials, ANSI Z39.48-1992

Library of Congress Cataloging-in-Publication Data

Harrison, Anthony Kwame.
   Hip hop underground : the integrity and ethics of racial identification /
Anthony Kwame Harrison.
        p.   cm.
   Includes bibliographical references and index.
   ISBN 978-1-4399-0060-4 (cloth : alk. paper) — ISBN 978-1-4399-0061-1
(pbk. : alk. paper)
   1. Rap (Music)—California—San Francisco Bay Area—History and criticism.
   2. Music and race.   I. Title.
   ML3531.H36 2009
   306.4'84249—dc22   2009006296

2   4   6   8   9   7   5   3   1

Contents

Introduction

A Walk in the Park

"Okay, the entrance to the park is two blocks that way *(pointing)*. Our job is to get there, rolling this deep, without being stopped by the police." And with that, fourteen young adults of various racial and ethnic backgrounds, several carrying backpacks containing forty-ounce bottles of beer, made their way down San Francisco's Fulton Street along the north end of Golden Gate Park. On reaching the park entrance, the collective enthusiasm quickly leveled under the encroaching darkness. Our guides, the two people who had "partied" there before, were quick to assure us that the spot where we were going was better lit. As we proceeded cautiously down the wooded trail, the sounds of a growling dog could be heard coming from a tent about twenty feet off the path. "So that's why all these homeless Haight Street kids have dogs," I thought to myself, "to guard their stuff." After a few wrong turns, we came to an opening and made our way to one of the distant picnic tables, as far as possible from the Park Presidio roadway.

I had come to San Francisco to conduct ethnographic research within one of the most racially diverse hip hop scenes in the world. "The SFC(ity)" is the commercial hub of Bay Area hip hop, which is one of the principal sites of a regional subgenre known as "West Coast underground hip hop."[1] For much of hip hop's thirty-year history as a commodified music form, the moniker "underground" has been claimed by many artists as an index to street authenticity. However, by the mid- to late-1990s, as the commercial popularity of hip hop (or rap) music began to swell to unprecedented heights—for instance, in 1998, after having six different rap artists hold the top spot on *Billboard* magazine's Top 200 album chart, the Recording Industry Association of America declared rap music its "biggest story of the year" (Watkins 2005, 61–62)—an independent movement specifically referred to as "underground hip hop" began emerging as an alternative to rap music's mainstream appeal. Since that time, underground hip hop has evolved into what is arguably the most dynamic, socially relevant, and racially/ethnically diverse subgenre of music in America.

Within seconds of arriving at our destination, bottles of beer were unpacked, distributed, and opened. Minutes later an impromptu, off-the-top-of-the-head rhyming circle, or what hip hoppers refer to as a "freestyle cypher," commenced. A locally prominent white emcee named Lord Top Ramen (Top R for short) began the affair, and T. Root, a heralded black (specifically Guyanese American) emcee in his own right, supplied a beat-boxed rhythm.[2] I was quick to arrive in the circle with my tape recorder in hand. My presence at several of these freestyle events had taught me that the introduction of a recording device was considered quite usual and, if anything, welcomed.[3]

Two weeks before arriving in the Bay Area, I attended a talk given by New York University (NYU) professor Britta Wheeler on conducting research within art worlds (Becker 1982). During her lecture, the single point that Wheeler most deeply impressed on me was the importance of researchers "putting themselves out there"—that is, displaying their own vulnerability when working among performance artists and similar groups. Clearly hip hop artists and particularly emcees fit this categorization. Yet, despite having written and recited raps years earlier (mostly while in high school), I was reluctant to enter "the field" with aspirations of rhyming alongside the people among whom I intended to conduct research. One immediate reason for my hesitancy was the apparent tendency among more established underground hip hop artists to take offense at the increasing numbers of would-be emcees in their midst. The following exchange between emcee Aesop of the then Bay Area collective Living Legends and journalist James Tai illustrates this:

> **AESOP:** But now every motherfucker I meet is talking about how he raps. Every motherfucker! No disrespect, I bet you probably rap a little bit too, though.

JAMES TAI: Nah. I make beats though (*joking*).

AESOP: Know what I'm sayin'? That's how it goes though. I could jump from this building and land on a rapper these days. (Tai 1998, 56)

Beyond a general predisposition against embarking on research with such performance ambitions, I specifically did not want to damage the rapport that I had established with artists like Aesop by suddenly announcing that I too had decided to become a rapper.

So, on my second night attending a weekly hip hop open-mic event at Haight Street's Rockin' Java Coffee House, when Top R approached me and asked if I was writing rhymes, I was very direct in clarifying that I was, in fact, writing field notes. Top R was neither the first nor the last person to inquire about my being an emcee or hip hop participant of some sort. Initially, I treated each of these inquiries as an opportunity to introduce my research. Furthermore, by mentioning my past experience writing raps, but explicitly saying that I no longer aspired to be a rapper, I felt that I was separating myself from the perceived masses of Johnny-come-latelies who had recently jumped on the underground hip hop bandwagon. However, the importance of Wheeler's words never left me. They, in fact, led me to make a deal with myself: that I would never be the only spectator in a group. More specifically, given my direct interest and past experience rhyming, I would not allow myself to be the only nonparticipant in a rhyming cypher. If such a situation were to arise, I would simply feel compelled to "put myself out there" and join in.

Back at the park, in his characteristically overbearing manner, Top R had taken it upon himself to orchestrate the sequence in which each person present that night would participate. On this particular evening, he was so dictatorial that at one point he even called out an emcee who was seated outside of the circle contemplating having to travel to his grandfather's funeral and bullied him into rhyming—which he somewhat reluctantly did. As one by one each individual took a turn holding the floor, it became clear to me that I was the only member of the gathered circle who had not yet rhymed; recalling my pledge, I felt a sudden urge to take part. Top R's failure to call on me was no personal snub. From our very first meeting, I had made it clear to him that I was an anthropologist, not an emcee.

Courtesy does not get you very far in a rhyme cypher. Under normal conditions, it is difficult to claim a turn without feeling like you are (at least to some extent) cutting someone else off. With the exception of cases like Top R's calling people out, typical transitions between emcees in cyphers feature either a definitive end to one emcee's freestyle verse, after which the next emcee to speak claims the floor, or a situation in which an emcee is struggling to maintain an appropriate vocal rhythm or "flow"—often acknowledged by the voice beginning to taper. At this point another rhymer will jump in with a louder voice that refreshes the sense of rhythmic punctuality. Sometimes two or more voices jump in simultaneously with the louder and more persistently forceful voice winning out.

When I finally did find the opportunity to grab the floor, Top R gave an approving yell of "Old Schooooooool!" into the San Francisco night. From there he proceeded to put his arm around my shoulder and bob his head rhythmically to my less than spectacular rhymes. Obviously this reaction was as much a response to who I was (the hip hop anthropologist) as to how I sounded. Minutes later Top R had reclaimed the floor and again had his arm around my shoulder. This display of support by the dominant persona in this cypher unmistakably marked my acceptance. I ended up taking a few more turns during the hour-long rhyming session. Interestingly, once the forty-five-minute tape was exhausted, and the tape recorder was put away, I felt much more at ease.

By local underground hip hop standards, the group that had assembled in Golden Gate Park that night was impressive: during my year in the Bay, I saw both Top R and another European American emcee, Dore One, perform in front of crowds of well over a thousand people at the Maritime Hall; a Filipino American emcee/producer named Destined released his own CD, which made a good bit of noise within particular underground hip hop circles; DJ Marz, who is also white, although not an emcee, was a popular deejay and member of the Bulletproof Scratch Hamsters/Space Travelers (a Bay Area deejay crew whose body of work was familiar to me well before my arrival); and T. Root was recognized by many as one of the best "unknown" (meaning he did not have a product out) emcees around.

When the rhyming had finally ended, one of the other cypher participants—a light-skinned African American producer/emcee named Dejá—immediately approached me and began explaining that he was in the process of putting together a compilation album and was interested in knowing if I "would like to be involved." Dejá might never realize the significance of this gesture. Beyond the possibility of being on his album, for even with my limited experience I knew enough to know that often nothing comes of such proposals, it was the fact that amid this group of talented artists someone had taken me seriously as an emcee and not just as an academic interloper that was so meaningful.

After being in the Bay close to four months, I came to realize that between the time demands of my employment at a popular in-scene record store (see Chapter 2) and the relative inaccessibility of some of the better-known underground hip hop artists (like Aesop), my research was gradually orienting itself toward the lesser-known strata of underground recording artists. Even Top R's and Dore One's Maritime Hall performances were as opening acts for Aesop's Living Legends. The value of this bottom-up perspective, particularly as an alternative to the top-down approach typically found within (cultural/media studies–influenced) scholarship on hip hop, was easy enough to rationalize. I was also finding that, for the most part, these up-and-coming artists, unlike Aesop, were not nearly as resentful toward newcomers in their midst.

One defining characteristic of Bay Area underground hip hop specifically, and translocal underground hip hop scenes (Bennett and Peterson 2004) more generally, is the erosion of barriers that have traditionally separated hip hop performers from audience members, or producers from consumers. As someone who regularly attended open-mic venues and frequently spent time with recording artists, yet insisted on acknowledging boundary lines where others saw none, my behavior was perplexing to many of the people I had come to know. "Why didn't you get up there?" emcees would sometimes ask me at the close of an open-mic. And after spending many evenings hanging out with several up-and-coming artists in their home recording studios, a few had begun to press me about either recording one of my old high school raps or writing some new ones.

Inspired by Dejá's endorsement, that night in Golden Gate Park I made the decision to completely change my approach to ethnographic research and thus to embrace the opportunity to participate in the Bay Area scene as an underground emcee. This meant that the very next Monday, at the weekly open-mic I had attended as an audience member close to a dozen times already, I would get on stage and (as was the underground hip hop standard) attempt to rhyme off the top of my head; and, regardless of how that went, week after week I would continue to do so. I would also approach those up-and-coming artists and insist that they let me experience the recording process firsthand. If ethnography can be thought of as researchers positioning themselves within a stream of unfolding experiences that define life in a given social context, then I had decided to jump from the calm and relatively predicable current of hip hop enthusiast/observer into the rapid waters of an emcee/participant.

Sometime during the summer of 1993, while looking out from a mountain vista at sunrise, I had (half jokingly) announced to a group of high school friends that if I ever came out with a hip hop album, I would go by the name "Mad Squirrel." Initially, this statement was greeted with a good deal of amusement, and for at least the next couple of weeks many of the people who had been there that daybreak would spontaneously say "Mad Squirrel" when in my presence. Shortly after making my decision to become a Bay Area emcee, I resurrected "Mad Squirrel" as my primary performing title.

*H*ip Hop Underground is an account of the ethnographic travels of researcher Anthony Kwame Harrison and emcee Mad Squirrel through various enclaves of the Bay Area underground hip hop scene. I put these two identities on equal terms because many of the people I performed in front of over the course of my time there knew me first and foremost as the latter, even if most of those I was closest with were introduced to me as the former. The transformations involved in my research experiences illustrate how ethnographic knowledge is a product of a network of situated social relationships and the events (observed or experienced) that they stimulate. Looking back, I can attribute my ability to participate in the scene to the degree that I did to two key factors: (1) the individual I was (an anthropology graduate student who had a background, albeit quite informal, in rapping) and (2) the context and focus of my research (a movement away from the gate-keeping practices that have traditionally defined hip hop participation). Basically speaking, if I had needed to rely on getting a recording contract in order to become a (legitimately received) Bay Area emcee, I would not have had this opportunity.

At the same time, *Hip Hop Underground* is an examination of the changing constructions and constitutions of racial identity among young Americans. By exploring the politics of authenticity and race within the world of Bay Area underground hip hop, this book sets out to address pressing issues of racial identification, interaction, and understanding. Despite the fact that no scientific basis for racial distinctions has ever been shown (Appiah 1986; Brace 2005), race remains a remarkably durable social category. As an organizing principle in American society, race stands on par with gender, class, and age. In fact, with its calls to stay vested in your own kind, racial allegiance can be paramount in shaping life plans and everyday activities. It is of great interest, then, to look at the interpersonal exchanges taking place within the social spaces in which racial heterogeneity appears to be the ideal. *Hip Hop Underground* takes a particularly micro-social focus, one that could not be achieved without the degree of ethnographic immersion that my forays into performing and recording facilitated. In these pages I share a handful of hip hop biographies, not for the sake of merely telling the stories of these individuals, but rather to present these episodes as illustrative of the social structures, patterned behaviors, and racial dynamics that young people participating in multiracial youth social scenes are perpetually negotiating.

Scenes oriented around hip hop music are pungent in their racial symbolism. The Bay Area's progressive politics and tremendous diversity make it a particularly fruitful location for exploring the contours of interracial accord and tension at the start of the twenty-first century. Yet, as the United States undergoes an unprecedented demographic shift and a post-post-soul generation (George 2004) comes of age in a world shaped through possibilities for audio, visual, and interpersonal communication that their grandparents could have hardly imagined, narratives of racial boundary crossing and issues of racial ethics and integrity will become more frequent aspects of all Americans' everyday lives. In this way, the subjects of this study can be viewed as young pioneers at the leading edge of a multiracial frontier.

Within the world of Bay Area underground hip hop, a professed color-blind mantra is celebrated. This ideal is upheld even in the face of frequent race-based assessments of hip hop legitimacy. In the chapters that follow, I contend that by looking at where and how race is of consequence within this local music scene, one can glean many of the evolving dimensions and emerging understandings of racial identity and American diversity that are occurring at a nationwide level. This position is premised on the notion of a fundamental relationship between hip hop "culture," demographic change, and racial and ethnic *performativity*.[4]

Strolling through a multiracial metropolis (Staiger 2006)—through cities like Los Angeles, Minneapolis, and Washington, D.C., or even places like Holyoke, Massachusetts, and Durham, North Carolina—it is obvious that young generations of recent immigrants are expressing both their Americanness and their experiences of growing up in America in no small part through the music and expressive culture of hip hop. Filipino American emcee Geo Logic (of the group Blue Scholars) aptly captures the essence of this young, interethnic, urban existence when he describes people in the neighborhoods of southeast Seattle as speaking "in the Beacon Hill[5] slang with a wonderful blend of black language and immigrant accents" (Blue Scholars 2005). Hip hop, fashioned through the experiences and outlooks of young members of a black (and brown) 1970s New York City underclass (Chang 2005; Perkins 1996; Rose 1994), has today become the canvas upon

which young people the world over craft their identities, voice their perspectives, and give shape to their politics. As America undergoes a dramatic demographic shift, the places and spaces that comprise the world of
underground hip hop offer an appealing vantage point from which to survey
the multiracial frontiers that lie ahead.

Before presenting the layout of *Hip Hop Underground*'s five chapters, I
should clarify a couple of points. The first concerns the time frame of
this research. In one of the few ethnographic studies on hip hop in America
(*Making Beats: The Art of Sample-Based Hip-Hop*), Joseph Schloss explains
that for Americans studying American popular music, "there is no formal
beginning or end to our research; our participant observation (i.e., experi-
encing popular music within the context of American society) covers our
entire lives, as do the relationships that we rely on to situate ourselves socially" (2004, 8). Although in the second chapter of this book I give a detailed disclosure of my twenty-five-plus-year relationship with hip hop music,
in terms of this immediate project a fitting starting point would be 1998—
the year when I first met the Living Legends and began an intense online
correspondence with their webmaster, Mystik Access, regarding many of
the ideas that are presented here. My official field stay in the Bay, which
forms the initial context of many of the experiences I discuss, occurred between April 2000 and May 2001. As with many academic texts dealing
with the rapidly changing world of popular culture, but perhaps even more
pronounced in this case, some of the examples given by the people I interviewed may sound tragically outdated. Since that official period of residence, I have returned to the Bay nearly every year—sometimes more than
once a year—and although these are usually short visits, during each trip I
have been fortunate enough to be welcomed to resituate myself within
many of the key relationships and activity patterns I participated in before.
For instance, on many of these return visits I have continued to record music with the same circle of artists (see Chapter 2). I have also been invited
to recording studios, video shoots, hip hop radio shows, deejay battles, and
b-boy/b-girl (aka breakdancing) events. In addition to participating in the
usual open-mic events and around-the-house rhyme cyphers, I have been
on stage at various hip hop shows (including a few in which my own group
headlined) and even once performed as part of a San Francisco State Ethnic Studies Conference. In the summer of 2004, three Bay Area hip hop
artists visited me in my East Coast university home, where together we
hosted a two-day hip hop event featuring lectures, workshops, panel discus-

sions, and performances. Throughout all these activities, there have been observations, experiences, and critical discussions that have furthered my evolving thinking on many of the issues presented here.[6]

In a 2003 paper presented at the Harvard Civil Rights Project "Color Lines Conference," I specifically talked about the emergence of Filipino Americans as a dominant voice in West Coast underground hip hop (Harrison 2003). Since I gave that paper, the increased popularity of West Coast Filipino artists like Blue Scholars, Native Guns (Kiwi and Bambu), Hopie Spitshard, and Power Struggle have confirmed this observation. While the accuracies of my (more nuanced) thinking regarding racial and ethnic identification are not nearly as cut-and-dry, in the years that have passed since my initial fieldwork, I believe that time and distance, tempered through regular return visits and observations, have enhanced my perspectives and theorizing. These dynamics continue to play out, and they continue to be relevant.

My second point of clarification concerns exactly what I mean by "underground hip hop." This is a discussion I have had with numerous people both inside and outside the scene in which I worked. Within the field of hip hop, the label "underground" can be applied to everything from Grammy-nominated artists like Common and The Roots[7] to groups like The Latter, who once boasted(!) of having sold only two copies of one of their CDs. Being that The Latter was one of the groups I initially worked closely with (see Chapter 2), it may be straightforward enough to locate "my" underground hip hop community somewhere closer to that end of the popularity spectrum. Yet to illustrate some of the complexities of this question, and hopefully work toward a more informed resolution to it, let me share a number of short vignettes.

On several occasions, when speaking with people who are familiar with both San Francisco and hip hop about my work, they have taken the initiative of describing the scene's racial dynamic to me. "It's all black artists and white audiences," the usual depiction goes. For example, an African American friend called me immediately following a Jurassic Five show at The Fillmore to announce that "hip hop [had] officially crossed over"—explaining that he had been there and that the audience had been "all white." During a September 2000 Solesides (Quannum) Reunion show at Bimbo's 365 Club, the nexus of racial and socioeconomic demographics found among the "typical" San Francisco underground hip hop crowd was brought to my attention by a co-worker of mine—who in no way fancied herself as a hip hop aficionado—when she pointed out how odd it was to be at a hip hop show and to see so many white people talking on their cell phones and a guy doing air guitar to DJ Shadow. A similar observation was made by Filipino American deejay King One, who pulled me aside at a January 2001 Coup show at Slim's to comment on the inconsistencies he saw between the group's revolutionary, Afrocentric politics and the fact that their audience appeared to be a bunch of "white yuppies."

Jurassic Five, Solesides/Quannum (which includes DJ Shadow, Lyrics Born, Lateef, and Blackalicious), and the Coup are all examples of what many of the hip hoppers I spent time among referred to as the "just about to touch the surface underground." When I asked Kegs One, owner of the Below the Surface hip hop shop, about the categories of customers who frequented his store, his immediate response was "I have a few different people that are into the more 'commercial underground' stuff, but then 95 percent of my customers are here for the literal four-track tapes. You know, dirty-sounding, low-budget, in-the-room, in-the-closet recorded tapes."

Clearly, the term "underground hip hop" can mean quite different things to different people. From the various comments presented above, we get a picture of a more commercial underground hip hop stratum in which relatively affluent, mostly white audiences predominate. This characterization is consistent with the observations of (commercially successful underground artist) Common who once famously said, "[At my concerts] all I see are coffee shop chicks and white dudes" (The Roots 1999). I want to juxtapose Common's line, which appeared on The Roots gold-selling *Things Fall Apart* album, with the lyrics of a comparatively obscure song called "Walking Fences," by the one-time Oakland duo Moonrocks (Bizarro and Nebulus): "Is there something about the things we do? / Is it the way we act that makes us exactly the same as you? / But different in a sense, we walk the fence, a thin line" (Moonrocks 1999).[8] This refrain, which is repeated several times throughout the song, was recognized by a few of the hip hoppers I spent the most time among as encapsulating a critical underground ethos introduced above: the idea of a blurring, thinning, almost imperceptible line separating artists and fans. I consider this phenomenon at greater length in later sections of the book (see especially Chapters 1 and 4). For the current discussion, however, it suffices to say that at the lesser-known end of the underground continuum, where audiences often consist largely of friends, family, and other associates, the racial and ethnic demographics of performers and "fans" tend to resemble one another more closely than where record label bureaucracies, copious album sales, and various other production-of-culture mechanisms (Peterson 1976) stand between them. Expressed a different way, the general pattern seems to be that as artists grow popular, and their underground hip hop fan base extends outside their more-or-less intimate circle of friends, audiences have tended to grow increasingly more white.[9]

In sum, people who describe Bay Area underground hip hop in general, and San Francisco underground hip hop in particular, as mostly black artists performing for mostly white audiences are not incorrect. The differences between their representations of the core scene and mine are largely a consequence of varying levels of underground hip hop notoriety and the intimacy of the fan bases they tend to attract,[10] although these levels are not entirely exclusive. Kegs One, who catered primarily to the "dirty-sounding, low-budget" end of the spectrum, set what I consider a fair dividing line with the twenty dollar show. In essence, only the more commercial underground hip hop acts had the ability to fill a venue charging twenty dollars or more to get in the door. The Latter, with their two CD sales, certainly were not attempting this.

Book Outline

The progression of analyses put forth in *Hip Hop Underground* is separated into five chapters. Chapter 1 focuses on establishing Bay Area underground hip hop as a valuable site through which to examine the changing integrities of race in twenty-first-century America. I begin this by presenting both Bay Area racial and ethnic demographic numbers and on-the-ground perspectives on racial and ethnic identification. Since the 1970s, California has gone through a "phenomenal demographic transformation" (Tafoya 2002, 102), and nowhere is that better represented than in the Bay. By looking at how these changes have been discussed by researchers and experienced by the people living through them, I situate young Bay Area residents within a wider conversation about U.S. population shifts. In the second part of the chapter, I outline the development of underground hip hop as both a national music subgenre and a local music scene. Through a variety of locally informed practices and sensibilities, underground hip hoppers in the Bay have worked to secure and sustain distinctions between their music/culture and its commercial counterpart. Within such a racially diverse metropolitan setting, where subcultural affiliations are at times more strongly felt than race, one result is an inclusive ideology of hip hop (racial) participation

that counters commercial rap music's near complete reliance on black performers. Contextualizing both the racial and distinctly underground hip
hop climates that young Bay Area hip hoppers move within is vital to later
analyses and assessments of their actions and inclinations.

Chapter 2 provides a first-person ethnographic account of the Bay Area
underground scene in which I immersed myself. Part research methodology, part autobiography, and part arrival story, the chapter paints a multidi-
mensional picture of my day-to-day experiences working at Amoeba Music's
San Francisco store (at the time the largest independent record store in
America);[11] experiencing the Bay Area hip hop nightlife; attending and performing at what was at the time the largest and longest-standing weekly hip
hop open-microphone event in the area; and recording music with a group
of emcees and producers who came to identify as the Forest Fires Collective. It was through these distinct yet integrated social arenas that I came
to know the world of Bay Area underground hip hop.

The remaining chapters of the book build on one another sequentially.
Chapter 3 sets a model for examining the racial ethics of underground hip
hop participation. I begin with a survey of the existing literature—and by
extension the available arguments—regarding hip hop authenticity and race.
After establishing this range of authenticity claims, I move to a more direct
discussion of how dynamics of identity and authenticity play out within
underground hip hop scenes. I must confess to a predisposition against the
idea that what is occurring represents legitimate color blindness. What I
propose instead is a race-based hierarchy of hip hop merit that allows underground hip hoppers to conflate dimensions of social and personal identity
as a means of negotiating their place on it. Building on Sarah Thornton's
(1995) concept of "subcultural capital" and John L. Jackson Jr.'s (2005) notion
of "racial sincerity," I argue that a genuine subjectivity, articulated through
the amorphous quality of "knowing what's up," becomes the key vehicle
through which Bay Area underground hip hoppers maneuver along hip hop's
racially symbolic landscape.

Chapter 4 presents various dynamics surrounding this racial maneuverability. Despite its color-blind mantra, the racial politics and scales of awareness that saturate the Bay Area underground scene compel people with
different racial identities to engage hip hop in remarkably divergent ways.
Throughout the chapter, I discuss how various understandings of, personal
relationships with, and sociopolitical investments in hip hop are leveraged as
bases for claiming underground legitimacy. The chapter includes specific
discussions of African American hip hoppers' inclusive dispositions, Euro-

pean American hip hoppers' heightened racial consciences, and Filipino Americans' embrace of hip hop as a means of fashioning new forms of identities and racial scripts. By narrating the life stories, defining moments, and situational politics of various individuals, I demonstrate the ways in which sincerity has come to trump authenticity as the primary sensibility through which underground credibility and racial integrity are pursued.

Finally, Chapter 5 poses a series of challenges to the optimistic tones that permeate earlier sections of the book. Through an in-depth reading of particular racially loaded episodes, as well as some pointed questions concerning underground hip hop's nexus of race, gender, and privilege, I ultimately argue that in considering the situational bases of contemporary youth identity constructions, there is as much cause for concern as reason for hope. As we embark on this new century, at a historical moment when shifts in the perception and performance of race in the United States appear to be quite monumental, we must remain attentive to the ways in which traditional axes of power continue to function. Underground hip hop celebrates a discourse of racial democracy and egalitarianism, but if the bases of racial distinctions (and possibly the integrity of race itself) are, in fact, becoming less scripted, then who benefits and why?

Notes on Methodology

Customarily, anthropology recognizes the confidentiality of its research subjects. In that many of the people I interacted with are commercial artists who would rather have their participation acknowledged than overlooked, by and large I did not follow this disciplinary decree. In a few delicate situations, I thought it wise to use pseudonyms for artists (these are all noted in the text). In addition, pseudonyms were regularly used for people in the scene who were not hip hop recording artists.

As Mica Pollock (2004a) explained in her wonderful study on race talk within a California high school, talking about race can be a very self-conscious methodological endeavor. Although I conducted twenty-four interviews, and use many of the quotes from them, I also must acknowledge recent methodological critiques of interviews as artificially and hierarchically constructed social exchanges that are secondary to the ethnographic project (Beaudry 1997; Borland 1991; Brand 2007; Kisliuk 1997). Interviews certainly provided me with quotable means through which to make my cases; however, many of my insights were gleaned from conversations and everyday interactions that fell outside the somewhat synthetic interview context.

The issues and understandings presented in this book come first and foremost out of my experience as both an ethnographer and an emcee within the Bay Area underground hip hop scene. Critical questions concern the various ways in which considerations of race impact the subcultural legitimacy and everyday activities of underground hip hoppers in the Bay and what this can tell us about the changing nature of racial identifications within America on the whole. My own position as an African American male[12] within this community allowed me to pursue these questions in terms of both ideological and practical considerations and to negotiate the relationship between what people say and what people do. Accordingly, this project is a product of knowledge gained not only through traditional ethnographic methods (including field notes, interviews, and conversational queries) but also through my participation recording music as part of a collective, performing at open-mic events and underground hip hop shows, and taking part in a variety of rhyme cypher exchanges.

Anthropologists continue to grapple with their prime directive not to intervene in the communities they study. Only recently has a "small revolution" within the discipline advocated the virtues of acknowledging and encouraging the fact that ethnographic researchers share the world with the people they work among (Turner 2007). This project should be looked at as part of that revolution in that it recognizes the methodological benefits of such inextricable involvement (see particularly Chapter 2). Throughout the pages that follow, I maintain that such a fully immersed ethnographic project allows for a more profound exploration of both what occurs within the world of Bay Area underground hip hop and the meanings that underlie and inform these actions.

I

Race in America and Underground Hip Hop in the Bay

The problem of the color line, or where and how distinctions between races are drawn, continues to plague American society. While multiculturalist initiatives and the conspicuous consumption of racialized popular cultures masquerade as remedies to racial issues (and in some cases even race itself), on close examination it is clear that the hangover of nearly two hundred years of legal white dominion will take more than a few generations to relieve. Beginning with legislative efforts initiated during the civil rights era, a number of congressional acts, legal precedents, and federal policies have sought to redress historical inequalities among Americans of different races. The effectiveness of some of these notwithstanding, by virtually all indications racial disparities, hostilities, and conflict are still with us.

Arguably, the most difficult race-related social ailments to cure will not be the laws and institutional structures that have historically restricted non-white people's opportunities and actions, but rather the less tangible racist ideologies that inform them; that is, the opinions and outlooks on racial differences that, as people say, "are of the mind." In this way, the metaphor of a racial hangover is apt. The foundations of American racism—and here I mean pervasive institutions of systematic material and symbolic inequities favoring people of (predominantly) European descent over those who trace significant portions of their ancestry to areas outside of Europe—are apparent in the language with which we speak about race, the notions of beauty and creativity we celebrate, the basis on which we recognize and measure intelligence, as well as the way we envision what it means to be American.

The beginning of the twenty-first century provides Americans with an opportunity to reassess the significance of the color line and to endeavor to embark on a new era of race relations. It was at the beginning of the last century that W.E.B. Du Bois made his now famous postulation about America's impending hundred-year struggle with race: "The problem of the twentieth century is the problem of the color-line—the relation of darker to lighter races of men in Asia and Africa, in America and the islands of the sea" (*The Souls of Black Folk*, 1996 [1903], 13). With the twentieth century behind us, and with the children of the post-civil rights (and post-1965 immigration reform) generation now having and raising children of their own, there seems to be a great hope (some would say wishful thinking) that America is poised to make its color line problem a thing of the past.[1]

It should come as no great surprise that some of the strongest proponents of the American multiracial success story are people whose racial identities have historically been the most privileged in this country. From atop the social ladder, the view of society as working well (i.e., offering equal opportunity) for everyone serves to rationalize one's own successes against others who have not faired as well. Perhaps more unexpected is the fact that many of these same people (of predominantly European descent) are among the most ardent supporters of a color-blind racial ideology (Frankenberg 1993), which alleges that race has, in effect, ceased to have any immediate salience in their lives. This is certainly not the case with all European Americans. In both rural backwoods and corporate backrooms good old-fashioned American racism lives on. However, a curious alliance between liberal idealists and conservative political pragmatists has formed around the post-civil rights conviction that it would be best if race as a social issue—and for some as an organizing principle in society—were to disappear (Guinier and Torres 2002; Williams 2006). At the same time, members of groups that have historically suffered as a consequence of being racially defined as "other" are far less enthusiastic about this prospect. Looking outward from our current vantage point, the forecast for the future of race in America would seem to stand at a compromise between these two opposing ideals.

The positions presented in this book are premised on the idea that the world of San Francisco Bay Area underground hip hop offers a particularly illuminating case study through which to consider how race in America will come to be conceptualized and acted on during the first part of the twenty-first century. Outside of the policies and practices that govern established social institutions, the way young Americans approach, rework, and reconsider the significance of race within their own social arenas provides a glimpse into its evolving, eroding, and enduring nature. By focusing on processes that I call *situational racialization* and the sensibilities that inform them, I address the dialectic relationship between ideology and social structure with greater attention toward the former. In doing so, my contention is that the participatory nature of underground hip hop fosters engaged performances of race that are likely to resonate beyond these transitory youth subcultural endeavors and impact broader (in both a spatial and temporal sense) aspects of social life. This, in conjunction with the particular dynamics of Bay Area diversity, forms a leading edge on which these emerging understandings of, and approaches to, race in America are initially most visible.

To begin this process, it is necessary to contextualize Bay Area underground hip hoppers' situationally racialized perspectives and activities at two levels. The first involves considering these particular dynamics against the broader historical and societal backdrop of race relations in America. Starting with an outline of current shifts in America's racial demographics, I specifically discuss how such changes have impacted the categories through which many Americans conceptualize and talk about race. My intent is to highlight the different ways young Americans today are able to make choices regarding how and to what extent they choose to identify and align themselves with particular racial and/or ethnic groups. This sets up later discussions that focus on practices used to leverage racial, ethnic, and national identities in accordance with vested interests, social aspirations, and self-conscious identity constructions.

In the second part of this chapter I approach the subject from an altogether different perspective: the specific factors that gave rise and shape to the Bay Area underground hip hop scene's formation. In particular, I discuss how key institutions, icons, and a powerful sense of local folklore contributed to the development of a distinctly underground hip hop ethos, which, in turn, engendered its own authentic hip hop identities. After providing a somewhat truncated description of the emergence of underground hip hop as a racially inclusive music subgenre, I move on to explore the unique set of circumstances that shaped its particularly vibrant and diverse manifestation within the Bay Area scene. For many aspiring underground hip hoppers, involvement in local multiracial scenes provides a meaningful basis for social grounding—a subcultural identity option, so to speak—that often surpasses racial and ethnic identifications. It is, therefore, particularly telling to examine when and how race continues to matter, as well as what the larger ramifications of these changes in identity formation might mean. The answers to such questions will be saved for later chapters; what is most vital here is to establish why a study of race within the world of Bay Area underground hip hop is at all important.

America's Multiracial Frontier: Inside the Numbers

One of the most obvious reasons for considering young Bay Area residents as representative of America's multiracial future is the strong parallel between current Bay Area demographics and what prognosticators have projected as mid-twenty-first-century population numbers for the nation as a whole. Many people with interests in American racial demographics are already familiar with the well-publicized forecast that by the year 2050 America will become a "majority-minority" nation (Chideya 1999): that is, that the percentage of white (non-Hispanic) Americans will drop to below half of the nation's overall population. During this period (2000 to 2050), the percentage of Latinos (or Hispanics)[2] is expected to more than double from 12.5 percent in the 2000 census to 30.2 percent; the Asian/Pacific Island population will grow from 3.7 percent to 7.8 percent; and the percentage of African Americans will drop slightly from 12.1 percent to 11.8 percent (U. S. Census Bureau 2001, 2008). Some commentators have suggested that even these numbers underestimate the growth of racial minorities on the whole (Bonilla-Silva 2004) and people identifying as racially mixed more specifically (Edmonston, Lee, and Passel 2002; Lind 1998). Statistically, the 2050 population projections can be seen already on the generational horizon. At the start of this century, less than 61 percent of Americans under the age of eighteen were white (U.S. Census Bureau 2002).[3] Many scholars have predicted that this imminent (majority-minority) transition will have far-reaching consequences, including shifting the alliances between races and reapportioning political and social power (see, for example, Bonilla-Silva 2004; Darder and Torres 2004; Gans 1999; Hattam 2007; Hill 2004; Sanjek 1996).

In both California—by far America's most populated state—and specifically its nine-county, seven-thousand-square-mile region known as the Bay Area, the racial demographics of today's population already look a lot like the mid-century projections (see Table 1.1). While the numbers are by

no means identical, several similarities and a few differences deserve attention. The most meaningful similarities include the aforementioned majority-
minority inversion, the conspicuous ascendance of Latinos into the largest
"minority group," and the preeminent growth of the Asian/Pacific Island
population. The most striking differences in these demographic compari-
sons are the relatively small numbers of African Americans found throughout California and the particularly large Asian/Pacific Islander population
in the Bay. My focus on hip hop, a cultural form that typically has been associated with African Americans, goes some way in addressing the first of
these; for, as we shall see, even within the supposed color-blind world of Bay
Area hip hop, black identities are represented as much, if not more, than
any other group. The high numbers of Bay Area residents with Asian and
Pacific Islands backgrounds certainly warrants attention. In later chapters,
I specifically focus on one Asian/Pacific Island group—Filipino-American
hip hoppers—to illustrate some of the ways in which racial and ethnic
identity has been leveraged by individuals and groups falling outside America's black-white dichotomy.

In much the same way that national demographic shifts are not uniform—
they are occurring more rapidly along the coasts and within cities than in
the middle of the American heartland (Frey 1996; Sanjek 2000)—different

TABLE 1.1   Population Percentages by Race*

	U.S. 2000	U.S. 2050 (Projected)	California 2000	Bay Area 2000
White (non-Hispanic)	69.1	46.3	46.7	50
Black (non-Hispanic)	12.1	11.8	6.4	7.3
Hispanic (or Latino)	12.5	30.2	32.4	19.4
Asian/Pacific Islander (non-Hispanic)**	3.7	7.8	11.1	19.3
American Indian/Alaskan (non-Hispanic)	.7	.8	.5	.4
Two or More Races (non-Hispanic)	1.6	3	2.7	3.3

*Because the U.S. Census treats race and Hispanic origin as two separate categories (meaning a person can
be racially Black and Hispanic), the racial percentages represented here include only people identifying
themselves as non-Hispanic. For this reason, Hispanic percentages may be slightly inflated relative to other
categories. Furthermore, because I have left out the small percentage of people identifying as "some other
race" (for consistency reasons), percentage totals are slightly below one hundred percent.

**This category collapses the "Asian" and "Native Hawaiian and Other Pacific Islander" census categories.

Sources: U.S. Census Bureau, "Census 2000 Brief: Overview of Race and Hispanic Origin," issued March
2001; U.S. Census Bureau Population Division, "Percentage of the Projected Population by Race and Hispanic Origin for the United States: 2010 to 2050 (NP2008-T6)," released August 14, 2008; Bay Area Census,
"California" and "San Francisco Bay Area," available online http://www.bayareacensus.ca.gov/ (accessed
October 20, 2006).

localities within the Bay Area exhibit vastly different racial demographics. The principle cities that provided the settings for my research were San Francisco, Oakland, and Berkeley. In cities like Oakland, the four major racial classifications (white, black, Hispanic, and Asian/Pacific Islander) are well represented, with each group making up between 15 and 35 percent of the populace. In comparison, San Francisco (just an eight-minute Bay Area Rapid Transit train ride from Oakland) is home to a population that is almost three-quarters white (43.6 percent) and Asian (31.2 percent). As the demographic comparison of each of these cities should make clear (see Table 1.2), the racial/ethnic diversity of the Bay Area varies tremendously depending on where one travels. The one consistency found within almost all places is the absence of a prevailing whiteness which, in terms of race in America, is in many ways most significant.

Regardless of the comparatively small African American population within San Francisco (7.6 percent), areas of the city such as the Fillmore and Hunters Point districts are considered predominantly black neighborhoods. Similarly, both San Francisco's Richmond district and parts of its Inner and Outer Sunset districts are known to be populated primarily by specific Asian American groups; Daly City, a city of over 100,000 located just south of San Francisco, is reported to be home to "the largest concen-

TABLE 1.2   Bay Area Cities Population Percentage by Race*

	San Francisco 2000	Oakland 2000	Berkeley 2000	San Jose 2000***
White (non-Hispanic)	43.6	23.5	55.2	36
Black (non-Hispanic)	7.6	35.1	13.3	3.3
Hispanic (or Latino)	14.1	21.9	9.7	30.2
Asian/Pacific Islander (non-Hispanic)**	31.2	15.6	16.4	26.9
American Indian/Alaskan (non-Hispanic)	.3	.4	.3	.3
Two or More Races (non-Hispanic)	3	3.2	4.5	3
Total Population Numbers	776,733	399,484	102,743	894,943

*Because the U.S. Census treats race and Hispanic origin as two separate categories, the racial percentages represented here include only people identifying themselves as non-Hispanic. For this reason, Hispanic percentages may be slightly inflated relative to other categories. Furthermore, because I have left out the small percentage of people identifying as "some other race," percentage totals are slightly below one-hundred percent.

**This category collapses the "Asian" and "Native Hawaiian and Other Pacific Islander" census categories.

***Although I did not spend much time there, I include statistics on San Jose (for comparison) because it is technically home to the Bay Area's largest population (although not as nationally known as San Francisco or Oakland), has its own thriving underground hip hop scene, and is generally recognized as the metropolitan center of the South Bay.

Sources: Bay Area Census, "San Francisco City and County," "City of Oakland," "City of Berkeley," and "City of San Jose," http://www.bayareacensus.ca.gov/ (accessed October 20, 2006).

trated Filipino population outside of Manila" (Eljera 1996; see also Vergara Jr. 2008). Even while acknowledging these ethnically specific districts, many Bay Area residents upheld an image of local cosmopolitanism that emphasized the social fluidity among different groups. I found this common among people of all races. African American deejay/emcee Rasta Cue Tip (who also makes up half of the group Various Blends) explained it in the following way: "Being in the Bay Area you are not secluded from other different types of people. Whether you try to or not, you're going to be dealing on a personal level with different types of people. People of different races, different class. You could be the poorest person, whatever . . . but in some part of the way you are going to cross paths with this rich person or might have a personal association with some type of rich person."

Rasta Cue Tip's decision to articulate his sense of Bay Area togetherness primarily through the example of class (the crossing paths of the "poorest" and "richest" persons) rather than race might not be the most common way this notion of social fluidity gets expressed; however, it does follow a noticeable pattern on the part of many African American hip hoppers to downplay the significance of race, particularly in their everyday hip hop–related dealings with others (see Chapter 4). As shall become clear over the course of this book, race continues to be important. If nothing else, this strong correlation between racial identity and the frequency and manner in which people discuss the significance of race is testament to that.

Racial Conventions and Complexities: Traditional Categories and New Identifications

Despite over four hundred years of people with a variety of racial backgrounds residing on this continent, racial diversity in America historically has been understood as a bipolar issue with black on one side and white on the other. At the dawn of the nation (and really since the founding of the colonies), race symbolized the difference between slaves and non-slaves. Even after slavery had been abolished the rise and reign of nearly one hundred years of Jim Crow institutions throughout the American South signified the enduring consequences of a racist American regime. In 1965, amid widespread changes in civil rights laws and enforcement, American immigration laws also changed to stress family reunification as the central criterion for admittance. Prior to this, entry into the United States had been organized around a quota system that benefited those hailing from what were considered "first world" nations. Following the 1965 Immigration and

Nationality Act, a new wave of immigration began, with many people coming from previously restricted parts of Asia, the Pacific, and Latin America. One direct outcome of this was the crystallization of the "Asian" and "Hispanic" racial designations, which came into common usage by the end of the 1960s and was further cemented by national standards for reporting on race in the late 1970s. In 1977 the U.S. Office of Management and Budget adopted statistical Directive Number 15, thus instituting what anthropologist Roger Sanjek (1996) has referred to as the five-race framework—black, white, Hispanic, Asian American, and (in some places) Native American—as the principal method of presenting federal statistics on race.

Although the five-race framework has become common in both "political and street-level discourse" (Sanjek 1996, 109), the black-white dichotomy continues to be America's most salient racial distinction, leading some speculators to predict that over the next several decades groups falling outside the black-white divide will either become assimilated into whiteness (Warren and Twine 1997)—as was the case with Irish, Italians, and Jews during early periods in American history[4]—or get grouped together into distinctly nonwhite "people of color" alliances (see Gans 1999; Sanjek 1996). Yet within many racially and ethnically diverse metropolitan regions, the Bay Area being the immediate example, we see signs of something altogether different taking place. Not only do we see the five-race framework giving way to a diversity of national distinctions, there also appears to be greater attention given to the variety of subjectivities that have been historically contained within each racial group. Where the cloak of racial designation fosters essentialist beliefs that serve as shortcuts to social understanding[5] by assigning certain attributes, agendas, and outlooks to persons of particular racial identities, within diverse social milieus such as the Bay Area hip hop underground the assumptions inherent in such generalizations are challenged daily. Still, it is precisely because race continues to matter that even the most seemingly divergent racial subjectivities cannot be thought of outside the framework of racial categorizations. In other words, it is a prolonged and prevailing awareness of racial identity—what I have referred to elsewhere as a sense of racial being (Harrison 2008a)—that creates the foundation on which all racialized acts (whether conforming to or defying racially essentialized behaviors) should be understood.

The preamble to Directive No. 15 acknowledged that the five-race framework is neither scientific nor anthropological; rather, the goal was to "develop categories that made sense in some general way" (Nobles 2000, 80). However, it is worth considering whether, or even why, melding four racial categories and one designated ethnic classification (Hispanic) made sense in any way (Hattam 2007). In the "principle case" in which the U.S. Supreme Court addressed the racial identity of a Hispanic group,[6] the Court ruled that Mexican Americans were racially white (Lopez 2000). Even at the time, this must have been seen as a puzzling decision given the fact that Mexican children in the community in question were required to attend segregated schools and on the courthouse grounds in which the ruling was served "there were two men's toilets, one unmarked, and the other marked 'Colored Men' and 'Hombres Aqui' ('Men Here')" (Olivas 2005, 4 fn. 4). Thus, prior to the 1980 census, Latinos were generally classified as white unless they could be identified as "definitely Negro or Indian" (Nobles 2000, 82). However, through the practice of adjacent reporting, Directive No. 15's five-race framework codified the ethnic category "Hispanic" with the other four racial terms; now the specific designation "white non-Hispanic" (the technically correct term of use for discussing census figures on European Americans) tends to sound awkward when used outside of census reporting.

Though many Americans have grown accustomed with reporting on and discussing race through the five-race framework, in truth this taxonomy is an overly simplified and quite problematic amalgamation of racial (i.e., black), cultural/ethnic (most notably Hispanic but also arguably American Indian and white as defined through Directive No. 15), and geographic (particularly Asian/Pacific Islander but to some extent all categories) qualifiers.[7] In a rapidly diversifying American landscape, the widespread acceptance of these categories as common sense is at odds with the complications, contradictions, and interracial tensions that the five-race framework (and I would add the concept of race as a whole) has never adequately addressed.[8]

The 2000 U.S. Census, for example, specified eleven racial (national) subclassifications for people falling into the Asian/Pacific Islander category alone; these included: Asian Indian, Chinese, Filipino, Japanese, Korean, Vietnamese, Native Hawaiian, Guamanian or Chamorro, Samoan, Other Asian, and Other Pacific Islander. The importance of this specificity rests on the recognition that each of these groups has a unique cultural legacy in America that is intimately tied to their period and conditions of arrival. As such, we see a variety of experiences and interests falling under the Asian racial umbrella.

Similarly, the various groups falling under the heading "Hispanic" show tremendous diversity in terms of their nations of origin, circumstances and times of arrival, and ancestral bloodlines; in fact, in just about every way except language.[9] Grouping all these people together under one collective label has lead to significant misrepresentations of the condition of "Hispanics" in America (Chavez 1991). To address this confusion, some scholars have advocated turning to a *colorism* model, defined as "the discriminatory treatment of individuals falling within the same 'racial' group on the basis of skin color" (Herring 2004, 3), as a means of acknowledging the diversity of Latino experiences. Sociologist Eduardo Bonilla-Silva (2004) proposed viewing Latin Americans in terms of two distinct racial groups: (1) "White Latinos," including Argentines, Chileans, Costa Ricans, and Cubans; and (2) "dark-skinned Latinos," including Puerto Ricans and Mexicans. Yet even the experiences of Mexican Americans, easily America's (and over-whelmingly California's) largest Latino group, can be divided between people of Mexican origin whose families were residing in the Southwest prior to its becoming part of the United States, those who have resided here for several decades, and more recent immigrants. The social circum-stances surrounding members of this last group, many of whom possess "relatively low levels of skill, inadequate command of English, and little formal education" (Aponte 2000, 165), differ significantly from those of native-born Mexican Americans who are steadily moving into the middle class (Aponte 2000).

The fact that recently arriving immigrant groups have greater levels of community cohesion and ethnic isolation is a well documented sociological phenomenon (Gordon 1964; see also Lee and Fernandez 1998; Tafoya 2002). Arriving immigrants tend to land in rich ethnic enclaves which foster an amplified awareness of cultural identity that, at least initially, often trumps race as a principle basis of identification. In turn of the century America, these dynamics have become even more pronounced as many newly arrived groups are shunning the traditional path of assimilation (see Branigin 1998), instead choosing to more doggedly hold on to their ethnic identifications and cultural roots. Some of the factors affecting this include advances and price reductions in travel and communications which have made it possible for members of immigrant communities to stay better connected to the people and places they left. This situation is complicated by the extent to which, through processes of globalization, the lifestyles within many of these places of origin have come to resemble (or at the very least relate to) certain aspects of America culture. In this regard, the strong ties maintained between communities of departure and destination might very well play a greater role in sustaining ethnic and national identities among immigrant groups than in contributing to the retention of specific cultural traditions. Amid this dialectic of increased transnational connections and accelerated (globalization-induced) change it should come as little surprise that more and more second and third generation Americans are preferring to identify with their recognized nation of origin (e.g., Mexican, Filipino, Bolivian, or Korean) as opposed to more broadly assigned racial groupings (Bonilla-Silva 2004).[10]

Such tensions between national and racial identifications were readily apparent in a study on racial discourse within California high schools (Pollock 2004a). In her book *Colormute*, anthropologist Mica Pollock described a six-category vocabulary—black, white, Latino, Filipino, Chinese, and Samoan—that merged racial and ethnic terminologies used by students to specifically discuss race (2004a, 7). Among Bay Area underground hip hoppers we see a similar ethnoracial[11] dynamic at play as what are thought to be traditionally ethnic forms of identification are often conflated with race in a new brand of identity politics. The conditional context in which this occurs and the extent to which these categories of collective identity (most notably race/ethnicity, but also class, sociogeography, gender, and the like) are embellished through personal qualities (articulated by way of ongoing individual biographies) are central to the arguments presented here.

The Integrity of Race Mixing

During the 1990s, prevailing notions of race in America came under considerable attack as more and more people began to act on the belief that existing racial conventions could not adequately account for their varied identities, ancestries, and senses of allegiance. Sociologist Mary Waters reported that in the 1990 U.S. Census one-third of all children having racially black mothers and white fathers were identified as white (quoted in Fletcher 1998). Such numbers seem remarkable in a nation which, for most of the twentieth century, defended the belief (and in several states the official policy) that one drop of non-white blood made a person not white. As late as 1986, the U.S. Supreme Court upheld an earlier Louisiana State Court ruling stating that Susie Phipps, a forty-eight-year-old woman whose great-great-great-great grandmother was a negress, despite having lived her entire life with a white racial identity, could not have her birth certificate legally changed to reflect this (Domínguez 1997).

Where Waters found a propensity among mixed-race children of white fathers to buck America's standard of white racial purity and hypodescent (i.e., identifying with the parent of the more socially subordinate race), throughout the 1990s white mothers of mixed-race children were leading a charge of a different sort. In her research on the multiracial movement and mixed-race census category lobbying groups, Kim Williams found that "white, liberal, and suburban-based middle-class women [having children with black men]" were the one's holding most of the leadership roles in those organizations (Williams 2006, 112). This movement ultimately resulted in the Mark One Or More (MOOM) race option on the 2000 U.S. Census, a monumental occurrence the significance of which is still being realized.

Since 1967, when the Supreme Court ruled that all remaining state-level miscegenation laws were unconstitutional, the numbers of recognized interracial couples in America have increased more than ten-fold. Notably, it has been Latinos and Asian/Pacific Islanders who have had the highest interracial marriage rates (Fletcher 1998; Sanjek 1996).[12] Today, mixed-race couples regularly appear on such historically conservative barometers of American values as daytime soap operas and talk shows. In Virginia, one of the last states to allow interracial marriages, a (white) partner in an inter-racial marriage was recently elected to the U.S. Senate.[13] And, arguably one of the most well-recognized offspring of an interracial union, Barack Hussein Obama II, is now the President of the United States.

As opposed to earlier times when the immediate consequences of racial designation would have been more profoundly felt, Waters' study and the MOOM option suggest that the possibility of inter-generationally outrunning less desirable aspects of one's "racial baggage" in the interest of climbing the racial hierarchy has become accepted. In an earlier study, Waters (1990) examined how selective ancestral identification was employed as a strategy of identity formation among people of European descent. Through a series of follow-up interviews with census respondents, Waters showed how, in the interest of not being too much of a "mishmash," white Americans hailing from multiple European lineages tended to identify with only two or three nationalities, selectively forgetting the others (Waters 1990, 236). While such practices have been customary within racial groups, the idea of selectively forgetting or concealing one's non-white racial ancestry— commonly referred to as "passing" (for white)—has been historically targeted as ethically suspect (see Appiah 1990b).

Presently, Americans of multiple racial backgrounds have the ability to make choices regarding the extent to which they want to embrace certain aspects of their national and racial identities. In other words, how and with whom they identify is no longer preset. Certainly Susie Phipps would have encountered a different set of assumptions regarding racial fluidity if her case had been tried today. Is it possible that the historical safeguarding of

white identity is giving way to the acceptability of hyperdescent (i.e., identifying with the parent of the more socially privileged race)? If this is the
case, has the notion of racial passing become obsolete? Furthermore, how
might these developments impact perceptions of distinctions between
group social identities and individual personal identities, particularly with
the latter becoming increasingly prominent in a time of accelerated identity
construction options?

The 2000 Census has profound implications in terms of both the reporting of racial statistics and the integrity of racial categorizations more broadly.
Throughout American history racial designation has been based on two factors, appearance and ancestry. Where the former (although somewhat ambiguous in that it is based on perceptual interpretations) gives social actors
some leverage to assigning racial identities (e.g.,"she looks white to me"), the
latter applies specific socially constructed rules to the project of determining
race; in the American case, these rules historically have been in the service
of safeguarding white racial purity and privilege. The option of marking
more than one racial category acknowledges that racial identity is not just a
matter of ascribed status; it is equally a matter of self-identification. People
who make the choice to identify themselves as multiracial are also deliberately declining the option to adopt one specific racial identity (Gooding-
Williams Jr. 2001). Some social scientists have estimated that by 2050 close
to 20 percent of Americans will be claiming mixed ancestry (see, for example, Edmonston, Lee, and Passel 2002; Kasindorf and El Nasser 2001). The
accuracy of this projection likely will be more a matter of racial politics than
interracial procreation.[14]

The mixing of racially distinct populations has certainly been a part of
America's demographic makeup, even if this went unacknowledged in fifteen of the twenty-two decennial censuses. The obvious impact of giving
respondents the option of marking more than one race on the census is that
it "challenges long held fictions and strongly held beliefs about the nature
and definition of race in our society" (Perlmann and Waters 2002, 1). As an
organizing principle, the concept of race in America has been largely predicated on a belief in distinct, exclusive categories that cannot be changed in
the course of one's lifetime or (in selective cases) through successive generations. The MOOM option acknowledges the fluidity and permeability of
racial categorizations and moves the general public toward what race theorists have long recognized: that race is a social construction and not a biological fact.

The Racial Foundations of Underground Hip Hop

Anywhere you go in America, you are bound to find strong opinions on these changing racial demographics and classification schemes. Within hip hop music and the social arenas that surround it, dialogues on race can be particularly contentious. The emergence of hip hop in New York City during the 1970s has been variously described as an expressive movement, a social coping mechanism, a means of protest created by young people living within economically decimated postindustrial communities, or as a combination of any of these (Rose 1994; see also De Genova 1995; Fernando 1994; Toop 2000). Common to all these explanations is the general view that hip hop began as a collection of cultural practices celebrated within predominantly black communities and fitting within black aesthetic and cultural traditions (see Chapter 3), and has since grown into a pop culture/music form that today profoundly impacts young Americans of all racial, class, and sociogeographic backgrounds. Even where hip hop has not been intentionally engaged or consciously identified with, its influence on the music, language, dress, attitudes, and, I would add, racial understandings (and misunderstandings) of young people is clearly visible (see Farley 1999; Tanz 2007). Popular music scholar Murray Forman offers the following list of consumer products that featured hip hop stylistic codes and images as evidence of its mainstream visibility during the 1990s: "soft drinks, snack foods, clothing, footwear, children's toys (including Mattel's Barbie® doll) . . . Campbell soup, McDonald's Chicken McNuggets®, and Pillsbury baked goods (with their trademark Doughboy recast as a conspicuously and literally white-bread rapping homeboy)" (2002, 214). As such, hip hop's growth and popularity can be looked at as a subtext through which many of the dynamics of race relations and meanings associated with race among young Americans can be read. Cultural critic Henry Giroux has referred to it as "the only popular culture that takes seriously the relationship between race and democracy" (quoted in Aaron 1999).

Despite rap's multiracial fan base, through most of its thirty-year history an enduring aspect of virtually all authentic hip hop musical performances has been their near complete reliance on black racial identities (Quinn 1996). To this extent, the racial dynamics within hip hop and rap music differ from earlier black music forms which became increasingly whitened as they moved from the "least culturally assimilated sectors of the Black cultural landscape" (Hall 1997, 33) into the American mainstream (Garofalo 1994). This enduring association between hip hop and blackness makes it a potentially powerful vehicle for both reinforcing and refuting existing racial stereotypes and assumptions.

Against the commercial ascendance of Music Industry[15] rap, during the mid-to-late-nineties a specific subgenre known as "underground hip hop" developed through networks of Do-it-Yourself (DiY) artists/entrepreneurs, home-based industries, and locally-focused collective movements.[16] While underground hip hop's emergence can be presented as the simultaneous appearance of several (seemingly distinct) local scenes, the widespread practice of spotlighting commercial rap music's inauthenticity as a means of making counter-authenticity claims (see Neate 2004), coupled with underground hip hop's early utilization of translocal communication channels (most notably the Internet), lead me to represent its emergence here as a single countercultural development.

Whereas Music Industry rap flourished through the proliferation of sensationalized images of black violent criminality, unbridled sexual potency, and conspicuous consumption, in both content and style, early underground hip hop artists sought to distinguish their music from major record label releases. During the subgenre's formative years (circa 1995–1999), pointed critiques of the Music Industry—particularly highlighting the commercial motivations and corporate interests governing its perceptions of good music— were requisite elements of nearly all underground hip hop songs. There were also extensive efforts on the part of underground hip hop artists to address topics that fell outside of commercial rap's dominant conventions[17] and to compose atypical rhyme schemes and lyrical cadences.[18]

Aside from these obvious thematic and stylistic differences, by refusing to conform to commercial rap's dominant (black) iconography, early African American underground artists were proposing alternative forms of hip hop blackness.[19] Notably, many artists sought to re-center what were rapidly becoming marginalized rap music varieties of an earlier golden age. Two of the more important of these were the subgenre of "conscious rap," epitomized by groups like A Tribe Called Quest, Arrested Development, and Public Enemy; and the "boom-bap" traditionalist sounds of artists like Gang Starr, Pete Rock, and Diamond D. Of course, these categories are not mutually exclusive (an artist like KRS-One, for example, is clearly positioned at the crossroads of the two) and adherents to both camps tend to recognize rapping as only one of a select number of branches falling under the hip hop cultural umbrella (see Chapter 3).

Contesting commercial rap music's one-dimensional presentation of black authenticity is only part of underground hip hop's racial story. While the Music Industry's standard formulation of commodifying hip hop through hyper-real expressions of blackness worked to restrict both the quantity and character of non-black participation, in places like New York, Los Angeles, Boston, Philadelphia, Minneapolis, and the Bay Area, local independent scenes were forming around increasingly multiracial circles of artists. Similar to the African American artists described above, the racially inclusive attitudes that pervaded these scenes were in no small part fueled by critiques of rap music's limited vision of black urban authenticity. Either intentionally or consequently, within these emerging underground enclaves the resulting terms of hip hop legitimacy came to not require blackness.

That hip hop's ghettocentric image (Kelley 1994) had a particularly voyeuristic appeal among suburban, white, middle-class consumers is well established (see Samuels 1991; Allinson 1994; Watkins 2005). As rap's popularity continued to soar and its most prominent commercial artists began to amass greater wealth, notoriety, and promotional support, the conspicuous exhibition of affluence became an essential element of nearly all commercial hip hop performances.[20] Media studies professor Christopher Holmes Smith describes this shift as hip hop's embrace of a more inclusive "commiseration with mainstream notions of upward mobility" (1997, 348). This collusion between hip hop and the corporate propagators of a certain version of the American dream narrative succeeded as a marketing strategy for both rap music and the brand-names that celebrated rappers consumed. Yet many longtime hip hop followers—scorned by the thought of "their music" going mainstream—sensed the invisible hands of Music Industry image crafters at work and were thus primed to celebrate competing versions of hip hop authenticity, particularly those which to a certain extent harkened back to an earlier hip hop era.

In this respect, the development of a distinct underground hip hop subgenre was a DiY response to the unsatiated demands of many one-time ardent hip hop consumers, brought about by the "increasingly atrophied, clichéd and repetitive" tropes and rhetorical conventions (Mitchell 2001, 2) that accompanied rap music's rise in commercial prominence. To clarify this premise, consider sociologist Glenn Carroll's (1985) theory of resource-partitioning. According to Carroll, business endeavors that set out with the intention of capturing the broadest possible consumer base are inherently inclined to develop generalist, middle-of-the-road products and operating principles. This phenomenon, common within oligopolistic industry arrangements, comes about through an interest in targeting the greatest common dominator within the mass market. In the case of corporate hip hop music, rather than simple blandness, it was the ubiquitous, formulaic convergence of ghettocentric authenticity and extreme consumerism that contributed to a significant subset of dedicated hip hop fans' increasing disillusionment. Carroll maintains that such generalist approaches to maximizing market share ultimately allow for the emergence of specialized niches and innovative dissent (Carroll and Swaminathan 2000). In this process, identity and cultural factors take on greater importance as consumption of smaller, more obscure products comes to be recognized as a form of self-expression. Thus, to the many African Americans who had grown frustrated with the extent to which commercial rap music misrepresented or failed to resonate with their own subjectivities, to the non-black enthusiasts for whom hip hop had existed as a means of alternative identity formation,[21] and to an array of people with identities and motivations falling both between and outside of these characteristics, the discovery of underground hip hop as a seemingly more organic alternative to the music being released by the corporate rap industry awakened new planes of subcultural identification.

I advocate a focus on underground hip hop music—a subgenre that by the year 2000 was thoroughly distinct from its commercial counterpart[22]—with the understanding that its appearance could very well signal the start of hip hop's transformation from an exclusively black music form (or a "race music") to a music that will soon come to be viewed as non-race specific (and could potentially, like rock 'n' roll before it, come to be seen as explicitly non-black).[23] With many of its African Americans constituents aspiring to what cultural theorist Stuart Hall has described as "the end of the essential black subject" (1996, 443), and with a high enough proportion of non-black artists consciously avoiding self-presentation styles that mimic black linguistic and performance aesthetics (opting instead to engage hip hop on their own racial and cultural terms), the racial compass of hip hop certainly appears to be changing.

Underground hip hop emerged at a time when developments and price reductions in music production and distribution technologies began carving out greater space for independent hip hop artists to commodify and circulate their music. Through local DiY practices and upstart record labels, a generation of independent hip hoppers succeeded in setting up viable alternatives to the commercial rap music industry. By the end of the 1990s, the Internet had become a catalyst in expanding independent hip hop's markets by providing both music makers and their fans with options outside the conventional yoke of major label distribution dependency.

The intersection of race and class in underground hip hop is significant, for as the subgenre's following expanded geographically its constituency became markedly more middle class. Subcultural theorists as far back as Paul Willis (1978) have recognized that a propensity to embrace alternative music and cultural forms as an aspect of identity construction issues largely from middle-class sectors of youth populations. During the early years of the digital divide, these inclinations were magnified through underground hip hop's utilization of the Internet as a principal promotion and distribution source. For non-urban hip hop fans, the Internet diminished the consumptive disadvantages of geographic isolation. It was suddenly possible for a teenager in Red Oak, Iowa, to access the latest Company Flow[24] release just as quickly as someone living in Bedford-Stuyvesant, Brooklyn. Underground hip hop's reliance on college and community radio—a strategy developed to avoid the politics of commercial radio—and its utilization of the college town tour circuit further cultivated its appeal in less urban areas and among college students of all races (see Rodriquez 2006). In February and March of 2001, I had the opportunity to serve as the assistant manager on a nationwide tour sponsored by (what was at the time) one of the most prominent West Coast underground hip hop labels, Nu Gruv Alliance. In addition to shows in cities like New York, Chicago, Los Angeles, and Houston, the twenty-eight "city" tour stopped in college towns such as Santa Cruz, CA, Chapel Hill, NC, Saratoga Springs, NY, Middletown, CT, Northampton, MA, Burlington, VT, Oberlin, OH, Lincoln, NE, Lawrence, KS, and Boulder, CO.

The technologies of underground hip hop production—including music production software, studio boards, samplers, keyboards, four- through twenty-four-track recorders, and costly microphones—also contributed to its distinctly middle-class character. I do not say this to suggest that the accumulation of (or access to) this equipment was beyond the reach of aspiring hip hoppers from poor and working-class backgrounds; that would be an oversimplification. However, where a lack of financial means is an issue, greater levels of diligence and resourcefulness are required. The folklore found throughout underground hip hop circles is rich with reports of college students funding their musical projects through sizable financial aid checks. It also includes biting criticisms of children of well-to-do parents who acquire expensive technologies as gifts. The following example, posted on a prominent underground hip hop discussion forum, illustrates this point: "'happy birthday jimmy, we got you your Mpc 2000[25] you asked for and those record players cost me and your father 1000 dollers [sic] plus the

700 doller [sic] mixer. We hope you don't lose interest like you did with your Chemist set or your breakaway portable basketball hoop.' . . . Get with the movement privileged suburbanites!"[26] While one can never be sure about the number of cases where something of this sort occurred, the fact that underground hip hoppers claiming to hail from more humble backgrounds frequently make such allegations speaks to the notable presence of privileged college students and spoiled rich kids in their worldview.

As will become evident throughout the remainder of the book, underground hip hop's racial and class inclusivity does not extend across gender lines. In this regard, there is a stark contradiction between the subgenre's liberationist ideal—the belief that all people should be able to take part in hip hop regardless of race, ethnicity, class, gender, or any other category of collective identification—and the existing opportunity structures for participation which significantly privilege men over women. Some of this is undoubtedly connected to existing gender socialization norms, which presume men are predisposed to greater mastery of the technologies necessary for independent music production (Rietveld 1998; Schloss 2004). In addition, the informal apprenticeships, which in terms of underground hip hop typically involve the diffusion of particular skills and knowledge within home and sometimes bedroom settings, tend to be activities of male bonding that often discourage female involvement (Cohen 1991; Rose 1994). A number of popular music theorists have also explored the different ways in which young men and women engage music (Gracyk 2001; Straw 1997; Thornton 1995), differences that I believe have a strong bearing on one's interests in and perception of available avenues to becoming a performer. Yet there are other reasons more specific to the competitive and racially gendered (that is, modeled after particular notions of black masculinity) image of hip hop which severely restrict and regulate female participation. Several of these will be explicitly discussed in Chapter 5; however, some recognition of underground hip hop's distinctly (if not overtly) masculine temperament should accompany readers throughout the book.

The emergence of the underground hip hop subgenre offered opportunities for hip hop music production to middle-class, non-urban, non-black (male) consumers with artistic ambitions and inclinations. Where Music Industry gatekeepers sought to preserve and profit from an image of hip hop culture as rooted in impoverished urban blackness, underground hip hop's DiY mantra tipped the scales of participation toward those who could best access the specific technologies and financial resources necessary to create and release music on their own. The existence of underground hip hop as a subgenre is a testament to the claim that after close to thirty years as a popular culture commodity, hip hop music can be acknowledged as "a legitimate part of [the] cultural heritage" of many young Americans regardless of race or class (Strauss 1999, 28; see also Chapter 3). Certainly race remains relevant. It is clear to me that even within the most integrated multiracial hip hop settings, race-based identities do not participate on even terms. Both how someone is identified and how someone self-identifies inevitably impact the ways in which they attempt to situate themselves and how these efforts are received.

At the heart of such dialogues are debates and deliberations over non-black hip hoppers' (more specifically, emcees') legitimacy and merit that are rooted in questions concerning the nature of cultural diffusion, racial ability, and entitlement. One contention of mine, which underlies many of the core arguments of this book, is that the racial dynamics surrounding questions of underground hip hop racial authenticity parallel the liberal-democratic tendencies of American race relations, which are supported by both the MOOM census option and ideologies of color blindness. Within the world of underground hip hop specifically and multiracial American social settings more generally, the idea that race should not matter and the false consciousness (for some) that race does not matter gets consistently confronted by the fact that it does.

The Making of the Bay Area Scene

Thus far I have been discussing underground hip hop as a national music subgenre that developed principally in response to themes and sentiments that dominated Music Industry rap during the 1990s. While there are certainly good reasons to begin with this (subcultural) explanation of the subgenre's emergence, including the importance of establishing its anti-commercial character and nationwide ascendance, both my ethnographic approach and my interest in examining the social relationships and interpersonal exchanges that characterize underground hip hop's social spheres lead me to narrow my focus to a detailed accounting of the specific factors that gave way to the San Francisco Bay Area underground scene.

Within popular music scholarship the concept of the music scene is generally credited to Will Straw (1991) who, building off Pierre Bourdieu's (1984) notion of fields of cultural practice, first presented the scene as a localized, interaction-based alternative to the structural paradigms that dominated earlier work on music subcultures (see Hall and Jefferson 1976; Hebdige 1979). Music scenes can be understood as social spaces in which producers, musicians, and fans come together to create and sustain structures and sentiments of social cohesion through galvanized tastes, practices, interest, and values (Peterson and Bennett 2004; Shanks 1994). Approaching the Bay Area underground hip hop scene through this conceptual lens enhances awareness and appreciation of the links between musical production practices (most notably the creation and circulation of music commodities and public performances) and the social exchanges that constitute group membership. Furthermore, it acknowledges the different ways that individuals negotiate their participation and identification within collective music-oriented social affiliations. It is here where I believe the most fruitful prospects for connecting the performance of race with the development of informed racialized ideologies lie. Although scenes can be translocal and virtual (Bennett and Peterson 2004), the concept inherently suggests a sense of rootedness—in place(s) and space(s)—which permits a more thorough accounting of the impact of contemporary social processes on the identity formations of situated individuals.

The conditions that facilitated the development of the Bay Area underground hip hop scene include instances of cultural agency, creativity, and vision which were linked to changes in technology and the evolution of commercial rap music (as discussed above). This rise was undoubtedly stimulated by the region's longstanding countercultural ethos (see Becker and Horowitz 1971), which for the parents of today's Bay Area hip hop generation was highlighted by Berkeley's student-led anti-Vietnam War protests, the radical politics of Oakland's Black Panther Party, and the hippie movement centered in San Francisco's Haight-Ashbury district. The legacy of this earlier generation has had a profound impact on local knowledge and sensibilities, both of which inform the way that today's young Bay Area residents see themselves. Again, Rasta Cue Tip explains: "The Bay Area just has so much history. You've got the hippies and you've got the Black Panthers, in the same town! We're children of that out here. We vibe off that."

Embedded in such sentiments of place and past are strongly felt anti-establishment and activist convictions which, within the arena of hip hop, manifest as something that many people refer to as "the Bay Area hustle." This notion of "hustle" seems to saturate all varieties of local hip hop. It suggests a savvy, independent-minded business approach to life that willfully embraces nonconventional means of pursuing artistic and career ambitions.

One hip hop enthusiast I interviewed expressed the essence of this hustle through a series of successive phrases such as: "handle your business," "stay on top of your game," "make your own rules," and "get that money."

The locally recognized archetype of this hustler mentality is unquestionably an East Oakland rapper named Too $hort. Virtually all Bay Area hip hop artists, regardless of race, city, or subgenre, acknowledge Too $hort as the progenitor of their local scene. According to legend, sometime in the early 1980s Freemont High School sophomore Todd Shaw (aka Too $hort) began making and selling custom-made rap tapes which he recorded in his bedroom on "mismatched stereo equipment and a Radio Shack mixer . . . 'out the trunk' of an old, beat-up hooptie with no reverse" (Jam 1999, 220–201). Shaw has credited his entrepreneurial brilliance of marketing himself through the creation of individualized rap songs to a neighborhood drug dealer named Hot Lips: "One day we were just rapping and Hot Lips was like, 'I'm really not interested in what you're doing. I don't want to hear that shit. If you had my name in that shit, though, I'd play it.' And the next day we had a tape with his name in it and twenty bucks in our pocket" (Jam 1999, 220). Through this innovative approach to targeting a highly localized fan base, Too $hort (and partner Freddy B) were soon overwhelmed with requests from "pimps and players" wanting their names immortalized on a song. It is this image of Too $hort making locally relevant music in his bedroom, and manufacturing and distributing it on ready to sell on the street cassette tapes, that dominates the folklore of Bay Area hip hop.[27]

By 1988 Too $hort had parlayed his independent music making achievements into a record deal with Jive Zomba Records (Orr 1995), which became a springboard to a tremendously successful commercial career.[28] Similar stories of locally independent to nationally recognized success surround later Bay Area artists like E-40, Mac Mall, Mac Dre, and Spice One; as well as one time Bay Area resident and later No Limit Records entrepreneur Master P.[29]

While nearly all longtime Bay Area hip hop fans give a nostalgic nod to the songs and albums of these past greats, there is a clear distinction between the subjects and sensibilities that mark this variety of rap and those which the vast majority of Bay Area underground hip hop enthusiasts recognize as their own. Each of the aforementioned Bay Area artists continue to release music and maintain a local relevance; their often violent and sex-laden pimp anthems have inspired later generations of Bay Area artists including Andre Nikatina (aka Dre Dog), JT the Bigga Figga, Cellski, and the numerous artists currently associated with the Bay Area "hyphy movement" (see Braiker 2005; Hix 2006), such as Keak Da Sneak and Mister F.A.B.

Yet the differences in sound, sentiment, and racial demographics between this (also largely independent) Bay Area scene and the underground hip hop scene that I moved within are profoundly felt and, at least from the latter perspective, regularly commented on. San Francisco's DJ Mizzo explains: "If you went down to Hunters Point, I don't know what you would find. But there seems to be an increasing divide between black hip hop and the underground sort of multiethnic hip hop. . . . It seems like the kids in Hunters Point and you know, down in Oakland,[30] they're listening to different things than you and I are listening to." This point is crucial, for on the national (commercial) rap music radar, the Bay Area is far better known for its "hyphy"—sometimes referred to as "Yay Area" rap—sound than for the subterranean world of underground hip hop that this ethnographic study explores. As Mizzo's quote reveals, some underground hip hoppers were very forthright in identifying this as a racial divide. For others, however, this division was more commonly explained through the vocabulary of subgenre, with "underground hip hop" being contrasted to a style of rap music that before the term *hyphy* came into fashion was often simply referred to as "thug rap." On one occasion, I witnessed the tension between the two become consequential enough to spark a confrontation which nearly escalated into violence, all because a house party deejay was playing too much hip hop and not enough rap.

The coexistence of underground hip hop and thug rap illustrates what is referred to as contested definitions of "the local" (Bennett 2000, 52). Both formats form a branch of Bay Area independent hip hop music, yet together they embody competing definitions of hip hop authenticity that cannot always be reconciled. Regardless, the two are not mutually exclusive since underground artists and thug rap artists do collaborate. They are rather mutually implicated in defining one another through notions of sameness and difference. San Mateo's Rasco (who together with Planet Asia form the hip hop twosome Cali Agents) elaborates on these distinctions: "The Bay has a sound, but then again, it has different sounds. . . . You might have that E-40 Click mafia, what they call mob music. You might have that and recognize that a dude is from the Bay, and that's Bay Area music. But then again, you got different sounds like myself or Hiero or Zion I that make it what it is. Being out here kinda allows you to just be yourself" (Folklore 2004).

In his richly detailed history of Bay Area hip hop, Eric Arnold describes underground hip hop as inspired by "literate, middle-class bohemianism, japanimation, children's fairytales, grassroots activism, spoken word poetry and artistic improvisation" (2006, 79). The earliest examples of music fitting squarely within this category include songs recorded and released by the Bay Area collectives Hieroglyphics, Hobo Junction, Bored Stiff, and Solesides. While these were not the only Bay Area artists making what came to be considered underground hip hop music during the first part of the 1990s, their popularity and the fact that all four have endured into the current era justifies mentioning them here.[31] Of these groups, the Hieroglyphics collective (comprised of the groups Souls of Mischief, Extra Prolific, and the Prose, as well as solo artists Del the Funky Homosapien and Casual) was the most successful in expanding the popularity of this new non-gangsta Bay Area sound outside the region. Through a series of critically acclaimed releases on Jive Zomba and Elektra Records between 1991 and 1995, Hieroglyphics' artists gained large followings throughout North America, Europe, and Japan. Bay Area emcee Dope Cigars, who was living in Minneapolis when he first heard Del the Funky Homosapien's song "Eye Exam," recalled that experience and how the decidedly non-ghettocentric lyrics appealed to him as a white Midwestern teenager: "The [emcee] was like 'I'm chocolate like a bar but my name is not Rosanne' and I was like, 'what is this?' Like, this guy is rappin' and he's not even talking about being hard, he's not talking about shooting people, he's being super funny . . . and I started seeking out more things that I could identify with at that level."

The same qualities that made Hieroglyphics's artists appeal to a select group of consumers like Dope Cigars, also contributed to their mediocre (by Music Industry standards) commercial success. By the early nineties, ghettocentric tropes of "hard" rappers "shooting people," and not material like Del's clever and creative lyrical wordplay (see Arnold 2006), were dominating both the commercial hip hop radio airwaves and record store cash registers. Hieroglyphics, along with Los Angeles–based acts like Aceyalone (of Freestyle Fellowship) and the Pharcyde, were some of the only West Coast underground hip hop artists at the time to release music of any notable consequence through major record labels.[32]

In 2006, it was reported that "not a single major record company has offices in the Bay" (Arnold 2006, 82). Rasta Cue Tip, in a tone that was very much in-line with his one-time bandmate Rasco's comment (above) about artistic freedom and being yourself, elaborated: "We've never had the major labels here so we've never had the influx of that political system. We've never had somebody telling us 'this is the shit, this is not the shit.' We've never had nobody tell us, 'you can't put this out, we're putting this out instead.' We've never had nobody telling us that so it's let us have our freedom of expression."

Over the years, this lack of Music Industry presence has forced local hip hop artists to embrace independent production and distribution practices as "a way of life" (Keast 1999).[33] In fact, since the days of Too $hort, the Bay Area scene has featured an informal network of music distribution that includes both hand-to-hand sales (aka "tape slangin'") and the willingness of prominent retail outlets such as Amoeba Music and Leopold's in Berkeley and T's Wauzi in Oakland to carry local music (Arnold 2006; see also Orr 1995). At the height of the tape slangin' era, some artists were reporting selling as many as forty to fifty underground hip hop cassettes in a day (Jam 1997).

By the late nineties, as the Internet became more prominent in many Americans' lives, Bay Area underground hip hop artists were quick to embrace it. San Francisco deejay Gammaray recalled that his first experience with underground tapes came via AOL.com:"I was on the Internet, on AOL. There was this hip hop room and I'd go there and someone was saying 'tapes for sale.' And I was like 'Whoa! That's cool.' I was like 'Yeah. Can I get one?' So I sent him five dollars and he sent me a tape. . . . [The person] was Karma [from Kemetic Suns]."

Not long after being released from their various record label contracts, Hieroglyphics resurfaced as champions of the early underground hip hop movement via a homegrown website (www.hieroglyphics.com) and the independent Hieroglyphics Imperium record label (see Ducker 2004b). In many respects, setting up a website or "hustling" tapes on hip hop discussion boards paralleled the DiY distribution practices most local artists had been raised on. Within the technology-savvy Bay Area, for many—including a healthy number of underground hip hop culture brokers—it was a small jump from the local to the virtual.

Underground hip hop's capacity to blur distinctions between musicians and fans, and thus serve as a genuine twenty-first century folk music (Harrison 2006), is unprecedented. At the start of 2001, the head hip hop buyer at Amoeba Music in San Francisco reported that an estimated 70 to 75 percent of all local music brought into the store by artists themselves (for retail sales) fell under the category of hip hop.[34] The Bay Area artists whom she and other underground hip hop retailers I interviewed credited most with establishing the blueprint which "all these kids have taken a page from" was not Too $hort, E-40, or Hieroglyphics, but a nine-member collective called the Living Legends.

During the latter half of the 1990s, "The Legends"—consisting of the duo Mystik Journeymen and solo artists Aesop, Arata, Bicasso, Eligh, Murs, Scarub, and the Grouch—used a relentless approach to recording and self-releasing their music to build one of the largest and most loyal fan bases in the Bay. Between 1994 and 2001, the collective released over fifty full-length albums. Combined with EPs, singles, sampler albums, and music recorded in conjunction with official members of the Legends' extended family, their total number of musical products released during this period exceeds one hundred; far and away the most prolific recording artists (to my knowledge) in hip hop at the time. Their ability to do this was predicated on recording practices which accentuated the virtues of limited music production capabilities through a minimalist aesthetic that was supported by promotional slogans like "unsigned and hella [very] broke" and "keep the four-track alive." By ardently championing the authenticity of gritty, low-fidelity recordings sold on crudely put together underground tapes (Harrison 2006), each Living Legends artist averaged over one release per year for a period of seven years.

The Mystic Journeymen, who were among the most visible "tape slangers" during the heyday of curbside cassette sales at key Bay Area sites like Telegraph Avenue in Berkeley, alone released seven full-length cassettes between 1995 and 1997. In addition to this, the group performed regularly at

FIGURE 1.1   Mystik Journeymen: "Fuck Commercial Radio" Sheeple Image. (*Artwork by GM5.*)

small venues throughout Northern California; continually expanded their fan base through a well-run website (originally www.mystik-journeymen .com, later www.llcrew.com); and self-funded several regional, national, and international tours (see Ducker 2004a). In the words of one Bay Area artist, by the late nineties the Legends had built "an empire the likes of which had never been seen in the bay area."[35]

The most celebrated version of the Living Legends' success, which is circulated in underground hip hop folklore throughout the Bay Area and beyond, was aptly captured in a 2001 article by James Dunn:

> Motley crew of emcee rebels throws middle finger to the evil record industry and eliminates the middleman, setting up shop on the Internet and selling its homemade albums on the streets. They roam the globe continuously, crashing venues from Europe to Australia to perform and slang tapes until they raise enough cash to cop tickets to their next destination. They have the time of their lives spreading their audio gospel across the world, each city greets them like returning royalty, record executives eat shit and everyone else lives happily ever after. (2001, 23)

While there were certainly enough people I met who did not care for (or in a few cases did not even know) the Living Legends' music, I still maintain that it would not be inaccurate to characterize the underground hip hop scene I moved within as comprised of the next generation of Bay Area artists to follow directly from the Legends. A majority of the people I spent time with (particularly many of those I was closest to) were, at one time or another, Living Legends' fans, and could therefore place many of their own DiY activities into a local tradition in which the Legends were pivotally situated. Several of the artists I was closest to had collaborated on songs with Legends' members. A few of them had even opened for the Legends at one time or another in their careers. Furthermore, a couple of people, in expressions of gushing fandom, spoke of a time when they considered themselves among the "biggest Legends' fans in the world." On the occasion of attending a Living Legends' show, I could be quite certain that I would see a lot of people I knew from my various ethnographic travels. And when Access, the owner and operator of the Living Legends' website, gave me a stack of "LL Crew" stickers to pass to select Amoeba Music customers, most of the people to whom I handed one immediately recognized the name (some even asked for extras). Still, I hesitate to simply describe this community as Living Legends' descendants. I believe it is more accurate to think of them as a group of people who can trace a direct lineage of DiY production and distribution, as well as certain aesthetic conventions, to a number of influential mid-nineties Bay Area hip hop artists (including the Legends, Hieroglyphics, Solesides, Bored Stiff, Kemetic Suns, Sacred Hoop, and Hobo Junction).[36]

Where the lines between producers and consumers blur, where "every emcee's a fan and every fan's an emcee" (Harrison 2004), the demographic characteristics of the community of artists begin to resemble those of the population at large. In underground hip hop this is true at least as far as race is concerned. Many of the foundational Bay Area underground hip hop collectives included prominent non-black members. For instance, the Living Legends featured two white emcees and a third who was Japanese; Solesides included members with recognizable Asian, Latino, and European bloodlines. In fact, with the exception of Hieroglyphics and Hobo Junction (both exclusively African American), all the Bay Area underground hip hop groups I have mentioned in this chapter have been comprised of racially mixed members.

I have already discussed how shifts that prioritized music-making technologies and finances over any strong sense of racial or cultural identification worked to racially diversify underground hip hop on the whole. Within the Bay Area, the presence of non-African American role models also played an important part in the scene's diversification. Racial role modeling has a powerful influence on many popular cultural forms. In professional sports, for example, there are numerous examples of athletes in a particular position or sport and of a notable race (e.g., a black quarterback) inspiring others of that same race to follow in their footsteps. The same dynamic holds true in music. Historically white artists with black sounds—think of Elvis, the Righteous Brothers, or the New Kids on the Block—have inspired large numbers of similar white performers. In the global competitive deejay scene, the successes of a handful of Filipino Americans in national and worldwide competitions at that start of the nineties inspired future Filipino deejays, thus "forever changing the racial path of hip hop" (Sue 2002).

Although white rappers like the Beastie Boys, 3rd Bass, and Eminem have all sparked significant followings of European American hip hoppers who resembled them in appearance and disposition, none have had any substantial long-term impact on the number of white emcees releasing music through the Music Industry. In Bay Area underground hip hop, however, the staunchly DiY ethos combined with the social proximity of artists to fans to facilitate a handful of non-black artists' (including: the Grouch and Eligh of the Living Legends [see Figure 1.2]; Equipto, Mint Rock, Mic, and TD Camp of Bored Stiff [see Figure 1.3]; King Koncepts of Kemetic Suns; and Lateef and Lyrics Born of Solesides) roles in diversifying an entire genera-tion of Bay Area emcees. As San Francisco State sociologist Andreana Clay remarked, in the Bay Area "hip hop's multiracial face . . . is simply accepted as a matter of fact" (quoted in Watkins 2005, 164).

The salience of identifications between Bay Area hip hop artists and fans is perhaps most strongly experienced in the interpersonal exchanges

FIGURE 1.2   The Living Legends. L to R: (standing) Aesop, the Grouch, Eligh, Luckyiam, Scarub, Bicasso; (crouching) Sunspot Jonz, (sitting) Murs. (*Photograph courtesy of Snap Jackson.*)

FIGURE 1.3   Bored Stiff. L to R: Dubstar, Mint Rock, Mic, TD Camp, Equipto, Big Shawn, and P-Way. *(Photograph courtesy of TD Camp.)*

surrounding the phenomenon of tape slangin' on the street or at music shows. Oakland Emcee Kirby Dominant expounded on the significance of these interactions:

> KD: To the consumer, in their head they were like "well, I see [the cassette tape] here [in the store] but I'm just gonna go to Telegraph [Ave.] and buy it from those cats. I'll catch 'em out there."
>
> AKH: And as a consumer did that mean more?
>
> KD: Yeah. Cause it was cheaper and you met the dude. You felt somethin'. You bought it right from the dude.

Similarly, DJ Gammaray recalled the sensations of profound connectedness that he felt while listening to his first Kemetic Suns underground tape, which he had purchased "right from the dude" over the Internet: "It was low quality but at the same time I could tell they really meant what they were saying . . . and it was from the Bay so I could identify with it."

As hip hop consumers venture into the realm of production, the experience of being "out there," of having their own product available, validates their sense of belonging to the scene by way of being an active agent within it. Popular music scholar Simon Frith (1987) has commented on music's remarkable ability to convey a sense of possession ("that's my music" or "this is our song") to fans. He attributes some of this to the circulation of music as a commodity form. Yet it is often the production of these commodities that creates the strongest sense of music ownership and entitlement. "Until you got an album out man, you can't really say nothing," Bored Stiff's Professor Whaley explained to me, "like, I'm not really one to be talkin' [on what hip hop should or shouldn't be] until I can put an album in your hands."

Starting at an early age, often through the influence of older siblings, today's underground hip hoppers came to regard specific music commodities and the technologies necessary to produce them as coveted objects through which participation within hip hop could be realized. In this way, the music-making practices surrounding underground hip hop can be thought of as activities of "self in process" (Frith 1996, 109). The commitment and shared narratives that underlie the creation of music within a given genre both individually and collectively distinguish music makers from other members of their local community. This identity as artist(s)/musician(s) operating within a specific field (Bourdieu 1984) gives way to new dimensions of authenticity forming around specific tastes, skills, and sensibilities; or, what has been called subcultural capital (Thornton 1995). As such, participation in music can come to supersede other aspects of social affinity (Fornäs, Lindberg, and Sernhade 1995). Within underground hip hop scenes particularly, these identifications are often oriented around a belief in the transformative and transcendent qualities of music to engender a color-blind ideology (Rodriguez 2006) that is in direct contrast to the integrities of race expressed within commercial rap music.

Frith commented that music both confirms and confuses social identity (1987, 149). Some of the most compelling democratic dialogues on race in American popular culture take place within underground hip hop, where largely middle-class, multiracial constituencies of young people navigate a transforming racial landscape. At the surface, Bay Area underground hip hoppers are able to bypass the tensions and anxieties that saturate discourses on hip hop and racial identity by cultivating a sense of belonging to a hip hop world in which race does not impact a person's ability to participate. Looking below the surface, however, it is clear that race is still important. With this acknowledged, what is most central to my project is understanding the ways in which participation in multiracial underground hip hop scenes facilitate novel and at times improvised approaches to racial identification and sociality.

Both the creation and consumption of music and its impact on the fashioning of identities need to be recognized as dialogic processes. The music scene, as a conceptual framework, allows researchers to contextualize the nexus of relations and transactions through which situationally racialized identities take shape. In order to best achieve this, these dynamics of identity formation and negotiation need to be explored through a reflexive ethnographic approach that acknowledges the researcher as an engaged participant in the meaning-making activities taking place within the social arenas they inhabit. In the next chapter, I paint a portrait of my own ethnographic experiences as a means of fleshing out this picture of the Bay Area underground hip hop world I became a part of.

2

Experiencing the Bay

The racial, ethnic, and (authentically) hip hop subjectivities that are at the core of this study involve dynamic and nuanced ongoing mediations. In representing these, *Hip Hop Underground* takes a critically reflexive ethnographic approach that situates the researcher as an interactive participant within the field of study. This "truly participatory participant-observation" (Cooley 1997, 4) facilitated countless instances of ethnographic disclosure, discovery, and understanding. Sharing in the everyday activities of underground hip hop artists and enthusiasts enhanced my familiarity and sense of affinity with this community, thus providing me with valuable insights into the contours of racial boundaries and how they are navigated. This closeness also compelled a persistent recognition of the ways in which my own identity was deeply embedded in the research process (Tsuda 1998; see also Bowman 1997; Narayan 1993; Slocum 1975; Srinivas, Shah, and Ramaswamy 1979). Critical ethnography has been described as a "culturally and socially active" type of research that explores the effects of sociological categories—such as race, class, and gender—on the lived experiences of researchers and the people they work among (Alsup 2004, 219–220). Inherently reflexive, such research pays particular attention to the intersectional dynamics (of such categories) that manifest through ethnographic endeavors. Like other critical ethnographers, I begin from the premise that the research process cannot and should not be separated from the interpretation and representation of findings (Babiracki 1997; D'Amico-Samuels 1991; Titon 1997). As such, this chapter serves as both a methodological treatise and a thickly descriptive (Geertz 1973) portrayal of the researcher and the underground hip hop world that he worked within.

The overarching principles that guide my research align with anthropology's post-positivist, postmodern, reflexive turn—what some have labeled "the new ethnography" (Denzin 1998)—the seeds for which were set during the late 1960s and early 1970s. Although understood as resulting from a confluence of factors, for many anthropologists this disciplinary shift begins with the 1967 posthumous publication of Bronislaw Malinowski's field diaries (made up entirely of entries written a half-century earlier and presumably never intended for publication). Remarkably, it was the appearance of what some have described as a "boring," repetitious, and otherwise unremarkable book (Firth 1989) which set off a controversy in the anthropological community that was responsible for pressing the issue of researcher subjectivity into the methodological foreground: "To discover that the founding father of modern fieldwork did not in every respect live up to [his own] methodological prescriptions . . . was bad enough; to hear him belaboring as 'niggers' the Trobrianders whose 'outlook on things' and 'vision of the world' he sought to represent seemed to expose an hypocrisy at the heart of anthropology" (Stocking 1990, 110).[1]

Fueled in large part by the rise of feminist anthropology (see, for example, Ortner 1974; Reiter 1975; Rosaldo and Lamphere 1974) and native anthropology (Jones 1970; Nakhleh 1979; Srinivas 1979),[2] over the next quarter century concerns arising from Malinowski's *A Diary in the Strict Sense of the Term* prompted "a loosening of attitudes about the publication of intimate details of [the researcher's] personal life" (Firth 1989, xxix) and caused anthropologists to take a more critical look at the relationship between ethnographic methods, observations, and intentions and the politics that surround them.

Although efforts like Dell Hymes's project to *Reinvent Anthropology* (1969) and Clifford Geertz's (1973) interpretive reading of culture are regarded as important works in the rise of critical ethnography,[3] for many (see, for example, Mascia-Lees, Sharpe, and Cohen 1989; Pool 1991) the seminal moment in this disciplinary shift occurred in the mid-eighties with the publication of James Clifford and George Marcus's edited volume *Writing Culture* (1986) and George Marcus and Michael Fischer's *Anthropology as Cultural Critique* (1986). Falling under the collective label "postmodern anthropologists," proponents of this approach mounted an attack on ethno-graphic objectivity by placing the rhetorical practices of ethnographic repre-sentation at the center of their analysis (Jacobson 1991; Marcus and Cushman 1982). Much of this work was founded on critiques of both the empiricist position that claims the existence of a reality independent of consciousness (Friedman 1987; Lopate 1979) and the positivist belief that such a reality is knowable (Rabinow 1986; Rosaldo 1989; Wolf 1996).

A second critical gaze fell on the politics of ethnographic research. Here the members of the "Rice [University] Circle"—as researchers Mar-cus, Fischer, Stephen Tyler, and their affiliates were also known (Pool 1991)—challenged the standard perception of a neat participant-observation dichotomy by calling attention to the dialogic nature of all ethnographic projects. This "intersubjective turn" (Jackson 1998, 6) underscored the rela-tionship between ethnographers' identities, the experiences they engender, and the processes through which researchers come to know about a society (Clifford 1986).

I would be remiss to not mention the considerable backlash against post-modern anthropology (see, for example, Fardon 1992; Kuper 1994, 1999; Sangren 1988). One of the most compelling critiques was lodged by feminist scholars, many of whom questioned the degree to which anthropological postmodernism succeeded in transcending the discipline's colonial (and male-dominated) heritage. Many feminist anthropologists found it notable that the end of objectivity (or Truth with a capital "T") was occurring at precisely the moment when women and members of traditionally studied communities began entering the dialogue (Di Stefano 1990; Harding 1987; Harstock 1987). Responding to *Writing Culture's* conspicuous failure to ac-knowledge feminist scholarship, Pat Caplin noted that "when women were using the experimental approach to ethnographic writing, much of it was dismissed as 'self-indulgence'" (1988, 16; also see Wolf 1992). Frances Mascia-Lees, Patricia Sharpe, and Colleen Cohen echoed these sentiments when they explained that "like European explorers discovering the New World, Clifford and his colleagues perceive a new and uninhabited space where, in fact, feminists have long been at work" (1989, 14).

None of this withstanding, the Rice Circle, perhaps owing to their privileged status as mostly white men, played an important role in shifting the debates over ethnographic subjectivity, reflexivity, and forms of repre-sentations from the margins of anthropology to the center of the discipline. Today even the most stodgily traditional anthropologists will accept what Raymond Firth, in a somewhat defensive tone, admitted over 70 years ago:

that "some account of the relations of the anthropologist to his [sic] people is relevant to the nature of his [sic] results" (1983 [1936], 10).

Joseph Schloss sees ethnography as a "grievously underutilized" (2004, 6) resource in scholarship on hip hop, not to mention popular music studies more generally (Cohen 1993). As a mode of research that recognizes sociality as shaped through ongoing communicative behavior (expressed through any medium, including speech), and acknowledges how continual assessments, modifications, and reorientations are fundamental to constructions of identity, ethnography offers a means to critically and analytically engage the dynamics of situational racialization that are fundamental to hip hop authenticity (Maxwell 2002). My contention that the integrities of racial distinction in twenty-first-century America are shifting from the objective to the subjective—from fixed race categories to contextually and circumstantially enacted performances of race—is supported through a detailed account of lived human experiences. Locating the researcher (myself) within the dynamic construction of the situations and circumstances where race gets performed results in a more meaningful representation of its implications and relevance.

Multiracial hip hop scenes present a particularly fruitful arena to examine these dynamics, in part because hip hop credibility also involves a dialogic negotiation and performance of self that gets reconstituted in each new social instance. The contested terrain of hip hop "subcultural capital" (Thornton 1995) is measured through forms of self-presentation—involving language, dress, attitude, and artistic proficiency—that get initiated anytime an awareness of hip hop subjectivity exists. Whether competitive or cooperative, hip hop sociality is a dramaturgical (Goffman 1959; see also Frith 1996) endeavor involving a measured assessment of self and others, particularly when the parties coming into contact have little to no history of interaction. For Bay Area underground hip hoppers, locating where race and hip hop intersect is often a highly personal, contingent, and elusive endeavor that cannot simply be mapped through standard social science categories and strictly empirical research methods.

Ethnographic data is gained through social transactions between researchers and members of the community they work within. In the interest of showing this, the remainder of this chapter can be viewed as an effort to both personalize the researcher and socialize the research process (Brown and Dobrin 2004, 9). In the following pages, I weave together various autobiographical and field narratives to form a series of ethnographic snapshots that detail the shifting positions and circumstances that shaped and defined my research experiences. Such radically reflexive (Best 2007) self-disclosure is important to establishing a sound basis for evaluating the interpretations and analyses presented in later chapters (Abu-Lughod 1988; see also Jacobson 1991; Tsuda 1998).

Situating the Researcher

The following patchwork of autobiographical episodes is intended to situate me, as both a researcher and subject, within the dynamics of race and subcultural legitimacy that saturate hip hop. Like other aspects of new ethnography, autobiography has a firm history in feminist anthropology. In the 1930s and 1940s, Franz Boas's student Zora Neale Hurston produced a series of auto-ethnographic texts—most notably *Mules and Men* (1990 [1935]) and *Dust Tracks on a Road* (1991 [1942])—that are regarded as "ancestors" of this tradition (Straight 2002, 3; see also Boxwell 1992; Domina 1997). As an African American who wrote about African American life, Hurston's "figural anthropology of the self" (Lionnet-McCumber 1993, 242) is an apt example in that her race and closeness to the subject of her work also epitomize the history of autoethnography among non-white and native anthropologists (see Jones 1970; Srinivas 1979). In presenting my own personal history, I highlight aspects of race, ethnicity, social class, gender, and geographic background. By framing my experiences within these conventional sociological categories, I hope to illustrate both their utility and limitations as analytical frameworks. Ultimately, I mean to show that contemporary social subjectivities are more fluid and conditional than traditional classifications allow (Narayan 1993).

Any disclosure of an ethnographer's personal background can be illuminating. This is especially true in projects where the researcher is a member of, or is close to, the community he or she works among (Davies 1999). The trajectories of most ethnographic endeavors invariably slope toward increased participation and belonging. My relationship to the underground hip hop scene I worked within can at once be described as outside researcher, marginal native, and fully integrated and implicated native anthropologist. Attempting to sort this out requires some understanding of the person I was when I first entered the scene.

MARCH 1992
"Ohhhh, so you're a country boy," Bekah said as her pickup truck reached the plateau of the hill. The last house we had passed was now a quarter mile back. Her insight seemed to be accompanied by a good deal of per-

sonal satisfaction at the recognition that we shared this in common. This occasion found me in the best of spirits: it was the start of a weeklong spring break during my final semester at the University of Massachusetts, Amherst; I was in the midst of celebrating a recent flurry of momentum within a courtship that I had been passively pursuing since the holidays; and I was now using the coincidence of our having grown up in the same part of the state to solicit a ride home and, more importantly, spend additional quality time with Bekah.

After another quarter mile across mid-mountain flats, the dark blue Ford resumed its ascent until it reached my parents home a thousand feet above the quaint western Massachusetts village of Shelburne Falls. The next morning, following a series of chance events, Bekah and I would meet again, this time in a bright café just off the Williams College campus in Williamstown. Waiting at a table near the window, I had no trouble spotting her—short crimson-dyed hair, dark sunglasses, three-quarter length black leather jacket, black stretch pants, and black Doc Martin boots—as she made her way across the wintry college-town street to join me. An award-winning painter (who had recently returned from a year in Rome), a high school state finalist in cross-country skiing, a hip hop enthusiast, and someone who was generally regarded as a "friend" of the UMass black community, Bekah did not fit my image of a "country girl."

Bekah and I were both kids from rural upbringings (she actually lived on a dirt road) who, upon entering college, were able to use the flexibility offered us by our parents' social class and cosmopolitan backgrounds to transcend this aspect of our identity. Both of us were able to position ourselves favorably within the urban/rural hierarchy that was the basis for popularity in many social circles at UMass, particularly the aforementioned black community. I distinctly recall one of the first times a group of UMass friends from the greater Boston area visited me at my parents' home. Upon greeting me, they mutually expressed their bewilderment about how a place like Shelburne Falls—a town of roughly 2,000 people—could produce a person like me. Of course, the very question rings of an uninformed perception of a homogenized rural experience that endures through existing stereotypes. Nestled midway between the five colleges of the Pioneer Valley (i.e. Amherst College, Hampshire College, Mount Holyoke College, Smith College, and UMass-Amherst) and Williams College, the population of western Franklin County (or the "hilltowns" as they are often called), for which Shelburne Falls is the largest village, includes high concentrations of academics, artisans, and other working intellectuals.[4] Together they make up a much worldlier and politically progressive community than typical views of the rural allow.

Bekah and I were among several people I knew at UMass who, through their social existence, challenged popular perceptions of this categorization. I had the explicit advantage of having an African American social identity, a marker that for most people on New England college campuses meant "from the city." However, this advantage was by no means a forgone conclusion. There were plenty of examples of African American students from much larger towns in the Amherst area who I had casually regarded as more urban, yet once they arrived at UMass were ruthlessly cast as "Uncle Toms" or "sell-outs" by a black community that made a practice of intensely scrutinizing their own.[5] For me, this marker of race was firmly supported by an interest in hip hop music (another perceived indication of urbanism). During my first semester at UMass, I acquired a reputation among my black friends as someone who had a lot of hip hop cassette tapes. In four years of campus living, my circle of friends regularly enjoyed spending time in my rooms in large part because I had music that people liked.

CHRISTMAS EVE 1984

My parents had a tradition of allowing my brother and me to open one gift on the night before Christmas. That year we both decided to open presents from our cousin Leslie, the daughter of my father's sister who at the time was living just outside of Boston. The Fat Boys and Whodini cassettes that we unwrapped that evening were the first of what for me would become an extensive collection of hip hop music; by the following summer, I was firmly committed to buying any hip hop album that came out. When I reflect on this period in my life, and how in less than a year two hip hop tapes turned into over a dozen, a couple of explanations come to mind. The first might simply be that for the area I grew up in, I had an early exposure and appreciation of a new music style that over the next fifteen years would become one of the most popular in America. The second, more socioanalytic explanation has to do with how hip hop came to shape my identity as an African American within a predominantly white high school. I am quite certain that these factors complemented one another. I would not have thrown myself into hip hop as I did had I not enjoyed it, and its rise in popularity strongly suggests that this enjoyment was not an act of self-determination. But hip hop, as a distinctly black urban music form, was congruent with an identity that I was interested in cultivating for myself.

OCTOBER 1981

On the Monday following a parents' weekend, Steven, a new seventh grader at the small private school I attended, came up to me and said, "I *saw* your father; he doesn't look anything like you." During his first month at school, Steven's irritability and terse classroom manner had cast him in the role of the new student my crew of sixth graders most enjoyed picking on. However, this one speech act effectively redefined the power dynamics of our relationship. In mentioning my father, Steven was not only revealing that he was aware my father was white but also making it clear that he recognized this knowledge as a potential weapon against me.

My father always maintained that he saw his interracial marriage and children as a social filter. "Anyone who has a problem with my wife and children being black is simply not someone that I want anything to do with," he would say. More than a set delineation between racists and nonracists, dad's words indicated a conceptual separation between what he saw as sophisticated cosmopolitanism versus redneck provincialism. As a young adolescent with a budding sense of self, I had difficulties embracing my father's philosophy. I was embarrassed by the contradiction between his white racial identity and my black one. I desired to be "normal." By the time I was in high school, however, my father's race had gradually stopped being the source of discomfort it had been. And by my freshmen year at UMass, I had come to terms with my interraciality enough to respond to an African American friend's jokes that "Kwame has a white man's mouth and a black man's lips" or "a white man's brain and a black man's jumping ability" with emotional indifference.

A high school guidance counselor once told my father that she thought the fact that my older brother was one of only two African Americans in his graduating class made him more popular among his peers.[6] Cobie was a football star; I was nothing close to one. However, I recall one time when as a freshman approaching the practice field with pads on and a freshly shaved head, all the older players (in admiration of my hair cut) commented that I looked like a member of a professional team. It was this isolated admiration of African Americans (even if primarily as athletes and entertainers) that made my association with hip hop a significant factor in the niche of popularity that I carved for myself while in high school.

Hip hop was not always so kind to me. When the break dancing craze reached the hilltowns during the mid-eighties, there were times when my racial identity drew an unwanted spotlight. One such occasion was during a summer festival held annually in the neighboring town of Rowe (population 351). It was late afternoon and my friends and I had been outside for the majority of the day visiting the various booths and activities. We had finally wandered over to the open doors of the elementary school gymnasium where inside there seemed to be a great deal of excitement. They were playing hip hop—Nucleus's "Jam On It." The song's introduction transformed what for most of the afternoon had been a typical daytime dance event into a break-dancing exhibition. In the middle of a large circle of people, two (possibly three) African Americans[7] took turns popping and locking in front of a crowd that *seemed like* hundreds.

What happened next, I can only place in the blurred realm that journalist Michael Ignatieff (1993) described as somewhere between memory and fantasy.[8] I remember standing in the back of the audience, just close enough to have a good view, when suddenly in mid-move one of the dancers noticed me (probably as the only nonparticipating black face in the room) and extended his arm as if to offer me entry into the circle. Instantly, without full recognition of if this was what had actually happened, I was out the door walking briskly toward the lake. The embarrassment of being singled out as a black person who could not break dance was terrifying enough to cause me to act as if I suddenly had a strong desire to see what was happening elsewhere. I did not say good-bye or explain my actions to anyone. I just turned and went. As I hurried to get as far away from the gym as possible, I hoped that no one else had noticed what had happened and, at the same time, wondered what the other kid would be thinking about our instantaneous exchange.

My relationship with hip hop as a consumer and collector of music was far more favorable. During the mid-eighties, with only a few hip hop albums coming out per year, it was possible to have a near complete collection. The local record store, in the neighboring hub of Greenfield (population 18,168), was good enough; and when traveling to larger cities, I took every opportunity to go music shopping. Most weekend evenings (particularly before many of my friends had a driving license) were spent staying up all night taping UMass and University of Connecticut hip hop radio shows.

One of my most telling high school experiences, an episode that highlighted my growing understanding that despite my rural isolation I had acquired a knowledge and interest in hip hop music that was comparable to teenagers from more urban backgrounds, occurred when our basketball team hosted a pre-season practice/scrimmage weekend with a team from the Eastern part of the state.[9] The general idea was to have players from our team host (including room, board, and other non-basketball time) players from the other school. Just prior to the visit, my coach approached me with the request that I host one of the African American players on the other team, who had specifically asked to spend the weekend with a black family.

Arnell and I ended up having a great time together. We mostly sat in my room and listened to hip hop. He was particularly excited when I played two brand new songs ("Going back to Cali" by LL Cool J and "Bring the Noise" by Public Enemy) off of the *Less Than Zero* soundtrack, which he had not yet heard. For our Saturday night project of filling a ninety-minute blank cassette with music, both songs were "must haves." Sunday, after our final scrimmage, as the other team prepared to board their bus and return home, I felt a strong sense of pride as I watched several of the Eastern Mass kids gather around Arnell and his boombox eager to hear these two new songs that he had told them about.

This experience, and others like it, impressed on me the degree of hip hop subcultural capital that I had accrued despite my rural background. I was fortunate to grow up in an area that had several boarding schools and colleges.[10] This influx of young people from more urban environments combined with college (and prep school) radio's general principles of patchwork programming—different genres of music in different time slots on different days—and commitment to playing music that commercial stations generally did not created a remarkably hip hop friendly radio environment. I spent my high school years idolizing the African American personalities of UMass radio, and spent my college years living among them.

AUTUMN 1985

As a high school sophomore, I wrote my first rap while lying in bed watching "The Cosby Show." Earlier that day, I had proposed the idea to my friend Jake. He agreed that it was a fine idea, and even offered a topic: "you catch your wife cheating on you with another guy and go crazy and kill them both."[11] Jake also provided me with what would become a locally legendary first line: "start it off like this, 'Listen to the story you might not care, but I was down to the office in my big armchair.'" Over the next few years, the "Armchair Rap" would receive positive praise whenever performed. One of the most spectacular episodes in "Armchair Rap" folklore happened when a good friend, who had transferred to a rival high school, performed the rap to what he reported was a standing ovation in front of his entire school during a football pep rally (apparently the hip hop taboo of using someone else's rhymes was completely lost on him).

Through the course of that school year, the success of this first attempt at rhyme writing led to an entire notebook filled with verses. Although my output slackened after that first year, I continued to write quite regularly throughout high school. And when I got to UMass, I was still writing a few rhymes each year.

As a hip hop performer, there were only a couple of phases in my undergraduate years during which I was active in any capacity. One started when I approached the stage at an off-campus house party with my hands raised in the air to show my support of an all-white funk band covering the song "Rapper's Delight." Immediately one of the band members got on the microphone and said, "we're not really good at this. If anyone out there can rap better feel free to come up." It was quite obvious that he was responding to my (one of conspicuously few African Americans at the party) sudden interest. Before I had an opportunity to decline, my roommate and another friend shoved me onto the stage. I ended up doing an extremely well received version of the "Armchair Rap," and for the remainder of that school year I was invited to perform with the band whenever they played locally.

A few years later, I entered the graduate program in anthropology at Syracuse University. My time in Amherst had provided me with sound intellectual foundations in both the social construction of race and the interpersonal and political dynamics of identity formation. This was shaped, in no small part, through advanced coursework with racial theorists like Robert Gooding-Williams Jr., Enoch (Helán) Page, and Robert Paynter. I originally went to Syracuse with the intention of studying the relationship between folk art and identity in Ghana, the West African nation where I was born and where half of my family still resides. The idea of researching hip hop in graduate school was suggested to me after a series of unforeseen events resulted in my giving talks on hip hop, first to several undergraduate folklore classes and later as part of the Syracuse Anthropology Department's lunchtime lecture series. At the time, I had only recently become exposed to the emerging world of West Coast underground hip hop, yet the conspicuous racial diversity of the Bay Area scene (and underground hip hop more generally) intrigued me and matched a longstanding interest in race and identity that I had developed back at UMass.

Situating the Research

The immediate settings and personal experiences that form the crux of my research occur at the intersection of four distinct, yet interconnected, strands of experience: (1) Amoeba Music, where I worked forty hours each week; (2) my frequent forays into the San Francisco nightlife with, notably, my two companions on most of these outings; (3) a weekly hip hop open-microphone event that I attended regularly; and (4) the crew of emcees and producers with whom I recorded music. By taking readers into *my world*—the underground hip hop world that I came into contact with and, through my own agency, helped to construct—my intentions are threefold. First, I want to convey a vivid account of my everyday ethnographic experiences in the Bay Area. Second, in keeping with the dialogic and reflexive nature of my approach, I aim to show how ethnographers both intentionally engage and unwittingly get caught up in the individual lives and communities of the people they work among (Shelemay 1997). And third, as a transition from the preceding autobiography into a more situated autoethnographic narrative, I hope to illustrate just how straightforward, seamless, and at times serendipitous it was to integrate myself into the world of Bay Area underground hip hop.

Anthropologist Irma McClaurin considers "autoethnography" to be a product of the "self-endowed" status as an insider within the community of study (2001, 67). When considering the shifting identities of both researchers and their subjects and the ways in which they are transformed through the ethnographic encounter, it becomes quite obvious that such insider/outsider delineations are never as clear as we imagine. Ethnographers exist in a space "betwixt and between" the (largely academic) worlds they come from and the communities they work within (Straight 2002; see also Schloss 2004). My goal here is to present the spaces and places where my research took shape and the personal circumstances under which it occurred; however, as an introduction to my fieldwork and in the spirit of classic ethnography, I begin with an arrival story.

Getting Settled

Once I chose the Bay Area as the place to conduct my research, my most immediate challenge was to decide on the appropriate course of action to organize the standard year (minimum) of field residence. Through serendipitous good fortune, within my first two weeks in the Bay I was offered a job at Amoeba Music's San Francisco store. Amoeba was not in the habit of hiring temporary employees. In response to an initial letter of inquiry into the possibility of my working there, Karen, the store's manager, had sent me a polite email stating that in retail "a year goes by in the blink of an eye and with the volume of [the] store, it is hard to even begin to get a feel and get in a groove by the first year." Still, she had noticed that my two previous bosses were also named Karen. "Do you think that is fate?" she asked in her message, "and if so, what does that mean for this Karen and Amoeba??" This was enough to get me an interview, which turned into a job. Widely regarded within the underground hip hop scene as "the place" to get music in the Bay, my job at Amoeba held the dual virtues of being a source of income and a position through which I could facilitate interactions with hip hop artists and fans. For these reasons, I interpreted the Amoeba job as an immediate sign of good fortune. The far greater challenge would be finding affordable housing.

"Exactly how are you intending to move into a city that already has a huge housing shortage?" a Syracuse friend had asked me at a crowded holiday party just a few months before I departed for San Francisco. Stumped by the question, in the following weeks I reluctantly explored the Bay Area housing market over the Internet. What I found, and what introduced me to the term "couch surfing,"[12] was not very encouraging. "If you are planning on residing within San Francisco itself, be prepared for the 'apartment-hunt' of your life!" one website warned.[13] According to a variety of sources, estimates of the 2000 San Francisco apartment vacancy rate ranged from as high as 2 percent to well below 1 percent, with the cost of a one-bedroom apartment starting somewhere around twelve hundred dollars (see, for example, Hartman 2002). Adding to my difficulties was the desire to find centrally located housing (meaning in San Francisco proper) to accommodate the late night activities that my research would entail as well as my reliance on public transportation.

Arriving in the Bay Area, I had initially settled on three couch surfing options: my cousin Leslie, who lived in the canyons just outside Mountain View in the East Bay; my cousin (yet another) Karen, who lived in the Inner Sunset area of San Francisco; and my longtime friend Owa, who lived just a couple of blocks from Karen. Although the family connections meant that I would never find myself "out on the street," of the three, Owa was a godsend. Throughout my initial two months in the Bay, despite the fact that he was in the process of arranging to leave San Francisco, Owa continued to assure me that it was okay for me to stay on his couch. Because he lived a bachelor lifestyle, my late night comings and goings were not a problem. Owa simply gave me my own key and let me do whatever I wanted. We also shared an interest in hip hop which led to several nights out together. During my first few weeks in the Bay, it was Owa who introduced me to the various clubs and people who shared some interest in hip hop. Still, there came a point (about six weeks after my arrival) when I started to grow anxious about finding my own housing.

Maggie entered my life on a Sunday afternoon while I was working in the Amoeba jazz room. "Are you Kwame?" she walked up to me and asked. Getting straight to the point, she reintroduced (we had met once before) herself as a friend of my cousin Leslie and explained that she had heard I was looking for a place to stay. She had an enclosed "back porch," which she described as nothing more than a place to put a cot. Seeing that I seemed interested, she invited me to stop by and check it out later that week.

The back porch was small and just off the kitchen at the end of a long railroad apartment. "It gets cold during the rainy season," Maggie explained. Owa described it as a typical "San Francisco backroom." It would work. What Maggie and her roommate Jay were asking for in terms of rent would also definitely work. For the rest of my eleven months living on the back porch, which involved rehearsing explanations in the event that the landlord should ever stop by unannounced,[14] I grew to celebrate the virtues of my modest accommodations. What the back porch offered was absolutely no reason to spend time at home. "I'm not here to sit around the house," I would explain to people. I either wanted to be out doing something hip hop related or at a coffee shop writing field notes.

What my digs lacked in terms of luxury they more than made up for in location. Technically in the Mission district of the city, the location of my apartment (on Sixteenth Street between Church and Deloris) was at various times described as the Castro or the Lower Haight area. To demonstrate the virtues of my new lodging, particularly for getting around the city on public transportation, consider the following: the apartment was two blocks away from Market Street, the city's major artery; all five municipal trains stopped within three blocks of the apartment; the Sixteenth Street BART (Bay Area Rapid Transit) station was just three blocks in the opposite direction; and there were four late-night diners located within five blocks, the only such clustering in the city.

The Amoeba Experience

I approached my job interview at Amoeba confident that I would get the position. Despite Karen's initial misgivings, I was optimistic about the way our first correspondence had ended. I also had previous record store experience, and was quite certain that in a face-to-face meeting I would come off as a mature and serious (although temporary) potential employee. Furthermore, as I walked toward the Amoeba information table that Tuesday after-noon ready to announce to them that I was here for my interview, perhaps my greatest source of confidence and security came from my understand-ing that, as a dreadlocked African American, I had a certain record store employee look that was firmly in line with the Amoeba/Haight Street aes-thetic. The fact that during my first few weeks working at Amoeba I was approached by several "cool hunters"[15] wishing to take my picture, for me, confirms this perception.

During my job interview, I was warned that my year there would involve a fast-paced, demanding work environment with no possibility of promo-tion. I would be behind the cash registers for forty hours a week. Was I ready for that? "Yes," I answered without hesitation, "I want to be as visible as possible. I want to be known as 'the guy who works at Amoeba.'" There were several occasions when this title accorded me near celebrity status. On one extraordinary night, I recall the first five people I met at a club all asking if I worked at Amoeba; included in this group was the doorman who let me slide by without having to pay the five dollar cover charge.

My job at Amoeba was crucial to creating a context of familiarity through which I got to know people and people got to know me. Occupying a space that was at one time a bowling alley (see Figure 2.1), the twenty-five thousand square foot store (see Figure 2.2) located on what has been described as "the world's most important counter-culture street" employs over one hundred and thirty people.[16] Since the mid-nineties, Amoeba (starting with the Berke-ley store and then in late 1997 spreading to San Francisco with the opening of a second Haight Street store) has been a place where independent hip hop artists have brought their music to be sold. The store's policy of purchasing music directly from the artist, as opposed to consigning it, makes it particu-larly attractive to independent musicians. Amoeba's philosophy of "giving people a chance" and "supporting local artists" encourages their independent buyers to take at least a few copies of "most things" (including music recorded on blank cassette tapes and CD-Rs) that are brought into the store. In 2000, the better-known underground hip hop artists were selling upwards of sev-eral hundred units to the store at one time, generating thousand of dollars of on-the-spot revenue. With both the San Francisco and Berkeley stores having sections dedicated to underground hip hop, Amoeba's reputation became well known throughout regional, national, and international markets.

Through Amoeba, I had the opportunity to meet and interact with many local hip hoppers. While employed there, I worked alongside four independent hip hop recording artists, each with music available in the store. Beyond

FIGURE 2.1   Amoeba Music SF (outside). *(Photograph by Jay Blakesberg.)*

these four, a number of interviews with artists were set up while at work. My daily interactions with hip hop fans, many of whom I crossed paths with on other occasions, were equally important. Finally, the more general environment of regularly being around music and people who were knowledgeable about music provided a wealth of information and insights.

It is no secret that an ethnographer's "apparent lack of activity" can lead to difficulties in the research situation (Hammersley and Atkinson 1995, 78). Typically, accounts of anthropologists' entries into fieldwork are structured around narratives of "finding a role" or "fitting in." By working alongside music enthusiasts and directly sharing experiences with them, I was accepted as a person with particular interests, idiosyncrasies, and views, and not merely as an inquisitive stranger whose regular presence required ex-

FIGURE 2.2   Amoeba Music SF (inside). *(Photograph by Catherine Cavey.)*

planation.[17] In terms of the "mutual construction of meaning" (Hutchins 2001, 2) and genuine rapport to which contemporary ethnographic research aspires, the benefits of my employment at Amoeba were immeasurable.

Out on the Town

An ethnographer's immersion into a research setting is shaped by the personal relationships one develops with members of the local community (Pandey 1979). Participating in San Francisco's underground hip hop nightlife (particularly since the East Bay was regarded as having few underground hip hop venues) was perhaps the most fundamental of all my research activities. Nightlife options—including going to clubs, concerts, open-mics, and house parties—provide the structure and stability for most local music scenes. During my first few months in the Bay, I met two people who became my regular partners on these outings.

The first was a Filipino American emcee/producer/b-boy/deejay/ex-graffiti writer going by the name Destined. Destined was familiar to me from a weekly open-mic that I had been attending since first arriving in San Francisco. Our official friendship, however, began on an evening in mid-July when he approached me with his CD and asked me to "peep it" (check it out). I asked him whether he was selling it, giving it to me, or just wanted me to listen to it. His answer was that I should just listen to it, "if you like it you can make a donation." Minutes later I handed Destined ten dollars, which I considered a fair going price, and in a gesture of friendship told him that if this was his CD I already knew I would like it.[18]

Later that evening, Destined offered me a ride home during which we shared our stories. Destined's family had recently moved from San Diego to Daly City, a bustling bedroom community just south of San Francisco (see Chapter 1). At the time when I met him, they were all staying with other relatives but it was his hope to eventually get his own place in San Francisco. Nineteen (with a fake ID), new to the area, unassuming, and on a constant quest for that elusive female who could make his outlook on life even more magical than it already was, Destined was intent on going out as much as possible.

My second companion was a European American self-defined snow-board instructor from Lake Tahoe who "summered" in the Bay Area in or-der to "couch surf and go to hip hop shows." Devorah was possibly the only person I met who had as keen an interest in finding a hip hop event to go to every night as I did. For a period of several months (before she returned to Tahoe for the winter) we would call each other early each week and go over—night-by-night—what our options were. Devorah's brother also hap-pened to be the leader of a well-known Northern California graffiti crew, which gave her considerable status within circles oriented around that as-pect of hip hop. Starting in late August and lasting through Halloween—shortly after which Devorah returned to snow country—the trio of Destined, Devorah, and I (or any two of us) became a fixture at many San Francisco underground hip hop nightlife events.

Destined stands about five feet, eight inches tall with a sturdy yet sur-prisingly slender build. Both agreeable and thoughtful in appearance, his family had come to Southern California from the Philippines. At the time of my research he wore his hair short, but at previous times had sported both the mullet and dreadlock hairstyles. Devorah is about five foot six, of eastern European descent, with an attractive slightly freckled face. She is quite slim, but has a dramatic head of long, thick dirty-blonde hair that she often wore wrapped. Where Destined's attraction emanates from his hum-ble demeanor and his strong soothing voice, Devorah exudes a self-assured charm, impeccable manners, and a raspy smoker's voice that many people found sexy.

Destined is what a few people have referred to as "a hip hop Renaissance man"; a person who participates (or has participated extensively) in each of hip hop's four principal elements (Rose 1994). He had an album out for which he was the featured emcee and produced (composed the music) for all but one of the songs. He was a regular at hip hop open-microphone events, and he was perpetually looking for opportunities to freestyle, whether at a club, a party, a more intimate gathering with friends, riding in the car, at work (midway through my time in the Bay, Destined also started working at Amoeba), while walking down the street, or even in leaving phone messages.

Despite all this attention to rhyming, one could quite easily make the case that Destined's true love was b-boying (breaking). Initially, I noted the number of times when he would hand me his car keys, beeper, lip balm, and other small items that might fall from his pockets while engaged in the various acrobatic maneuvers of his dance repertoire. On the evening when I first introduced Destined to Devorah, our disparate paths had converged at the Hotel Utah where DJ Short Kut (of the Invisible Skratch Piklz) was spinning. It was a memorable night out. There was a sizable crowd and "positive vibe" as just about everyone seemed to be enjoying the musical selection of classic hip hop (from the 1987–1993 period), seventies funk and soul, and an occasional Jamaican dancehall set. As a result of its small size, physical layout, and intimate feel, the Hotel Utah was one of my favorite places. For these same reasons, and specifically the fact that it had several poles in the middle of what would otherwise be a small dance floor, Destined did not share my opinion. On this particular night, I noticed that he had a disappointed look on his face. When I finally asked him if he was enjoying himself, his response was, "it's cool, but there's nowhere to dance." This was my first realization of just how important being able to b-boy was to him. He went on to explain that the last time he was there he tried dancing and nearly kicked a girl in the face.

Before that particular night ended, Destined approached me, handed me his various things, and said, "fuck it! I'm going to dance." Minutes later, I saw him on the small stage talking with Short Kut. After they had come to some understanding, Destined proceeded to clear the assorted microphones and equipment out of the way. He then stood against the wall and started his routine of stretching out, "feeling" the beat, and gathering himself. Suddenly his signature off-beat (yet on-beat) style of quick foot movements, leg extensions, and body sways was under way. As these grew more rhythmic and more pronounced, he would spring into a handstand "freeze" pose, holding it for a couple of seconds before resuming his upright dancing.

Oakland emcee Dream Nefra once paid Destined what he considered a huge compliment when she described his dancing style as "smooth but powerful." That evening's repertoire also included occasional one-handed cartwheels and a sprinkling of various spins, kicks, and twists executed with both hands and feet on the floor.

Despite the fact that he did not practice deejaying a great deal, Destined was a very capable record mixer and scratcher. I can recall several occasions when the question "can I scratch for a minute?" transformed a two-minute stop at someone's house to grab a jacket or drop something off into an hour delay. This same request was frequently made at house parties and other informal gatherings where deejays were present.

Finally, although Destined confessed to have not done any tagging[19] since arriving in the Bay, he was very aware of the Bay Area graffiti scene— who the big names were and who "got up" a lot. When he realized that I did not know much about graffiti, he strongly encouraged me to educate myself and insisted that it was "the language of the streets." He also told stories of his junior high school days in San Diego when several times a week he would sneak out of his house after 2:00 AM in order to "hit up" various spots and how, on nights that he did not go out, he would ride the school bus the following morning feeling exasperated every time he saw a spot that he could have tagged.

I first met Devorah at a Tuesday night hip hop event known as "Beat Lounge" at a club called Storyville. That night I had ventured out to Storyville on my own specifically in support of a Latino emcee named Wonway Posibul's (of the group Secluded Journalists) twenty-first birthday. The previous evening, while freestyling at a packed open-mic, Wonway had worked into his performance the details that he would be turning twenty-one at midnight, was planning on going to Storyville the following evening, and that he would be appreciative of anyone who wanted to show up and buy him a drink. Not only did this fit into my game plan of having something to do every night, it also seemed like a perfect opportunity to get to know an emcee who I really admired. Upon my arrival that night at the club, I purchased two drinks, one for me and one for Wonway, and began looking for him. At some point during this initial inspection of the crowd I noticed Devorah, in part because she stood out as one of the more attractive women there, but more so because of how her style of dress seemed to clash with the rest of the crowd.

The first time I went to Storyville, my friend Owa had made the astute comment that one of the things he liked most about the club was that while there, one temporarily forgot that they were in San Francisco. What he meant by this was that in a city so driven by particular scenes and cutting edge fashion, the crowd at Storyville resembled the kind of crowd one might expect to find at a hip hop club anywhere in America (from Kansas to Colorado to Ohio to Central New York). At this time, common fashion included tight black (stretch) pants and halter tops for women, and baggy jeans, cargo pants, and T-shirts sporting labels like *Tommy Hilfiger*, *Timberland*, and *Ecko* for men.

This was particularly true for "Beat Lounge." Once an exclusively hip hop event that featured guest appearances by many of the Bay Area's top deejays and frequently drew a large number of b-boy's and b-girls, Tuesday nights at Storyville had become just another hip hop club night. The Invisible Skratch Piklz (and other well-known deejays) no longer spun there, and breakers were finding themselves increasingly squeezed out by a crowd that preferred drinking and dancing as a means of cozying up to the opposite sex. I was once privy to a discussion between two club deejays in the Amoeba record aisles in which one was explaining to the other that as a club or weekly event grows popular it reaches a certain "girl quota" at which men no longer attend out of enjoyment for the specifics of the venue, but rather simply because there are going to be a lot of women there. According to this deejay, this marked the beginning of the eventual deterioration of the venue into a "meat market."

On the night when I first met Devorah, the scene at Storyville could accurately be described as a meat market. She stood out, however, due to her head-wrap and loose ankle-length print dress, both of which seemed far too neo-bohemian for the crowd. Over the course of the evening, we acknowledged one another several times, typically through a meeting of eyes and a head nod. Finally, after handing Wonway a second drink, in an indirect effort to find out more about Devorah, I approached her companion—a dark-haired Bostonian named Meagan whose fashion taste was far less conspicuous—and asked, "do you know what we're listening to?" This seemed like a fair enough question, for both women appeared displeased with the music. To my surprise, Devorah turned around and took the initiative in answering my question by shouting, "some commercial bullshit!"

Caught off guard by her forthrightness, I reacted by inquiring about their specific music tastes and was pleased to find that we shared a great deal in common. A half-hour before the club closed, Devorah informed me that they had grown tired of the scene there and were going next door to have a beer and talk. She asked if I would like to join them, which I did.

Next door, where things were much quieter, Devorah and I quickly discovered that we had a number of mutual friends and acquaintances. When we finally said goodbye that evening, I left with the pleased feeling of having established the beginnings of what would be a strong friendship.

Devorah was different from Destined in that she did not actively participate in any elements of hip hop. Also, unlike Destined, who the first night I met him spoke of several families sharing one house (five people to a room with him on the floor) in Daly City,[20] Devorah was a native of Marin County, the posh county located on the other side of the Golden Gate Bridge which has one of the highest per capita incomes in America (Waller 2000, 79).

In Chapter 1, I discussed underground hip hop's markedly middle-class character. Through the various panels, presentations, and conversations that I have had regarding my research, I have learned that this descriptor often calls to mind images of white picket fences, private school attendance, and unquestioned economic and social privilege—the kinds of things that stand as the antithesis of hip hop's authenticity and street credibility (see McLeod 1999). In reality, this middle-class encompasses a vast range of economic circumstances and social experiences, which, together, the class backgrounds of Devorah and Destined effectively represent.

On the surface, Devorah in many ways typified the secure, middle-class image from which underground hip hoppers sought to distance themselves (see Chapter 1). During the time I spent with her, I had the privilege of enjoying rides to shows in her late-model Jeep Cherokee, and, on occasion, I also took pleasure in her father's San Francisco Giants season tickets. During the (roughly) two and half months that we spent as nightlife companions, Devorah took a ten-day trip to Egypt and twice took weekend trips with her family to the Miami Hurricane's (her father's alma mater) home football games.

Destined, on the other hand, described himself as having grown up in the "best part of the rough section" of San Diego, and had an adolescence that brought him precariously close to Southern California gang life:

D: In the ninth grade, dude, I was trying to [gang] bang . . . like, my brother was a Crip, and I was getting sucked into that a little too. Like, wearing a lot of blue and even rolling with fools. Just like getting in fights and shit. But then I realized, that shit's not gonna get me anywhere. Like those kids right now are probably still doin' it. (*pause*) And there was another kinda conflict in that, with one of the kids, I used to always fuckin' get in fights with him. Like the kids I used to kick it with. And like, he was kind of one of the main kids. You know wha' I mean?

AKH: Yeah, so it wasn't gonna be a pleasant trip for you to be kickin' it with those dudes everyday.

D: Yeah, Yeah. So I just gave that shit up, and like, that's when I started getting more into [graffiti] writing and rhyming and like, getting more hardcore. And like, that's when I started getting more into underground hip hop, and just started listening to shit and just like getting real focused.

Destined's longstanding involvement with hip hop's expressive forms and proximity to street life combined with his Filipino identity to produce a firm and self-assured sense of hip hop belonging that few, if any, people questioned. Devorah's status, however, as what might crudely be described as a relatively well off white girl, with no direct involvement in hip hop outside of being a consumer, needs further explanation.

Once, following a sold-out Aceyalone show at Slim's that Devorah and both attended, I was surprised (and I must admit slightly affronted) to read an online poster's complaint about too many white girls wearing hair kerchiefs at the show. This was definitely Devorah's style. Although I had not noticed an unusually high number of European American women with this look, in recalling what Devorah had worn that night, it was clear to me that this poster could very well have been talking about her. But "Devorah's different," as Top R was quite fond of saying; her longstanding interest in underground hip hop,[21] her personal charisma, and the subcultural status of her brother as the leader of a prominent graffiti crew all combined to make her a known person within the Bay Area hip hop scene. As my reputation as a friend of hers grew, I was surprised to find other hip hoppers, many of notable repute, approaching me and in an almost bragging fashion explain that they were also connected to her in some way.[22] In fact, when I left that show at Slim's, a deejay friend of mine who had recently moved to the city went on at length about how he sees "a lot of girls at hip hop shows," but how Devorah came across as "someone that really knows what's going on."

In both this instance and the "girl quota" example mentioned above, one can glimpse the distinctly male temperament of underground hip hop which I spoke of briefly in Chapter 1. One area where I believe these gendered dimensions and intentions become particularly visible is in the construction, maintenance, and (at times) vigorous defense of underground hip hop spaces as masculine social settings. In both public venues and private home studios, the key sites of musical activity within the scene, certain factions of underground hip hop's male constituency show considerable interest in limiting the access of and restricting the roles available to young women. These issues will be explored in greater depth in the book's last chapter.

While it is not inaccurate to describe the general constituency of Bay Area underground hip hop as middle class, by examining the differences between Devorah and Destined one gets a better idea of just how broad a range of experiences this category includes. In her study of black middle-class neighborhoods in Chicago, Mary Pattillo-McCoy (1999) effectively argued that residents within these communities often have quite precarious levels of middle-class standing, and that middle-class youth tend to orient their behaviors and aspirations simultaneously toward what sociologist Elijah Anderson (1994) calls "street" and "decent" lifestyles.[23] Whereas the experiences of Destined—who (owing to his mother's bad credit) recalled needing his J.V. basketball coach to cosign the loan with which he purchased his ASR 10 sampler—would seem to have some important parallels with those of the young people in Pattillo-McCoy's study, Devorah's experiences more closely resembled the several underground hip hop enthusiasts I met, who, when September came around, returned to school at places like New York University, the University of Chicago, and Brown.

Arguably, the most telling point about this confluence of middle-class statuses is that, at the interpersonal level, no one seemed all that concerned with it. Only occasionally did I get a glimpse of Destined's (or others') street savvy and this was never anything he made a point of foregrounding as part of his hip hop self-presentation. Similarly, Devorah, who once explained to me that she would rather "chill under the Redwoods" in her parent's outdoor hot tub than come into the city to attend a Dead Prez show, was seldom questioned by anyone *who knew her* with regards to her class status and hip hop credentials. Racially, as an African American, a European American, and a Filipino American, there was nothing particularly remarkable about our trio at all.

So, for a period of about ten weeks that define my immersion into the Bay Area hip hop scene, it was Destined, Devorah, and me, or any combination of us, who stayed out together past 2:00 AM four to five nights a week. Over the year that I spent in the Bay, club nights, open-mics, and other weekly events changed regularly. Table 2.1 provides a listing of a typical week's options for nightlife. There were also shows and monthly special events to attend. These

TABLE 2.1 A Typical Week's Nightlife Options

Monday	(a) Hip Hop Open-Mic @ the Rockin' Java Cafe (b) Hip Hop Open-Mic @ the Java Source Coffee Shop (c) Hip Hop Music* @ Blondie's
Tuesday	(a) *New Roots to Hip Hop* @ the Last Day Saloon (b) Hip Hop Open-Mic @ the Hotel Utah (c) *Beat Lounge* @ Storyville
Wednesday	(a) *Elephunk* @ the Justice League (b) Hip Hop Music @ Nikki's (c) Hip Hop Music (Open-Mic) @ The Boomerang Club
Thursday	(a) Hip Hop Music @ Hotel Utah
Friday	(a) *True Skool* @ Storyville (b) Hip Hop Music @ the Justice League
Saturday	(a) Hip Hop Music @ Storyville (b) Hip Hop Music @ Sacrifice

*I use the generic label "Hip Hop Music" when I do not know the specific title of the event. In considering these options one of us might say to another, "I know they've got hip hop at Blondie's."

seemed to come in waves. Sometimes it would seem like a whole week would go by without a show or an event, and there were other times when there would be four straight evenings of successive shows.

Rockin' Java Open–Mic Night

A local music scene is typically sustained through key venues which provide a context for its various constituents (musicians, fans, and others) to come together and "share their common musical tastes" (Peterson and Bennett 2004, 1). Of all the different hip hop-oriented events that I attended, the Day One DJ's open-microphone event at the Rockin' Java Coffee House (see Figure 2.3) deserves specific mention (see M. Austin 2001). According to DJ King One, Rockin' Java open-mic was one of the few locations in the Bay where the semblances of what could be called a cohesive hip hop community existed.[24] I know of no other place in the Bay where a sizable collection of hip hop artists (regularly numbering above twenty-five) were able to gather on a weekly basis in a forum that existed for nearly four years.

I first heard about the Rockin' Java open-mic from an Amoeba co-worker—a drum and bass deejay named Baxsmackwards—who suggested that I might find going there useful in terms of my research. He also told me that although

FIGURE 2.3   The Rockin' Java Coffee House on Haight. *(Photograph by Anthony Kwame Harrison.)*

he personally was not a huge fan of underground hip hop, it was mostly his friends who put on the event. Months later, when I interviewed DJ Mizzo (one of the open-mic's regular deejays) about its history, I would learn that Baxsmackwards had actually been one of the founders. The following history of the Day One Open-Mic is a collection of excerpts from that interview:

> **DJ MIZZO:** Originally Baxsmackwards and Long came up with the idea. It didn't start off exclusively as hip hop, it was just a bunch of deejays who were just like "we want somewhere to play, anywhere we can just play our music publicly." I'm not sure how Long got the hook up. It was at Fifth [Avenue] and Clement and the guy was like, "Okay. Sure. Yeah! Just come down. If you bring your own equipment you can spin. I can't pay you anything." But we were like, "yeah, cool.". . . . That was over two years ago. So it started on Friday nights and it was deejays. Fools would just come up. There was Root (different from T. Root), Long, Baxsmackwards, [and] this other guy Mike who lives with Root. And like Mike and Baxsmackwards, they spun jungle, drum and bass, you know, etcetera.

And Long and Root were spinning hip hop. And I started coming down with them, spinning hip hop, and Root knew Halo from [San Francisco] State, he started coming down.

I mean, for almost two years before that Root and I pretty much learned together. I really never spun with Long or any of those other guys. I spun with Halo a couple of times in Root's basement but mainly it was me and Root in his basement, every week staying up till four in the morning, just by ourselves practicing and it was like, "Dude. We need to get out." You know? Cause you can mess up here and if you're feeling frustrated you can just quit, but if you're in public you really need to come on strong. I think we needed that kind of motivation. . . .

It was just deejays at first, the way it became an open-mic is this dude Prince Lou. I'm not sure if he just showed up or if Root met him on campus at SF State. He just showed up and started freestyling like "Yeah. Yeah. Can I bust some flows?" And he was *really* good. . . . He's really charismatic. He has stage presence. You know? It started off on a really good vibe and after that more and more people started coming and the rest is history.

But initially there was a little bit of a conflict as far as what direction it was going. After Prince Lou started rapping it was kind of clear that it was going in more of a hip hop direction. But I think because it was Baxsmackwards' equipment, he was supplying the speakers, I think he felt he was being edged out a little bit, which was true, I mean there were just more and more hip hop heads. People really weren't feeling . . . [the] dance stuff. I mean you can't really . . . [*pause*]

AKH: Dance at a coffee shop?

DJM: Yeah. And it's a little hard to just sit there and listen to drum and bass. So I think it eventually just got more and more hip hop as time went on.

In the beginning it was just our friends. You know . . . it was just neighborhood. Clement Street. That's where we all grew up. . . . [But then] more and more people started coming through . . . we were getting cats from Vallejo, San Jose, the East Bay, coming out every week. . . . The talent was just like exploding. Kids would come out and there'd be new people every week, and it was just like "Who's going to show up this week?"

Apparently the open-mic became so popular that the owner of the coffee shop wanted to start charging five dollars to enter. This, according to Baxs-mackwards, was at odds with their intention to "provide something to do for the broke college kids." Thus, at some point just prior to my arrival in the Bay, the decision was made to move the open-mic, and it eventually landed on Monday nights at Rockin' Java.

Rockin' Java is a neo-fifties-looking café that includes a pool table, Web TV connections, and a small stage area. During my time in San Francisco, weekly events at Rockin' Java included the hip hop open-mic on Monday nights, a singer-songwriter open-mic on Tuesday nights, and a poetry/writers workshop for teens on Fridays. Rockin' Java also hosts regular performances by local artists. Located on the upper part of Haight Street, not far from Golden Gate Park, the sidewalk in front of the coffee shop is usually crowded with panhandling young people, many of whom sleep in the park at night. Just two doors down from Amoeba, a popular destination for anyone who walks the Upper Haight, the area outside Rockin' Java is a center of sidewalk traffic activity.

On a typical Monday night, the deejays would start spinning music shortly after seven. For the next few hours people who enjoy listening to hip hop gather, some just to have a cup of coffee and talk, others in anticipation of the emcees who would get on the microphone sometime after nine. The deejays' activities range from simply playing music (classic hip hop, funk, soul, and more recent underground hip hop records) to performing intricate impromptu routines sometimes involving as many as four people on four different turntables. Generally, one deejay would spin and mix music while another scratched on a side turntable or "scratch station." Deejays usually took turns doing one of these two activities while the others watched, conversed with one another, or went through each other's records commenting on rare, recent, or unknown titles. Usually between 8:30 and 9:15 PM a crowd would start to assemble,including several locally known and lesser-known emcees. A typical crowd would be quite diverse racially, about three-quarters male, and predominantly under the age of thirty (the majority were college aged). For much of the time leading up to the opening of the microphone (generally around 9:30), many of the emcees would gather outside on the sidewalk and engage in freestyle cyphers. The start of the open-mic was typically signaled by Halo (the only regular deejay who also freestyled) coming out from behind the turntables with microphone in hand, and calling all emcees to the front, after which he proceeded to freestyle for a couple of minutes. Once finished, the microphone was passed to the next emcee to step up, and so on until about 10 PM when the whole event and the coffee shop closed down.

During most evenings that I recall, there were so many emcees that the allotted thirty to forty-five minutes only allowed each person to go once. There was no sign-up sheet or set order, people simply gathered and positioned themselves in order to be given the microphone next. Generally, each emcee performed for a couple of minutes. Emcees who continued for more than three minutes (unless exceptionally entertaining) would often start to hear jeers and calls of "pass the mic!" from the crowd and some of the waiting emcees. On several occasions, in the interest of giving everyone a chance to perform, a "two minute time limit" was explicitly stated by Halo at the beginning of the open-mic; however, this was a difficult rule to enforce. If anything, such a statement was most effective in alerting the crowd and other emcees to the fact that their heckling of a "mic hog" was sanctioned. There was a general understanding that everyone should get a turn before someone went twice, but this was not always followed. Furthermore, on many evenings there were a number of emcees who did not appear or make it known that they wanted to "get on" the mic until the final ten minutes. Inevitably, at the time of closing there were almost always several people waiting who did not get a turn. It seemed like every week DJ Root would close the mic by saying, "if you guys show up earlier, we'll open the mic earlier next week." When the coffee shop closed, the scene moved to the front sidewalk where freestyle cyphers would resume and conversations between performers, between audience members, and between performers and audience members would take place. These gatherings lasted at least until 10:30 and sometimes past 11:00.

For emcees, the open-mic provided an opportunity to practice freestyling and performing in front of a crowd. The open-mic also offered a setting for networking. As a site where at least fifteen emcees consistently came together, it was a space in which collaborations originated, groups were formed, and, as important as anything else, friendships and recognitions between fellow emcees were made. Cyphers at other clubs like the Justice League or Nikki's often originated through a group of emcees who knew one another from Rockin' Java. Beyond emcees, there were also a number of hip hop producers (or people who made beats) in attendance. A producer might be an emcee, a deejay, or an audience member. The Rockin' Java open-mic provided a place where these two necessary elements of hip hop recording (music and vocals) had an opportunity to connect. Lastly, a popular open-mic such as the one at Rockin' Java was a place where an emcee could gain confidence and make a name for his or herself. Performing in public is crucial to having a social identity as an emcee. At Rockin' Java, an aspiring emcee could be assured the opportunity to perform in front of several dozen people each week. In this way it was a port of entry for many. I can attest to all of these aspects firsthand, for from the moment I decided to put down the notebook and pick up the mic (i.e., participate as an underground emcee), Monday nights at Rockin' Java became my main performing venue.

The Rockin' Java open-mic was not the only hip hop open-mic that I attended. However, considering its duration (it had been going on for more than a year before I arrived and continued to go on well past the end of my official "field stay"), crowd size, and the number of emcees who regularly performed, it easily outdistanced any of the others. Many hip hop open-mics lasted only a couple of months and then, due to low turnout, faded away. For this reason, Rockin' Java deserves a special place among nightlife destinations.

The Forest Fires Collective

The story of the Forest Fires Collective (FFC)—the hip hop group I started with an Amoeba co-worker named Feller Quentin—is significant to my research in several ways. Hardly a household name in underground hip hop circles, the six-person (plus several peripheral members) crew's official catalogue of releases[25] includes two full-length CDs and two twelve-inch records. In May 2002, the FFC held the number one album and number one overall position on U.C. Santa Barbara's KCSB 91.9 FM "Urban Beatbox Top 30" chart—above artists like Blackalicious, DJ Shadow, Atmosphere, and will.i.am (see Table 2.2). In pointing this out, I am not suggesting that the quality of our music or the importance of its impact should be considered anywhere close to these far more accomplished artists; however, in this era of GarageBand home recordings and MySpace pages, the fact that virtually anyone can present themselves as a hip hop recording artist (see Chapter 4) motivates me to mention such accolades. In 2001, the Forest Fires Collective's self-titled debut CD was an Amoeba Music hip hop album pick of the year.[26] The following February, the FFC was the featured "Artiste du Mois" on the French webzine *Hip Hop Section*. Students of mine have purchased FFC 12-inch records while traveling in France and Japan. And, over the years, I have received dozens of fan emails and have had several serendipitous encounters with underground hip hoppers (from all across America) who know our music. Nevertheless, it was particularly within the Bay Area between the years of 2001 and 2003 that the FFC had its strongest underground hip hop presence.

TABLE 2.2 KCSB Urban Beatbox Top 30 for the Week of May 27, 2002

	Artist	Title
1	Forest Fires Collective	Forest Fires Collective
2	J-Live	All of the Above
3	Fat Jon the Ample Soul Physician	Wave Motion
4	Blackalicious	Blazing Arrow
5	Infectious Organisms	Human Experience
6	Atmosphere	Modern Man's Hustle
7	Non Phixion	Future is Now
8	Asheru and Blue Black	Truly Unique
9	Herbalizer	Something Wicked this way Comes
10	Labtekwon	Song of Sovereign
11	Sage Francis	Personal Journals
12	Procussions	All That It Takes
13	W.A.R.	Fix Your Face
14	RJD2	Let the Good Times Roll
15	Diverse	Move (single)*
16	DJ Shadow	You Can't Go Home Again (EP)
17	Slum Village	Tainted
18	Emanon	For What You Live
19	Strict Flow	The Genuine Article
20	Sonic Sum	Rocket
21	Jel	10 Seconds
22	El P	9mm
23	Weathermen	Same as it Never Was
24	Will.I.Am	Will.I.Am
25	Automator	Wanna Buy a Monkey
26	Emanon	MCs Like Me
27	Diverse	Move (single)*
28	Non Phixion	Rock Stars
29	Count Bass D	Dwight Spitz
30	Princess Superstar	Is

Playlist provided courtesy of Quinn Chaloeicheep. See also "KCSB's Hip Hop Top 10," available online at http://www.dailynexus.com/article.php?a=3266 (accessed July 16, 2008).
*Unexplained double appearance

Perhaps more remarkable than any of this, was the group's description appearing in the liner notes of the *Independent Sounds: Amoeba Music Compilation Vol. III* CD (an album on which we were featured): "In the true west coast indie hip hop tradition the Forest Fires Collective is an assembly of talented emcees and DJs/producers who are dedicated to the art of hip hop" (2001). The *Independent Sounds* compilation was put together and released by longtime Bay Area hip hop aficionado Billy Jam's *Hip Hop Slam* label. Clearly, the author of this group bio (quite possibly Jam himself) did not see the FFC as some anthropologist's sideshow or experimental foray into the world of recording. Nor did my fellow FFC members; Feller was quite blunt in sharing his initial dissatisfaction with my decision to leave San Francisco and return to Academe. While I never made an effort to conceal my anthropologist identity, to the countless hip hoppers who came to know me through my music with the FFC or my regular participation in the Rockin' Java open-mic, I was first and foremost emcee Mad Squirrel.

I met Feller Quentin at the start of my first full-day working at Amoeba. Midway through that Monday morning, a six foot tall, lanky white "dude" with a scraggly unkempt head of hair and goatee approached me apparently looking to confirm that I was, in fact, "an anthropologist studying hip hop." It was customary for Amoeba to post memos announcing its new employees. In a music store with over 130 workers this was one of many small steps taken toward cultivating an environment in which people knew one another. Feller, who had started cashiering there about a week earlier, had apparently seen the latest memo in which I was described as "an anthropologist and a cool guy." He had also spoken to Baxsmackwards, whom I had discussed my research with at some length during my training period. My first conversation with Feller was relatively short. After learning that I was in fact what he suspected, Feller promptly suggested that since he was a hip hop artist we should do an interview right there and then. I did not immediately take him up on his offer, explaining that I needed time to formulate some questions, but as Feller pointed out other employees who might be worth interviewing, I felt satisfied that I had chosen the right place to work.

Of the new Amoeba employees who were assigned to work behind the cash registers, Feller and I immediately connected through our mutual and long-standing interest in hip hop. Two years earlier, Feller and his roommate Edison Victrola (Eddie Vic)—a fellow European American, Wesleyan University alumnus, and East Coast transplant—had formed a hip hop duo called The Latter (see Figure 2.4). The Latter had an EP out entitled *1983*, and, at the time when Feller and I first met, they were putting the finishing touches on their follow-up full-length album entitled *Hearing Aids*. About a month after starting at Amoeba, I began making regular Sunday evening visits to The Latter's Western Addition district apartment/recording studio—affectionately called "the Cabin." At first, these visits were mostly spent listening to their unreleased (often recently recorded) songs. Feller also played me songs featuring an African American emcee who lived a few doors up the street named Just One—soon to start going by the name Prego with Zest—as well as a couple of songs by an emcee called Simile, who Feller explained was from "Africa" and had not been rhyming over beats for very

FIGURE 2.4   The Latter: Feller Quentin (top), Eddie Vic (middle), The Latter (bottom). *(Photograph courtesy of Jacob Buehler.)*

long. The five of us, plus a reggae connoisseur, deejay/producer going by the name Dr. Lester, who was sleeping on The Latter's couch when I initially met him, made up the original six FFC members.[27]

In truth, the bulk of the FFC's music making involved just four of us: Eddie Vic, (who owned all the equipment we initially recorded on) made beats and deejayed; Feller (who used the name Smif Carnivorous for the project) also made beats and emceed; Prego and I (the two African Americans) just emceed (although Prego did make beats for his own solo projects).[28] Although the Forest Fires Collective concept was unquestionably inspired by my—Mad Squirrel—emcee handle, the actual name and many of the themes that marked our debut CD came from Feller. Initially, neither Eddie Vic nor Prego seemed particularly enthusiastic about the madcap idea of writing hip hop songs about the forest, but they were willing to go along for the ride and as time passed they gradually became more enthusiastic about the project (see Figure 2.5).

Recording music and performing as a member of the FFC had three important methodological virtues. First, being a member of an interracial hip hop group gave me a firsthand perspective, or an integrity of experience

FIGURE 2.5   The Forest Fires Collective performs in Oakland. L to R: Mad Squirrel
(wearing helmet), Prego (rocking the mic), Feller Quentin (wearing backwards baseball
cap and holding microphone). *(Photograph courtesy of Tim Cohen.)*

(Rosaldo 1989), in understanding how dynamics of race play out within
specific hip hop recording and performing contexts. All music groups are
social units governed by negotiated codes of conduct, as well as convictions
about, and commitments toward, the music its members are collectively
involved in making (Bennett 2001). The gravity of race can be particularly
palpable in circumstances where African American and European American musicians endeavor to create music within as racially loaded a genre
as hip hop (see Chapter 3).

Second, my status as a member of the FFC allowed me to flesh-out my
overall identity as an emcee, which I was developing through regularly freestyling at the Rockin' Java and other local open-mics. None of the other FFC
members ever performed at Rockin' Java, although they were connected to a
wider affiliation of artists including Substance Abuse, Slumplordz, Meanest
Man Contest, and the Connoisseurs. Thus these two activities—publicly
freestyling and recording—mutually impacted one another and helped to
legitimize my presence (not only to others but also to myself) in both realms.
This obviously facilitated rapport with the many hip hoppers with whom I
spent time. On one particular evening, I was both astonished and honored

when several of the emcees I admired most from the Rockin' Java open-mic cornered me at an Anticon house party (see Chapter 5) and explained "we've been talking . . . and decided that of all the emcees at the Rockin' Java you're the most on the come up." Establishing a role as a participating emcee in the scene enhanced virtually all my relationships. As with my job at Amoeba, having a position, putting myself "out there," and showing my own vulnerability encouraged the people I spent time among to regard me as a person who shared their world rather than simply as an interloping observer who was "working on his paper for school."

Finally, being a recording artist (and a freestyler for that matter) allowed me to enter into genuine dialogues with other artists about recording and performing experiences. This was particularly evident in interviews where I consistently made a conscious effort to uphold dialogic principles. For instance, when Kirby Dominant spoke to me about the virtues of his simultaneous affiliations with several distinct hip hop collectives, I could relate to him by talking about what I liked and disliked about the particular style of hip hop that we were making in the FFC.

In addition to these research benefits, I feel it is also important to express just how much I enjoyed and cherished having the opportunity to create and record music with such a talented group of artists. Although I have continued to engage in music making activities with Feller, Prego, and (while he still resided there) Eddie Vic on return trips to the Bay, the FFC no longer exists in any official capacity.[29] Cultural historian Robin D. G. Kelley has criticized much of the existing scholarship on hip hop for its failed to acknowledge the "deep visceral pleasures" that come from making and consuming music (1997, 37). Being a part of a collective that left its mark (however small) on the Bay Area underground hip hop scene was incredibly meaningful for me and continues to be a tremendous honor.

The Forest Fires Collective concept emerged out of my relationship with Feller Quentin, an Amoeba co-worker, literally while talking behind the cash registers one morning at work. I also first learned about the Rockin' Java open-mic through an Amoeba co-worker. I met Destined at Rockin' Java and met Devorah on a night when I went out with the specific intention of meeting up with someone I knew from Rockin' Java. Many of Devorah's friends were familiar with me through Amoeba or Rockin' Java. With the help of my recommendation on his behalf, five months after meeting Destined, he began working at Amoeba. Less than two weeks after introducing

Destined to Devorah, she commented to me about how ironic it was that the two of them spent more time on the phone talking together than either of them did with me. And although my fellow FFC members rarely attended the Rockin' Java open-mics, through connections with me, several Rockin' Java emcees developed friendships with Feller, Eddie Vic, and Prego, a few recorded songs in the Cabin, and one (T. Root) was featured on three FFC releases.

As I have highlighted in this chapter, my familiarity with Bay Area underground hip hop and the dynamics of race within it came about through my employment at Amoeba Music with its diverse staff and cliental; my excursions into the Bay Area underground hip hop nightlife as an African American male who primarily went out with a Filipino male and a European American female; my participation (first as an audience member and later as a regular performer) in open-microphone events, which consistently brought together a racially diverse audience and group of emcees; and my involvement recording and releasing music as a member of an interracial hip hop collective. Anthropologist Takeyuki Tsuda makes the point that ethnographers are often forced to "subordinate their inner self"—or the person they envision through their self-conception—in order to conform to the cultural expectations of the people they work among (1998, 116–117). In describing my own research experiences, I think it is just as important to acknowledge how within a "close-to-home" (Pattillo-McCoy 1999) ethnographic situation the ethnographer's inner-self is often accepted and even embraced. Through my welcomed involvement in the world of Bay Area underground hip hop, I was able to experience the nuances of the transformation from audience member to performer and from observer to participant that is at the crux of the concerns of both reflexive anthropologists and the experiences of the people that I lived among.

3

Claiming Hip Hop

Race and the Ethics of
Underground Hip Hop Participation

Hip hop, more so than any other music style, has been mired in deliberations over authenticity. As a genre of music that teeters on the edge of anti-establishment radicalism and corporate co-opted commercialism, it often straddles the line between extremes of street credibility (poverty) and pop celebrity (wealth) (Watkins 2005, 5). In an essay entitled "Authenticity within Hip Hop and Other Cultures Threatened with Assimilation," Media studies scholar Kembrew McLeod (1999) argued that during the latter part of the 1990s, what came to be understood as authentic hip hop oriented itself around sets of binary oppositions occurring along various semantic dimensions. These included "staying true to yourself" versus "following mass trends," being "underground" as opposed to "commercial," and originating from "the streets" and not "the suburbs." McLeod was equally attentive to the importance of race, where he definitively presented "real hip hop" as associated with blackness and "fake hip hop" as marked by its connection to whiteness (1999, 139). It is precisely this last issue, the relationship between race and authentic hip hop, that has dominated scholarly debates and everyday discussions about the music genre since at least the early 1990s (see Harrison 2008b). The fundamental question, in my opinion, is whether hip hop, as McLeod's binary suggests, should be regarded as a distinctly black music form in which participation by other groups requires some qualification, or whether hip hop should be viewed as a more racially inclusive musical domain.

Over the last decade the underground hip hop subgenre, with its droves of white emcees, has offered one of the most readily available objections to McLeod's racial schism. Any listing of underground hip hop's most prominent white emcees should surely include figures such as Slug[1] (of Atmosphere), El-P, Evidence (Dilated Peoples), The Grouch (Living Legends), R.A. The Rugged Man, Vinnie Paz (Jedi Mind Tricks), Sole (Anticon), Copywrite, Sage Francis, and Eso Tre (Substance Abuse).[2] Even Eminem, who today is regarded as one of hip hop's most popular artists, has roots in this multiracial underground tradition. What is perhaps most notable about this collective influx of white emcees has been the ability of so many of them to claim a level of underground hip hop legitimacy without having to resort to transparent efforts at "figuratively passing" (Ogbar 2007, 38), such as adopting speaking styles inspired by African American Vernacular English (AAVE) and modeling their clothing and self-presentation after popular black rap acts. That so many white emcees have achieved underground hip hop authenticity, arguably on their own terms, certainly complicates the common association between whiteness and hip hop fakeness. Ignoring their presence in the interest of promoting some sort of hip hop black essentialness is, in my view, shortsighted and intellectually flawed.

In this chapter, I directly confront the issue of racial authenticity with regards to underground hip hop. While distinctions between blackness and whiteness remain pivotal to my theorizing, I extend the discussion to include and account for hip hoppers identifying outside this racial binary. My objective here is to propose a race-based model for underground hip hop's participatory ethics which will serves as a theoretical and structural basis for the ethnographic examples and analyses that make up much of the remainder of the book.

I begin with an overview of the key debates and deliberations concerning hip hop, race, and authenticity found within hip hop scholarship. These arguments largely orient around the question of whether hip hop is a black music, art form, and performance activity (see, for example, Touré 1999) with non-black (and particularly white) performers being relegated to less than authentic status, or whether, after thirty years as a popular cultural form, hip hop can be legitimately claimed by young people of all racial and ethnic backgrounds (Strauss 1999). Rather than arguing one way or another—as if to imply that there is a single, straightforward resolution to this most monumental of all hip hop authenticity debates—I acknowledge a certain truth to each reading, and in doing so mean to direct attention toward how the very concept of *authenticity* gets marshaled in the service of specific individual and collective social interests.

Acknowledging that authenticity in music is socially and politically constructed does not diminish that fact that within virtually all music scenes the power of the authentic is extremely and pervasively real. As musicologist Adam Krims has reminded us, what is authentic and consequently real to one hip hopper can be the epitome of fakeness to the next: "fans of each [rap] genre not infrequently tout theirs as the true rap genre asserting likewise that fans of other genres have somehow betrayed something essential about rap music, perhaps hip hop culture as well" (Krims 2000, 48). Lucius Outlaw made a parallel observation about race when he explained that the fact that "'race' is without a scientific basis in biological terms, does *not* mean thereby that it is without any social value" (Outlaw 1990, 77). These two points, taken in conjunction, are important to understanding the manner in which tropes of racial authenticity and hip hop authenticity have been historically interwoven. Underground hip hop threatens to rupture the connection between racial and hip hop essentialism, and in doing so, at times puts forth the progressive postulation that extending the racial scope of hip hop authenticity is tantamount to transcending race itself.

For reasons that I will elaborate on shortly, underground hip hoppers make up a remarkably historically and intellectually informed segment of the hip hop nation. This knowledge of hip hop history and scholarship— and the extent to which it gets disseminated from the most schooled and well-read members of underground hip hop communities to others—serves as one pillar of "subcultural capital" (Thornton 1995) that is frequently leveraged in constructing authenticity claims. Thus, the different lines of scholarship that I discuss here amount to more than simply ivory tower ruminations. Each of these positions on hip hop and racial identity contributes to the ongoing deliberations and dialogues regarding legitimacy in which hip hoppers actively participate.

In the second part of this chapter, I propose a framework for understanding the interpersonal dynamics and subcultural assessments that saturate social exchanges within multiracial underground hip hop scenes. Part of this process involves presenting a preliminary map of hip hop racialism, which appears as an inverted version of America's existing race hierarchy (with allotted statuses being commensurate with each group's perceived level of historical persecution and contemporary lack of privilege). Legitimate participation within underground hip hop is also contingent on individuals having certain (subculturally valued) experiences, competencies, sensibilities, and outlooks. Starting from sociologist Sarah Thornton's concept of subcultural capital (1995), I explain how both empirically verifiable criteria and ideologically inferred ethics impact underground hip hop community membership. In considering the two, I put greater emphasis on the latter, most specifically how notions of "racial sincerity" (Jackson 2005) serve as a means through which non-black hip hop enthusiasts circumvent the limitations of their racial identity. In this way, the dialogic nature of authenticity claims and identity constructions combine to enable a malleability and maneuverability that is experienced as occurring along racial lines. Such dynamics of agency and structure shape the racial contours and enable the processes of identity formation which are the subject of the remaining chapters.

Hip Hop Scholarship and the Great Race Debate

As I prepare to explain why hip hop scholarship is uniquely central to the underground hip hop worldview, I am reminded of two bits of knowledge regarding hip hop consumption and the media that over the years have been passed on to me. The first came during my initial week at Amoeba by way of a Latina co-worker who joined me out one night for an after-work drink. As we sat at the bar discussing my project and the state of hip hop more generally, one theory of hers, which she made a point of stressing to me, was that there existed a fundamental difference between the older generation of hip hop enthusiasts (she placed both herself and me within this group) who had grown up engaging it within interpersonal community contexts, and the younger generation who connected with hip hop primarily through television, magazines, and films—often in isolation. The particular example she used was a new dance move which could either be learned at a house party from those around you or while sitting in your living room watching Black Entertainment Television's (BET) *106 & Park*.[3]

The second piece of wisdom came via an after-class conversation I had with a student in a *Hip Hop Music, Culture, and Society* course I taught in 2003. This particular discussion took place following a heated in-class exchange between said student, who fancied himself as a hip hop expert, and what is probably best described as a distinctly underground hip hop inflected group of his classmates. That day, while walking out of the building together, he shared his view that there was a "big difference" between people who knew all about hip hop because they had "read every book ever published on it" and those who actually "lived it." As an African American, he even racialized the tension between himself and his all-white classmate adversaries by (quite astutely) explaining that whenever he heard a black rapper he could immediately tell which region of the country they were from (East Coast, West Coast, or the South), yet "these white underground rappers" regardless of their region "all sound the same."

At the heart of these comments lies an important point, not so much about black authenticity and white inauthenticity, but about the extent to which, even within anti-corporate underground hip hop circles, the media plays a central role in defining the constituents' understanding of what it is they are taking part in. While most underground hip hoppers harbor severe skepticism toward popular media outlets like VH1, BET, the *Source* magazine, and other bastions of commercial hip hop commentary, their charge to know where hip hop came from, the nostalgic legitimacy given to all things "old school," and their middle-class (often college student) standing (see Chapter 1) make them particularly receptive to more highbrow media forms such as scholarly texts and documentaries. During the course of my fieldwork, I visited several hip hoppers' homes where I found canonical texts such as David Toop's *Rap Attack* (1984), Nelson George's *Hip Hop America* (1998), and Tricia Rose's *Black Noise* (1994) on the bookshelves. While teaching the abovementioned course on hip hop, I was surprised (a little) to find that the three or four students within the underground-inflected group were familiar with many of the books and documentaries used in class. Murray Forman insists that this emerging canon of hip hop studies needs to be viewed as an integral part of what hip hop has become: "These texts and their content do not exist outside the culture—they do not provide externalized objective views. Rather, they, too, are internally significant facets of what today is recognized as hip-hop culture" (2002, 36).

Within underground hip hop circles these canonical hip hop texts are particularly salient. Even those who do not know the name of scholar Tricia Rose have a basic grasp of her analysis of hip hop's postindustrial New York City formation (discussed more extensively below). As underground hip hoppers move in and out of variously discriminating subcultural contexts, this demonstrated understanding of hip hop as it was meant to be is selectively employed as a basis for claiming legitimacy.

Within hip hop scholarship, debates regarding the relationship between race and authenticity have taken several forms. The one constant is the centrality of black identity and culture. In presenting this overview, I have chosen to divide the work into three fundamental themes.

The first focuses specifically on the formation of hip hop in New York City during the 1970s and considers the racial identity of those who should be correctly thought of as hip hop's founders; I refer to this as the *formative* line of argument. The second involves situating hip hop historically within a continuum of cultural influences which may or may not (as the debate goes) be associated exclusively with black people. Where these first two themes surround issues of hip hop "originalism" (Perry 2004), the third considers hip hop in its contemporary manifestations. Although the question of where hip hop came from will always lend itself well to authenticity claims, my discussion of hip hop in the present is based on an understanding of culture as an ongoing, historically unfinished process (Clifford 1988). As such, I make the case that there is more to authenticity than just origins, and that tradition is, in fact, socially constructed through time. To paraphrase the familiar hip hop adage, my approach recognizes that it is not just where hip hop is from, but also where hip hop is at.

How Hip Hop Began: Formative Claims

For the last decade, perhaps longer, the trend in hip hop scholarship has been away from fixed notions of an essential blackness and toward a more multicultural, hybrid understanding of both hip hop's origins and its current makeup. So much so that law professor Imani Perry, in *Prophets of the Hood* (2004), described her re-assertion of hip hop as a definitively black American music form as quite "radical"(2004, 10). In actuality, declarations of hip hop's essential and exclusive blackness, although common enough in everyday conversations, rarely appear within the existing scholarship on hip hop's formative period.[4] Surely a good deal of early research took this general, if not absolute, position. An illustrative example would be Tricia Rose's *Black Noise*—quite likely the most influential work ever published on the socioeconomic context of hip hop's beginnings. One need look no further than Rose's title to grasp her general position that a firm connection between hip hop and blackness is apt and appropriate.[5] In fact, throughout the book's second chapter—described by Rose as a "sweeping exploration of hip hop" and "some primary factors contributing to its emergence" in her introduction to the book (1994, xv)—hip hop is presented as a form of "Black urban renewal" (p. 61) rising out of a postindustrial New York City environment. Yet, if one interrogates the pages of *Black Noise* more thoroughly, specifically the second chapter, it is clear that Rose shows great diligence in continually including Hispanic communities along with black communities as the core sites of hip hop's initial resonance. This results in a curious, yet quite common, phenomenon of balancing some acknowledgment of hip hop's hybrid (cross-ethnic) origins against a prioritization of its distinct blackness.[6]

Certainly Puerto Ricans and other non-black ethnoracial (Rivera 2001) groups (e.g., Chicanos in Los Angeles [Kelly 1993]) have contributed to hip hop's development (Rose 1994; Thompson 1996). However, the formative line of debate insists that one consider whether these contributions occurred early enough and were influential enough to justify a group's status as hip hop founders. Some commentators have suggested that because of their socially, economically, and racially marginalized position in 1970s New York, not to mention their partial African ancestry, Puerto Ricans—the chief Hispanic group to which Rose refers—should be considered "virtual blacks." For example, hip hop historian/journalist Davey D once asserted: "When I say Black, I am including my Latino Brothers and Sisters. . . . They are and have always been a part of Hip Hop culture. . . . To me Puerto Ricans in particular are akin to Black folks, they just happen to speak Spanish" (1999).

However, I would caution against such a simple solution to this Puerto Rican dilemma—that is, how and where to place Puerto Ricans within the context of hip hop's formative moments—on several grounds. Since the publication of *Black Noise*, a number of works have come out which specifically address the oversight or historical amnesia of not putting Puerto Ricans on record as pivotal players in hip hop's emergence (del Barco 1996; Flores 1994; Guevara 1996; Jenkins 1999; Rivera 2003; Verán 1999). Certainly the identity politics that motivated these scholarly contributions suggest that for many Puerto Rican researchers, writers, and hip hop enthusiasts the presumption of being included within the descriptor "black" was not enough. Nor should we assume that Rose's dutiful mention of "blacks and Hispanics" (at least fourteen times in Chapter 2 alone) in a book that was entitled *Black Noise* stood as sufficient recognition.

Raquel Rivera argues that during this formative period, youth culture within the South Bronx (hip hop's formative environment) featured a racial and ethnic fluidity and a sense of interracial allegiance—between African Americans, Puerto Ricans, and African Caribbean immigrants (most notably Jamaicans)—that would be "hard to conceive of" in most American contexts (2001, 240). In support of this, William Eric Perkins suggests that much of the dynamic percussion within early hip hop was the product of "Latin music's powerful influence on New York . . . popular culture" (1996, 6; see also Chang 2005; Hebdige 1987). Such straightforward understandings, however, are undermined by works that highlight the initial outsider status and struggle for acceptance that many Puerto Rican hip hoppers had to endure. Juan Flores, for example, discusses how pioneering deejay Charlie Chase was often greeted with a "What the fuck are you doing here, Puerto Rican?" challenge during his early forays into emceeing (Flores 1996, 89).[7] A similar testimony can be found in the documentary film *The Freshest Kids* (Israel 2002), a definitive history of b-boying, in which Richie "Crazy Legs" Colon[8]—one of the original members of the Rock Steady Crew—reflects on his earliest days as a Puerto Rican b-boy and recalls that when he first started breaking in predominantly Puerto Rican settings people would refer to it as "moreno [black] style" (see also del Barco 1996, 68; Verán 1999, 54). Perry (2004) takes this a step further by insisting that overly romanticized notions of harmonious connections between African Americans and any Caribbean group—black or Latino—belie the tensions and conflicts surrounding those relationships.

I agree that simply collapsing Puerto Ricans or other Latinos into one notion of blackness is an unsound and therefore unwise endeavor. This was as true for 1970s New York City as it is today. Categories of race already impose crude, perceptually based generalizations on members of what are increasingly diverse and culturally complex societies. Furthermore, outside the context of claims to hip hop authenticity, there are certainly enough cases where Latinos appear to be more strongly oriented toward images of whiteness (see, for example, Darity, Dietrich, and Hamilton 2005; Dávila 2001; Mills 1998).[9] Overall, my concern is that any uncritical pairing of racial and ethnic identity ultimately conceals far more than it reveals.

The question of whether the Puerto Rican youth who resided in the South Bronx during the 1970s should be seen as hip hop originators or as early adopters amounts to more than merely splitting hairs. By proposing that the authenticity of a cultural practice should be defined strictly in accordance with those who created it, all claims of origin are inherently excluding endeavors. To make an issue of black exclusivity by acknowledging the authenticity of an early adopting ethnoracial (Rivera 2001) group opens the door for legitimacy claims from additional (later) adopting groups. In other words, if we are to recognize late-seventies Puerto Rican b-boys and b-girls as authentically hip hop, then why not do the same for the European American b-boys and b-girls who just a few years later could be found breaking in malls throughout suburban America? Surely there are compelling arguments for why a white, suburban, b-boy should not be considered authentic;[10] however, my point is that such deliberations can become far more complicated and convoluted than most originalist advocates are comfortable with. And they reveal a notable shortcoming in the formative line of argument.

The formative position is based on the idea that there is a bounded period of time in which what we now consider hip hop was initiated and crystallized. Placing hip hop within an historical continuum of cultural traditions, as my second category of authenticating debates does, begins to address the issue of this period's beginnings. Even if we are unable to plot the exact moment when hip hop began, we can at least argue that things which resembled hip hop—the politically conscious jazz poetry of the Last Poets[11] and Gil Scott-Heron for example—are, to most hip hop historians, part of an earlier and distinctive enough to be called something different tradition. My concern here, however, has more to do with the arbitrarily decided moment in which hip hop's formation is purported to have ended, for I have yet to encounter an altogether convincing argument for exactly when that would be.[12] This commonsense idea of a formative period in which a neat set of traditions were established is certainly familiar, yet as any critical cultural theorist can tell you, traditions are, in fact, never fixed, but rather constantly changing and going through continuous processes of revision (Handler and Linnekin 1984; see also Clifford 1988; Friedman 1992; Glassie 2003).

Decisions on when and where to set hip hop's formation and how stringently to recognize and honor divisions between racial and ethnic groups are ultimately more perceptual than natural. By this I mean that they are shaped by the forces that guide our interpretation of reality more so than by any empirically verifiable truth. As such, all authentic claims that are rooted in arguments over "how it was" during hip hop's formative moments are subject to dispute.

Where Hip Hop Came From: The Historical Continuum

A second approach to the origins of hip hop involves presenting it as one of the most recent in a long line of musical and cultural traditions that, for the most part, can be situated within a trajectory of African diasporic experiences. In what is widely regarded as the first serious effort to explore these cultural origins, British journalist David Toop (1984) utilized an African cultural survivals approach (Herskovitz 1941) which highlighted direct linkages between New York City emcees and griots of the West African savanna. Over a decade later, in an effort to explore "Africanisms that are part of the rap music tradition," Cheryl Keyes (1996, 223–224) highlighted both the concept of *"nommo"*—defined by her as "the power of the word" (Keyes 1996, 234)—and the African perception of outer and inner (nonlinear) time as fundamental to hip hop's African ethos. However, as with the formative testimonies I have discussed already, many declarations of hip hop "having started in Africa" come in the form of passing comments which are rarely elaborated on through detailed or well-researched linkages (Yasin 1999).

Scholarship on African American expressive cultural practices often emphasizes the connections between North America and the Caribbean, particularly the confluence of cultural influences from southern African American, northern urban African American, and Caribbean cultural traditions, while relegating the African continent to a distant, mystified, and seldom discussed source of original cultural materials (Chang 2005; Cobb 2007; Fernando 1994; Keyes 1996; Perkins 1996; Rose 1994; Szwed 1999). Although such treatments do little to address my aforementioned concerns about tradition as an ongoing reinterpretation of the past, and even less in terms of Perry's critiques of romanticized diasporic relations, they are nonetheless worth considering in that they put forth a representation of hip hop that can be used in the service of legitimizing its black racial and cultural situatedness.

Toop (1984) provided the prototype for hip hop scholarship's recognition of its African American lines of descent. These span a range of:

1. *Musical Traditions*—including blues, jazz, rhythm & blues (R & B), bebop, soul, funk, and an array of associated dance steps;
2. *Orature*—including a variety of "good talkers" (Abrahams 1964) such as storytellers, poets, preachers, comedians, and black radio deejays;
3. *Aesthetic Conventions*—combining theoretical analyses of repetition, rupture, percussion, and re-signification (see also Gates 1988).[13]

In reviewing the range and breadth of Toop's historical treatment, it is notable that he pays relatively little attention to Caribbean influences on hip hop. Dick Hebdige more than makes up for this oversight by dedicating a chapter of his book *Cut 'n' Mix: Culture, Identity, and Caribbean Music* (1987) to New York City hip hop. The majority of work that has since been published on hip hop's Caribbean roots can be placed under one of two analytical and rhetorical approaches. The first builds on the fact that large numbers of Caribbean immigrants—starting in the early twentieth century and then increasing rapidly following the 1965 changes in immigration laws (see Chapter 1)—resided in New York. I call this direct linkage between Caribbean and hip hop cultural practices the "Caribbean survivals approach."

Within this approach, arguably the most widely circulated origin story, or "creation myth" (Chang 2005, 67), regarding the formation of hip hop in the South Bronx connects it to the 1967 arrival of a Jamaican immigrant named Clive Campbell, aka DJ Kool Herc. Kool Herc's testimony that there were "a lot of things from Jamaica" (Fernando 1994, 4; see also Yasin 1999) that he incorporated into his early hip hop deejaying in America is one of hip hop folklore's most durable and effective references to its Caribbean lineage. These "things" included his utilization of the massive (bass heavy) mobile deejay sound system,[14] which had functioned as a community-based alternative to the elite-centered Jamaican national radio broadcasts since the late forties (Fernando 1994); his practice of soaking off record labels in the bathtub in order to conceal their identity from curious onlookers (Chang 2005; Nelson 1999); and his transplanting of the Jamaican style "talk over" (popularized by artists like U Roy) into a 1970s New York City funk context—a practice that eventually gave way to emcees rapping (Fernando 1994; Hebdige 1987). In addition to these directly Jamaican-inspired practices, scholars have drawn a connection between Kool Herc's way of extending particularly pungent percussive segments of a song (i.e., break beats) by alternating between two copies of the same records and the sound manipulation practices of using echo effects, reverb, and instrumental b-sides for "chanting 'pon the mic" within Jamaican dub music (Chang 2005; Fernando 1994; Keyes 1996).

The stories of Kool Herc are what people call "the stuff of legends." They form the core of a body of folk knowledge that virtually anyone claiming to know something about hip hop's origins can recite. Whereas this emphasis on hip hop's Jamaican ties advances the notion of hip hop as an essentially black yet culturally hybrid form, a good deal of Caribbean scholarship, including the work of Hebdige (1987), Guevara (1996), and Rivera (2001), point to the sizable Puerto Rican and Cuban presence that had existed in New York City since the 1920s. Perkins, for instance, alleges: "The Cuban son, Puerto Rican salsa, and Dominican (and Haitian) merengue were all driven by percussion-based bands, and many black *and Puerto Rican* young adults freely borrowed from this source in developing their own musical styles" (1996, 6, emphasis added).

Rather than tracing specific cultural survivals, the second approach to hip hop's Caribbean roots, which is best represented in the work of British cultural theorist Paul Gilroy, locates the Caribbean at the core of a series of fluid transnational movements of people, commodities, cultural practices, and aesthetic sensibilities. This "Black Atlantic" (Gilroy 1993) model is predicated on a sophisticated conception of black modern subjectivity as emerging out of complex, fractured, and often multidirectional linkages and mediations between Africa, Europe, and the Americas.

One of the more notable applications of the Black Atlantic approach was offered by George Lipsitz, who used examples of work by hip hop pioneering DJ Afrika Bambaataa to suggest a transcontinental "diasporic intimacy" within the Black Atlantic world (1994, 27). Lipsitz specifically detailed how colonially mediated African imagery (e.g., Bambaataa's "the Zulu Nation"), Hollywood film scores, and European electronic music (e.g., the German band Kraftwerk) are combined in the creation of Bambaataa's aptly titled 1982 hit "Planet Rock."[15] One critique of the Black Atlantic model alleged that its complex and fractured presentation of black subjectivity ultimately detracts and distracts from the importance of hip hop's black American situatedness. In this regard, Perry goes so far as to question the centrality of Caribbean cultural experiences within hip hop when she pointed out, quite astutely I believe, that within their own families many of the young Caribbean immigrants who most ardently submersed themselves within the emerging hip hop subculture would likely be seen as becoming "too American" (2004, 18).[16]

Where Perry's focus is on a cultural (and sociopolitical) distinction between black Jamaica and black America, Lipsitz's utilization of the Black Atlantic approach allows for a reading of hip hop as part of an international dialogue:

> To be sure, African and Caribbean elements appear prominently in U.S. hip hop . . . but these claims place value on origins that distort the nature of Black Atlantic culture. The flow of information and ideas among diasporic people has not been solely from Africa outward to Europe and the Americas, but rather has been a reciprocal self-renewing dialogue in communities characterized by upheaval and change. The story of the African diaspora is more than an aftershock of the slave trade; it is an ongoing dynamic creation. (Lipsitz 1994, 39)

Lipsitz insists that the original citizens of Bambaataa's "nation" included African Americans, Puerto Ricans, Afro-Caribbeans, and European Americans (Lipsitz 1994, 26). This position is endorsed by Bambaataa himself who has said that initially hip hop was not about race but rather about ideology (see Israel 2002).

A good deal of the hip hop scholarship which has utilized the Black Atlantic approach has focused on hip hop's hybrid origins as a means to legitimizing its global proliferation. Nonetheless, one is left asking if a model that locates hip hop within the international crosswinds of aesthetics, identity construction, and economic processes of capital accumulation goes too far in devaluing the importance of hip hop's blackness and Americanness (Perry 2004). The Black Atlantic model is probably best viewed as a series of historically patterned relations of diffusion, exchange, and identification through which contemporary black cultures and consciousnesses continue to be constituted. However, by placing their analyses within the realm of black consciousness, Gilroy, Lipsitz, and other followers of the approach are appealing to a kind of postcolonial essentialism that is ultimately transferable to other (non-black) disenfranchised subjects. In this regard, Gilroy's model has certainly lent well to scholarship on hip hop outside the United States (Bennett 1999a; Hesmondhalgh and Melville 2001; Levy 2001), where many local scenes have few, if any, regular black participants.

In presenting these aspects of Black Atlantic hip hop scholarship, I am not suggesting that any significant proportion of underground hip hoppers are familiar with the work of Gilroy or Lipsitz in the way that most self-professed hip hoppers can recite the stories of Kool Herc. However, since its publication, the Black Atlantic model has weighed heavily on many works that attempt to understand hip hop through a diasporic paradigm. Even when Gilroy is not directly referenced, the prevailing focus on transnational essences soaked in the trappings of modernity flows from Black Atlantic waters.

By centering their debates over race and hip hop authenticity on questions of origin, scholars and commentators are seeking to socially and historically establish the terms of hip hop's initial expression as a measure to be used for assessing the legitimacy of its contemporary manifestations (Moore 2002). The strength of such arguments lie in their matter-of-fact reliance on a stable notion of hip hop culture "as it was intended to be," which transparently follows from a progression (in the case of cultural survivals approaches) or a confluence (as with the Black Atlantic model) of cultural, sociopolitical, and psychological experiences—most often involving black people. But history, by its very nature, is contingent and selective. It involves an ongoing interpretation of the past that gets enlisted in shaping relations of authority in the present (Hobsbawm 1983; Stokes 1994). For someone immersed within these debates, a proper understanding of hip hop's history becomes a sound basis on which to gauge the authenticity of hip hop in any form. Thus, both the individual who follows Perry's steadfast declaration that "hip hop music is black American music" (2004, 10) and the one who adheres to George's claim that the belief that "at some early moment [hip hop was] solely African-American created, owned, controlled, and consumed" is little more than "an appealing origin myth" (1998, 57) take firm reassurance in the idea that they understand the essence of hip hop in a way that anyone who disagrees with them simply does not.

Hip Hop Today: Contemporary Manifestations

The third significant area of discussion surrounding hip hop culture and racial authenticity acknowledges its origins—the specific version is not so important—but places greater significance on the racial composition and legitimacy of its contemporary forms. The key question here is whether the full breadth of hip hop's history has involved non-black people to enough of an extent that, at some point, these individuals and communities were able to legitimately claim their connection to (and sometimes, by extension, "their ownership of") hip hop. In other words, has hip hop evolved to the point where a Chinese American living in Brooklyn (to use an example explored by Taylor 2005) can today genuinely refer to it as "my music"?

Whether New York City Puerto Ricans are considered among hip hop's originators or not, that they were proximately positioned relative to hip hop's formation is enough for most scholars to grant them some degree of insider status (Ogbar 2007). By locating Puerto Rican identities in an ill-defined ethnoracial middle ground between blackness and its Latino equivalent, which she refers to as "latinidad," Rivera (2001, 2003) draws attention to the manner in which this acceptance has been achieved and precariously maintained. Similarly, the "parallel discourses" of marginalization shared by African Americans and Chicanos (Delgado 1998) and "employed" by large numbers of Asian American youth (Ogbar 2007, 53) have enabled each group to construct a claim to hip hop authenticity around the notion of its fundamentally oppositional politics. But should such recognition be extended to those non-black groups who are more generally regarded as being heirs to the dominant institutional structures that hip hop is typically presented as emerging in response to (namely, white youth)?

An early charge to this effect was leveled by David Samuels who, in his oft-cited *New Republic* article "The Rap on Rap: The Black Music That

Isn't Either" (1991), pointed out that, since at least the early nineties, both a significant proportion of the key movers and shakers within the rap Music Industry (with the obvious exception of rappers themselves) and rap's predominant consumer base have been white. This understanding of the relationship between identity and music is predicated on what music scholar Keith Negus calls "articulation," and describes as the "web of unmediated connections" between processes of production and consumption (1997, 135). Negus insists that a proper understanding of cultural production should move beyond simple notions of linear channels from producers to consumers. Hip hop's musical, artistic, and social performances are all consciously enacted with an audience (even just an audience of peers) in mind. This intention and understanding of audience expectation and reception has always been a crucial element in hip hop creative production. Even hip hop's original emcees first took to the stage with the clear intention of "moving the crowd."

By highlighting the reciprocal impact of producers and consumers, articulation, as a concept, directs attention toward production of culture (Peterson 1976) processes, which by their very nature challenge organic, primordial, and/or essentialist links between hip hop and specific social groups. This is not to say that hip hop, as a popular cultural medium existing within a field of cultural production, cannot retain an essentially black character; in fact, Samuels would quite likely agree that much of hip hop's Music Industry production has been done with exactly this intention in mind. However, such a reading of hip hop is predicated more on the symbolic construction of social boundaries than on some naturally occurring relationship between musical forms and specific racial or cultural groups.[17]

These issues can be unpacked further by considering the degree to which black subjectivities (as opposed to an objectified blackness) are understood to be active agents in the production of hip hop culture. By McLeod's reading, hip hop's ghettocentric turn (Kelley 1994; McLaren 1995; Smith 1997)—its emphasis on hypermasculine urbanity, blackness, and a certain street-situated outlook on life—should be viewed as a response by the hip hop community (read black) to the threat of assimilation via the mainstreaming of hip hop (read white). Thus, an awareness of hip hop's white market encouraged its music makers and cultural producers to actively take on a more culturally exclusive message and aesthetic. Evidence supporting this line of reasoning can be seen in the slogan "It's a Black Thing, You Wouldn't Understand," which appeared rather suddenly on college campuses and other places where young black and white people came into contact at precisely the moment when hip hop's mainstream appeal was becoming too obvious to ignore.[18]

Indeed, hip hop's turn toward ghettocentrism was soaked in a strong sense of post-Reaganomics inner-city black authenticity that could not have succeeded without a level of popular black endorsement (see Ogbar 2007).[19] Still, it is equally valid, I believe, to recognize that such spectacularized images of blackness have been highly profitable entertainment commodities within the white consumer market for nearly two centuries, since Thomas "Daddy" Rice first developed the popular minstrel character Jim Crow (see Jefferson 1973). Many underground hip hoppers are well aware of how these sensationalized expressions of ghettocentricity have served as commercial strategies aimed at appealing to a mainstream market (see Chapter 1). This was precisely Samuels's point: "[that] the more rappers were packaged as violent black criminals the bigger their white audiences became" (1991, 25). Furthermore, Samuels stated, many of hip hop's most pivotal taste makers— for example, Rick Rubin (who along with Russell Simmons founded Def Jam records), David Mays and Jon Shector (who together started *The Source* magazine), and Barry Weiss (president and CEO of Jive Records)—were also white (see also George 1998).[20]

Starting in the early 1990s, numerous reports began to surface that claimed upwards of 70 percent of all hip hop music fans were white suburban teenagers (Aaron 1999; Leland 1992; Light 1992; Lusane 1993). Since that time, many of the most popular books, articles, and films dealing with hip hop have featured European American authors, protagonists, and/or lead characters. These include books like William "Upski" Wimsatt's *Bomb the Suburbs* (1994), Patrick Neate's *Where You're At* (2004), and Jason Tanz's *Other People's Property* (2007); Hollywood films such as *Bulworth* (1998), *White Boys* (1998), *8 Mile* (2002), and *Malibu's Most Wanted* (2003); as well as notable articles like Wimsatt 's "We Use Words Like Mackadocious" (1993), which became, at the time of its publication, "the most responded to article in the history of hip-hop journalism" (Wimsatt 1994, 22).[21] Although many of these were satirical it does not diminish the fact that their appeal lay in their representing a phenomenon which increasingly more Americans could identify or identify with.

In his 1998 book *Hip Hop America*, Nelson George dedicates a chapter specifically to the question of white nurturing and belonging within hip hop. Reminiscent of Samuels, he begins by making several challenging claims about where hip hop would be without white involvement. For example, George comments that "scores of white stepmothers and [step]fathers adopted [hip hop] as their own and many have shown more loyalty to [it] than more celebrated black parental figures" (George 1998, 57). This is certainly provocative stuff. Even more telling (for my purposes), is that George's chapter ends with an anecdote about attending a 1995 Labor Day Run DMC concert in the Hamptons (Long Island, NY) in which the "99.9% white audience" exuded a profound sense of connectedness with and reminiscence for mid-1980s hip hop: "'My Adidas,' 'Rock Box,' and 'King of Rock' are not exotic to this crowd. It is the music they grew up on . . . for these twenty-somethings Run-D.M.C. is '80s nostalgia. . . . It may not be what many folks want hip hop to mean, but it is a true aspect of what hip hop has become" (George 1998, 75).

Hip Hop has been part of the American youth popular cultural land-scape for at least a quarter century. Twenty-first–century young people, regardless of their racial, ethnic, economic, or geographic background, have lived their entire lives with hip hop as a readily accessible cultural resource. Even within the least black, least urban "hoods," a fascination with hip hop has become something of an adolescent rite of passage (Roediger 1998).[22]

The phenomenon of white enthrallment with black musical and cultural forms has a history that extends farther back than the origins of hip hop. Since at least the 1957 publication of Norman Mailer's essay "The White Negro," this uniquely youth-driven mode of musical miscegenation has attracted the attention of scholars on both sides of the (black) Atlantic (see, for example, Chambers 1976; Grossberg 1984; Hebdige 1979; Jones 1963; Rudinow 1994). One of the more ambitious treatments on the subject was proffered by Simon Jones who, in his book *Black Culture, White Youth* (1988), describes a uniquely transformative "cultural dialectic" resulting from complex relations of power, appropriation, innovation, and commerce. According to Jones:

> Those relations turn on the contradictions of using forms inherently op-posed to white hegemony and forged out of the experience of racial op-pression, as sources of meaning and pleasure. At the heart of them lay a fundamental tension between white youth's struggles for more respon-sive and articulate modes of cultural expression, and black musicians' struggles against white cultural and economic power to redefine their music. (1988, xxi; see also Back 1996)

The trajectories of hip hop's multicultural, interracial, and global spread fol-low from the same processes Jones effectively outlined. However, allusions to its hybrid origins, appropriative modes of expression, and hyper-mediated contemporary transmission[23] all suggest that hip hop exists as a more adaptive and malleable cultural resource than earlier black music varieties.

There is no question that hip hop is experienced differently within various social contexts. As my Amoeba co-worker attested, it can take on disparate meanings when consumed in relative isolation as opposed to within a vibrant local scene. It should also be remembered that each distinct audience approaches hip hop through its own interpretive frameworks (Gracyk 2001). In light of these differences, it surprises me that, within the United States at least, a greater variety of socio-spatial contexts are not viewed as noteworthy sites of hip hop resonance.

Forman (2002) points out that as the organizing tropes surrounding hip hop authenticity shifted from the cultural to the spatial—from the arena of black experience to the inner-city and ghetto (see Smith 1997)—the boundaries of hip hop affiliation became more racially and socioculturally permeable. Rivera echoes Forman by describing this as the "slight relaxing of blackness's ethnoracial scope," which by her account allowed for a recognition of the "virtually indistinguishable . . . experiences of class and ethnoracial marginalization" shared by African Americans and specific Latino groups (2001, 249). As with the origin claims discussed above, outside of hip hop's persons-of-color alliances (and at times even within them), there is a certain danger in overstating the affinity between these groups; for, as cultural critic Jeffrey Ogbar reminds us, "the popular understanding of what it means to be 'Latino' exists outside the parameters of the popular understanding of being black" (2007, 41).

Hip hop's expanding inclusivity can also be explained through what Christopher Holmes Smith describes as its "'keep it real' . . . engagement with American commercial culture" (1997, 348); that is, the rise of hip hop's "ghetto-fabulous" or "bling-bling" aesthetic. Smith argues that despite hip hoppers predisposition to stand in opposition to all things mainstream—what McLeod lists as mass trends, commercialism, the suburbs, and whiteness—the foregrounding of materialism, which has always been a part of hip hop (Rose 1994) but which reached unprecedented levels as the music became more commercially viable, actually functioned as "camouflaged means of negotiation" (Smith 1997, 348). I state all this to illustrate what should be an obvious point: that the mainstreaming of hip hop opened up legitimate avenues and spaces for engagement by young Americans from a variety of racial, ethnic, class, and geographic backgrounds.

In moving forward, I think it is useful to temporarily set aside conventional critiques of white, or non-black, hip hop as appropriation (something I will return to in Chapter 5) and instead focus on considerations of hip hop's cultural diffusion;—specifically, the diffusion of aesthetics, activities, politics, and social sensibilities that has occurred both through and in response to commercially sculpted presentations of urban African American youth culture. I believe Forman (2002, 61) was correct in stating that the prevailing tendency to associate hip hop with black authenticity has come at the expense of a more dynamic picture of hip hop's place within today's multiracial urban youth spaces. Furthermore, I would advocate for the inclusion of predominantly white spaces, Latino social events, Asian American community centers, and a host of other manifestations and permutations into our existing understandings of sites where contemporary hip hop culture flourishes.

Nothing I have written should be taken as the definitive answer to questions of hip hop authenticity and racial identity. I can at once wholeheartedly agree with philosopher Paul C. Taylor's assertion that when "we start to attend to the complexities of history, to the details of cultural borrowings and cross fertilizations, it becomes hard to say when a culture really belongs to a single group" (2005, 91), yet still find wisdom in Perry's claim that "America's love-hate relationship with" hip hop stands as arguably the single greatest testament to its position as black music (2004, 27). What is most critical here is the interpretive process by which such questions get answered. Through the existing body of scholarship on hip hop, a variety of different readings of its connection to race have been put forth. And, as a subset of the hip hop nation that pays homage to its traditional practices and is acutely aware of its historical scholarship, underground hip hoppers are prepared and at times eager to enlist any combination of these arguments in asserting their authentic claims.

In a terrific ethnographic account of hip hop authenticity in all-white Newcastle upon the Tyne in northeast England, Andy Bennett (1999a) identifies two patterned responses by white Newcastle youth seeking to validate their connection to hip hop. As one might expect, one of these responses involves asserting that hip hop is not a black thing, but a class or a street thing; or, I might add, whatever the person making the assertion sees as their legitimate connection to it (maybe a "youth thing"). The second position, perhaps more surprisingly, acknowledges hip hop as black music and uses that recognition as an avenue for claiming a personal understanding of it and, by virtue, a connection to it. A quote from one of Bennett's subjects, a hip hop record store owner named Jim, makes the point: "There's no such thing as white hip hop. . . . Because hip hop is black music. As white people we should still respect it as black music . . . I went to New York, well actually to Cleveland near New York and stayed with a black family. It was brilliant, it changed my life. You can't talk about white hip hop, it doesn't exist" (Bennett 1999a, 11).

While non-African American San Francisco Bay Area underground hip hoppers' connections to blackness tend to be more substantive than Jim's brilliant visit to Cleveland, the practice of understanding hip hop's essential blackness as a means to legitimizing a place within it is common enough (see Chapter 4). Whereas Bennett presents his two case-study responses as distinct, I propose that they actually represent two poles along a continuum and that among sophisticated, less isolated, and more subculturally attuned constituents of multiracial underground hip hop scenes, amalgamations of the two approaches are quite normal. In other words, acknowledgments of hip hop's essential blackness and non-essential inclusiveness can and do occur simultaneously. My aim is not to support or refute the position that hip hop is or is not essentially black music, but to illustrate how the multiple voices in this dialogue provide various resources and lines of argument from which hip hop enthusiasts commonly draw in making their own claims to understanding "real hip hop" and justifying their relationship to it.

Subcultural Capital, Racialism, and Underground Hip Hop's Ethical Code

The vast majority of Bay Area underground hip hop enthusiasts that I met—regardless of race, class, or geographic background—could recount relationships with hip hop that extended back over most of their lives. DJ Mizzo, for example, was certainly not alone in his recollection of hip hop being a part of his earliest school years:

> DJM: I just think that with anyone growing up in San Francisco in the eighties, hip hop was probably like the first popular culture that anyone remembers, even if you went to private school. I went to public school. I went to a Japanese bilingual school, so most of the kids were Japanese, Japanese American, but everyone listened to hip hop. That was like the big thing. When I was in kindergarten, I just remember all the older fifth

graders. They would come to school and they had their boomboxes and stuff, and they'd be breaking in the schoolyard, and I just thought it was the coolest thing. I wanted to break dance so bad. Break dancing was like huge.

Perhaps more important than elementary school break-dancing battles, influential recordings—or what Theodore Gracyk (2001) refers to as musical "texts"—serve as conduits through which a variety of understandings of hip hop circulate and meaning-making occurs. San Francisco emcee Dope Cigars recalled his first cassette tape being the Beastie Boys *Licensed to Ill*, purchased for him by his older brother when he was in third grade. "It was one of the first influences I had," he explained. The first album Feller Quentin ever bought was Run DMC's self-titled debut (1984), purchased when he was just eight. A third white emcee who goes by the name Black Santa Claus recalled Run DMC's *Raising Hell* (1986) album, which came out when he was in fourth grade, as his first rap music experience. Within just a few years Black Santa Claus was making rap songs on a practice drum pad with his suburban California friends.

The model of underground hip hop participatory ethics that I put forth in the following pages is intended as a means to organizing the varied identities within this multiracial hip hop scene. Although my model was formed through insights gleaned within the Bay Area and its underground hip hop corridors, because it is founded on broadly applicable understandings of race, ethnicity, and hip hop, as well as sociological processes of identification, self-presentation, and inclusion, wider inferences can be made regarding similarly diverse settings where racial and hip hop authenticity come into play. In Table 3.1 (see below) I present my "Preliminary Map of Hip Hop Racialism," which forms the groundwork for the complex cultural dynamics that I describe below. *Racialism* is the belief that the social world we inhabit can be accurately divided into a series of distinctly identifiable racial groupings (Appiah 1990a). Thus, this preliminary map serves as an index to the default statuses assigned to hip hoppers based on their racial identities. Without denying any individual or collective group their license to hip hop authenticity, this mapping of race (and ethnicity) stands as an indication that such legitimacy is not doled out on equal terms (which is probably quite clear from all that I have said already). The Preliminary Map of Hip Hop Racialism simply sets the landscape that each individual must initially negotiate.

All underground scenes feature social logics that are characteristically skeptical of, if not downright adverse to, a perceived mass population or mainstream (Thornton 1995). Thus, a premium is placed on subcultural distinction and boundary maintenance. In this effort, the interactions taking place within underground scenes are often strewn with evaluative assessments intended to keep this ever encroaching mainstream at bay. In the following passage, emcees Dope Cigars and Dialex explain to me how such (inclusive/exclusive) evaluations pervaded even their work environments, where they chose to listen to (what was at the time relatively commercial) underground hip hop music.

DOPE CIGARS: With some of these people, I have a problem with letting them in on what [a particular piece of music] is. . . . Like I work at this fast food restaurant place and we serve shit all day. It's like takeout lunch food . . . and I'll play a lot of things that people will ask about, like Blackalicious and Jurassic Five. When I play that, everybody always asks, "Is this the Jurassic?" "Is this the Jurassic Fives?" "Is this the Five Jurassics?" You know that shit? "Juraawssics?" Like, they don't know how to say it. And I'm like "this is the Jurassic Five." And they're like, "Really? Where are they from?" and I'm like "Los Angeles." "What is this called?" "It's called 'Quality Control'" "I gotta get this album!!"

AKH: And you don't want to give [the information] to these people?

DOPE: Some of these people, especially if they pronounce it wrong or they're just trying to guess it, I'll be like, this guy's a fuckin' idiot, and they're trying to make small talk with me, and I don't give a shit what you have to say; especially if I'm annoyed at work.

AKH: You don't think they really want to get it?

DOPE: No. They're trying to make small talk. If someone comes in and they look like they're about my age, and if they're dressed like a student, or something like that, especially if I'm listening to something obscure . . . you can tell if it's just in passing or if it's genuine. Like then I'll go out of my way and tell them what it is. I don't know. It just seems like some of those people are trying to get music to play at their parties on weekends.

AKH: In order to be hip?

DOPE: Yes! Yes! Completely.

AKH: But they don't really love it?

DIALEX: No, they don't really love it. They don't understand it either. Like, "this song's cool! I bet a lot of people will think I'm cool if I listen to this and they heard me listening to it." I'm like, fuck that!

DOPE: Go listen to some DMX![24]

Clearly both Dope Cigars and Dialex recognized that their knowledge of (what were at the time) the latest underground hip hop releases was a valuable social resource, which provided anyone who possessed it with a level of "hipness" (my word) or "coolness" (theirs). Knowledge of this sort—being aware of good music, understanding underground terminology, being familiar with the latest dance steps—is just one of several spheres of influence that Thornton (1995) locates within her framework of subcultural capital. Building off of Pierre Bourdieu's (1984) notion of cultural capital, Thornton describes *subcultural capital* as an "alternative hierarchy" within the terrain of youth culture in which status is conferred through the elusive aesthetic of "cool." In addition to embodied qualities such as knowledge, behaviors, and attitudes, such capital can be objectified in the form of clothing, haircuts, and record collections (Thornton 1995).

This concept serves as a useful means for beginning to make sense of the assessments and evaluations that are constantly taking place within underground hip hop scenes. I do not mean to imply that all underground hip hoppers are constantly on the lookout for "fuckin' idiots" searching for "music to play at their parties." In this regard, the San Francisco lunch crowd might be a particularly suspicious bunch. But subcultural spaces are so thoroughly saturated with symbols signifying degrees of insiderness— particularly within hip hop, which is regarded simultaneously as popular music and an anti-commercial subculture—that, even without being consciously aware of it, constituents are constantly reading their social worlds as texts. The form of greeting, a reaction to a particular song, an awareness of a specific artist, and certainly a person's racial identity all communicate subtle bits of information which underground hip hoppers use to round out their initial sketches of one another and to decide the extent to which they are interest in "being down with" someone.

At this point, I need to be clear in saying that rather than using Thornton's concept in the usual framework of subcultural analysis, I am applying the notion of subcultural capital specifically to the kinds of microsocial evaluations that take place within music scenes. The key difference being that the subculture model presumes a single commonly shared set of measurements with regard to subcultural capital, whereas the music scene perspective allows for relative measures, multiple cores of association, and varying degrees of salience (Peterson and Bennett 2004; see also Bennett 1999b).

This notion of sociality through processes of ongoing assessment has been a standard of sociological research at least since Erving Goffman first sketched the contours of his dramaturgical approach. Indeed, Goffman opens his classic, *The Presentation of Self in Everyday Life,* as follows: "When an individual enters the presence of others, they commonly seek to acquire information about him [sic] or to bring into play information about him [sic] already possessed" (1959, 1). The flipside of this postulation is the dynamic and ongoing presentation of self, informed by an understanding that in the same way an individual makes subtle yet consequential appraisals of others, his or her social performances are also being assessed. Navigating one's way through the subcultural terrain of hip hop authenticity often involves a particularly animated self-presentation. Still, outside of obvious considerations like deciding what shirt to wear to a photo shoot, I would caution against attributing too much conscious intentionality to many of these choices. It is not as if underground hip hoppers stand in front of the mirror for hours figuring out just the right outfit to wear or attempting to master the perfect subcultural gesture (at least I don't think so).

Just prior to traveling to the Bay to begin my official fieldwork, I found myself in a Pittsfield (MA) clothing store trying to decide between a relatively nondescript black messenger bag and a bright yellow Ecko Unltd. one. In a moment of vanity I chose the more ostentatious of the two, not realizing the extent to which, within the backpack-saturated world of underground hip hop, my yellow Ecko bag would come to be one of my most defining accessories. At that time (maybe still) the Ecko brand name was popular within many underground hip hop circles.[25] By branding this logo to my person virtually everywhere I traveled, I was signaling, or at least strongly suggesting, to anyone literate in reading the subcultural codes, that I was "down with the underground." The frequency with which I was asked whether I was an emcee or a deejay testifies to this. A few other "accessories" which undoubtedly contributed to my underground hip hopper image were my headphones, my dreadlocks, and of course my African American racial identity.

Mapping Hip Hop Racialism

At one time it might have been thought that non-black people were incapable of successfully or convincingly mastering the aesthetics of hip hop performance (i.e., "white people can't rap"); today, the question is no longer about who is innately or culturally capable but rather what gives someone the right. My Preliminary Map of Hip Hop Racialism (see Table 3.1) addresses this question by presenting a right-based hierarchy grouped through collective categories of racial and ethnic social identity. It is modeled after a tri-racial stratification system proposed by Eduardo Bonilla-Silva to explain what he describes as an emergent hierarchy of racial classification within the United States (see Bonilla-Silva 2004, 225). Following Bonilla-Silva, my aim is to articulate a complex structure of racial stratification that recognizes the presence and importance of the millions of Americans who fall outside the traditional black–white binary. Also like him, my framework features a "categorical porosity-fluidity" (Bonilla-Silva 2004, 226) that allows individuals to move up or down the hierarchy by elaborating on dimensions of their personal identity (Appiah 1994). Lastly, Bonilla-Silva and I agree that the recognition of multiple racial and ethnic groups should not distract us from the enduring significance of blackness and whiteness, which continue to stand at opposite ends of the hierarchy and thus define the trajectory of all racializing dynamics.

Our models differ, however, in two important ways. First, because I am presenting a map of underground hip hop racialism, rather than mapping ra-

TABLE 3.1   Preliminary Map of Hip Hop Racialism

"Black"	Blacks/African Americans Recent Caribbean and African Immigrants Part African-descended Multiracials More Racialized Latinos*
"Collective People of Color"	Filipino Americans Other Pacific Islanders (e.g., Hawaiians) Korean and Japanese Americans (and by default other Asian Americans) Arab Americans Native Americans Non-African descended Multiracials Less Racialized Latinos*
"White"	Recent White Immigrants (Eastern Europeans) One-time Marginalized White Ethnics (Jews, Italians, Irish, etc.) Anglo-Americans ("ordinary" whites)

*The distinction between what I am calling "More Racialized" and "Less Racialized" Latinos is admittedly imprecise. Generally speaking, I am using the latter term to refer to Latinos who, through language use, dress, and other (both cultural and phenotypic) forms of self–presentation, do not appear all that different from white people. Bonilla-Silva makes a similar distinction between "Dark-skinned and Poor Latinos" and "White middle-class Latinos" (2004, 225).

cial privilege more generally, my hierarchy is inverted. For even within this supposedly color-blind hip hop world, in the quest for legitimacy black identities are most privileged and white identities have the most to overcome. Second, where Bonilla-Silva takes care to mention most, if not all, significant racial and ethnic groups within the United States (he lists a total of twenty levels of racial strata), I limit my categories to the specific identities that I feel in someway qualified to comment on. This will surely leave out many Bay Area hip hoppers whom I simply did not cross paths with in any meaningful capacity. In an essay examining Bay Area hip hop's global consciousness, Eric Arnold (2006) points out that fifty-seven different languages are spoken in Oakland alone. To the extent that many of these groups might include young people who identify with hip hop, most of them will not be represented here. Still, as a point from which to begin, I think the map illustrates important contours along underground hip hop's multiracial landscape.

For individuals falling under the "Black" racial grouping, hip hop credibility is almost a given. Surely an exhibited lack of subcultural capital or competence can lead to its loss, yet in many cases, the mere presence of a person falling within the "Black" grouping at an underground hip hop event—with an added sprinkling of subculturally appropriate (yet not overly commercial) accessories and symbols—is enough to grant them a de facto level of legitimacy. For example, despite any confidence that I might have in my own hip hop performing abilities, I would not fool myself into believing that I would have been so quickly embraced by so many underground hip hop enthusiasts, so strenuously encouraged to start emceeing, or so well received as a novice public performer had it not been for my black racial identity.

Underground hip hoppers who are identified as falling under the "Collective People of Color" grouping have more to prove. However, through displays of subcultural capital (the details of which are outlined below) it is not all that difficult for them to establish the legitimacy of their hip hop self-presentations. Still, for some I interviewed, the understanding that hip hop originated within black communities led to a level of uneasiness about their place within it. This was particularly true of those who regularly reflected on issues of race and thus chose to confront the possibility that their participation in hip hop might not be viewed as all that different from white people who have historically been accused of appropriating black music forms.[26] DJ Mizzo, who identifies as having one white parent and one parent who is part Japanese and part Chinese, quite poignantly expressed his ambivalence regarding this:

DJM: Anyone can be in hip hop now pretty much. It's just about your skill, you know? It's not about whether you're black or whether you're whatever, you know? But at the same time, I think we have to come to grips that there is a split between underground and like the mainstream, and in the mainstream it's all black artists and in the underground it's really diverse. . . . Before it was just the black community, the black community created the music and the black community consumed it. Now it's like, sorta becoming like Jazz . . . I'm not sure what it's gonna become in the future. If what we call hip hop is gonna be something else . . . I'm not really sure if I'm part of the solution or part of the problem in the whole thing. I can only do what I feel and I definitely feel a connection to hip hop.

For persons within the "White" racial grouping, the onus is on them to demonstrate to others that their forays into the underground hip hop lifestyle are genuine and that their position within it is legitimate. That so many white hip hoppers have successfully done this tells me that for the "true" underground hip hop enthusiast it is not a tremendously difficult challenge. This frequency of success also allows for the existence and continuation of a color-blind ideology (Rodriquez, 2006). However, for this group particularly, legitimacy is often contingent on who is doing the assessing. Some hip hoppers I spoke with tended to be particularly weary of "all these white emcees tryin' to front." Conversely, several European American emcees shared their struggles about feeling unaccepted: "The last couple of weeks [at the Rockin' Java open-mic] I've tried to talk to people and I feel like when I'm trying to talk to them they're not understanding where I'm coming from. They haven't seen me around or they just don't know me so they're just like, 'who are you?' and they keep their distance more or less." Although some were hesitant to come out and say it, the question of race, specifically the issue of their white identity, was everpresent in their reflections on these struggles.

RONNY CEE: I don't really want to say it, but this is something I have to address within hip hop. . . . This is such a crutch. I don't even want to bring it up. But I think it might be a little bit about race.

AKH: Do you think that you get flack as a white emcee?

RC: Oh yeah. No one has necessarily said shit to my face but I mean, like I said, a lot of times people will hear my shit and they'll like it.

And like, I don't really think that they want to work with me because of that. I don't know. Like, sometimes I think about that. It makes me wonder.

I want to reiterate that these subcultural evaluations and presentations of self are, on the whole, neither calculated nor conscious. I believe that most of the underground hip hoppers who professed to thinking that an emcee's race does not matter were being truthful with me, but perhaps not with themselves. At moments of ambiguity, for instance when trying to make sense out of a Latino emcee repeatedly drifting away from you when you try to engage him in a post open-mic conversation, many white hip hoppers are pressed to confront the likelihood that the issue of their race may come into play

In addition, I think it is important to consider that the scope of one's perceived authenticity or lack thereof can subconsciously impact the confidence exuded during social performances. Those who have racial identities that historically place them under greater scrutiny, whether they recognize it or not, are invariably more pensive in seeking out the right balance between activity and disinterest that gets understood as the ever elusive "cool."

This becomes something like an inverted form of W.E.B. Du Bois's famous "double consciousness" postulation. Where Du Bois contended that being black in America yielded "no true self-consciousness," but rather an existence rooted in "always looking at one's self through the eyes of others" (1996 [1903], 5), white hip hoppers participating within multiracial underground hip hop milieus cannot, or should not, lose sight of the ways in which their racial identity impacts their pursuit of hip hop authenticity. During an early conversation I had with Top R, he practically echoed Du Bois in explaining that "you have to be aware of how your role as a white hip hop artist is viewed by both the black community and the white community."

As a final word of explanation about my Preliminary Map, I should make clear that I have organized the hierarchies within each racial grouping with the same attention to perceived hip hop legitimacy (or de facto right) that structures the entire model. For instance, Filipinos, who have been referred to as "brown Asians" (Espiritu 1992, 32; see also Balce 2006), are located closer to "Black" status than other Asian groups. These delineations are arrived at through a consideration of four principal factors:

1. A group's history (or awareness thereof) of persecution through colonial or neocolonial regimes. It is here where allusions to a Black Atlantic–inspired postcolonial understanding of hip hop carry the greatest weight.
2. A group's current experiences with racism and discrimination in America.
3. The extent to which a group is already identified as actively engaged in hip hop. The West Coast awareness of the tremendous popularity of hip hop in Japan (Condry 2006; Wood 1998) and Korea (Morelli 2001) results in Korean and Japanese American hip hoppers being placed above Arab Americans, even if the latter (in the post 911 era) experience greater racism.
4. My own impressions of the extent to which, given the other three factors, members of each group struggle with being accepted.

Of course any listing of this sort is ripe for discussion and debate. Given their history of persecution, should hip hoppers identifying as Native American be higher on the list than some of the other "Collective People of Color" groups? How can there be such a great distance between the two (somewhat ambiguous) categories of Latinos? Since this map is merely a basis from which to begin, with the greater point being the racial mobility with which non-black individuals ascend this hierarchy, I can only ask that readers not dwell on their issues with my rankings too stringently.

Dimensions of Underground Hip Hop's Subcultural Capital

Earlier in this chapter I explained that Thornton divides subcultural capital into the categories of objectified and embodied attributes. While this distinction is obviously useful, because my discussion here is concerned more with underground hip hoppers' situational assessments of one another and how these are connected to processes of racialization, I want to highlight a dichotomy of a different sort. Some aspects of subcultural capital are readily discernable and can be verified through empirical inquiry. This includes all forms of objectified capital, for instance: Do you wear a Living Legends t-shirt? Do you have Bored Stiff's *Ghetto Research* CD? Do you make beats on (i.e., own) an E-mu SP1200 sampler? Many of Thornton's embodied characteristics can also, more or less, be confirmed through direct examination: Do you know the song that Bored Stiff's Big Shawn sampled on track number four? Do you greet fellow hip hoppers in the subculturally appropriate manner (or have the knowledge to)?[27] Do you have a mastery of the national and local underground hip hop vernacular?

I only once recall witnessing someone blatantly attempting to administer such an "underground hip hop test." It occurred outside the Rockin' Java open-mic a week after a white emcee named Tré Nice[28] (actually his entire multiracial crew—The Sultans of Style) had suffered a humiliating defeat in a showdown with, what one witness described as, a pair of "battle-ready Latino emcees" named Jay Star and Protégé. To no one's great surprise, the following week neither Tré Nice nor any of the Sultans were anywhere to be found, at least initially. As the open-mic came to a close and people started filing out of the coffee shop onto the sidewalk, Tré suddenly appeared stumbling through the crowd with a forty-ounce bottle of malt liquor half-concealed in his jacket. When he finally came face-to-face with Jay Star, amid much commotion and slurred speech, Tré started to quiz him about whether he or Protégé could name "the second graffiti writer to come out of Oakland," all of which caused Jay to turn and walk away muttering something in disgust. My lasting memory of that evening, one which in the weeks to come would be recounted many times by several of the people present, was of a lone, drunk, Tré Nice standing in the middle of a crowd repeatedly yelling "who was the second graffiti writer to come out of Oakland?"

As rare and unsuccessful as Tré's effort may have been, it offered a telling glimpse into the kind of underground hip hop jockeying that usually occurs at a more implicit level. It is during disruptive events, when individuals' definitions of the situation break down, that key dynamics about self-presentation and status maintenance are revealed (Goffman 1959). For Tré Nice, the blend of alcohol and emotions—which included humiliation, anger, confusion (about why he had been attacked the previous week), and the urgency of needing to save face—combined to momentarily lift the veil of tactful subcultural posturing. There was no concealing the fact that, for Tré, this confrontation was all about proving he was "more underground hip hop" than his rivals. And, in his state of mind at the time, he was willing to go to transparent extremes to demonstrate this was so.

There is yet another dimension of subcultural capital that is not so easy to empirically observe. I am speaking of an ideological element that is often thought to be exhibited through certain political and social predispositions. If we accept that a good deal of most subcultural capital revolves around the elusive notion of "coolness," I propose that in the realm of underground hip hop the ideological complement to coolness is an equally elusive concept that can be referred to as "knowing what's up." I choose this particular terminology because of the frequency with which I heard it used either in describing a person ("she knows what's up") or as a statement of approval in response to a particular thought or idea that was introduced ("that's what's up"). To an extent, "knowing what's up" is synonymous with "coolness." For instance, I am quite sure that almost anyone who feels that a particular person "knows what's up," would also agree that said person "is cool." However, it seems to me that relative to "knowing what's up," assessments of "coolness" focus largely on external, projected, or image-based considerations. "Knowing what's up," on the other hand, gets more at the core of someone's outlook on the world, from which such things as personal tastes, goals, and ideas about how to engage other people flow. For this reason, in the interpersonal quest for underground hip hop acceptance and legitimacy, having the appropriate sensibilities and worldviews (i.e., knowing what's up) ranks far ahead of being able to name all the members of a particular music group.

As opposed to more tangibly grasped aspects of subcultural capital, the determination of whether or not a person "knows what's up" is primarily made through inference. It is not so much what someone says or does, but rather what those acts of self-presentation and social performance are seen as implying about the individual. Thus a specific piece of knowledge, like knowing the history of the Oakland graffiti scene, is never in and of itself a qualification of "knowing what's up." However, having such knowledge can be indicative of a person being entrenched within the political struggles over aesthetics, recognition, and ownership (J. Austin 2001; Rose 1994) that graffiti has historically addressed.

Early one Sunday morning, while making my way up Haight Street toward one of my usual coffee shops to write field notes, I spotted my friend Devorah's brother Quake's graffiti tag[29] on the back of a street sign. At the time, Devorah and I had been friends long enough for me to be well familiar with her brother's *nom de plum*. "Quake's your brother?" I had heard her asked on several occasions; however, up until then, I had never seen (or more accurately, recognized) any of his work. Noticing his tag for the first time, I was surprised by the immediate rush of warmth that came over me. At one level, I felt a bond with Quake through Devorah. Seeing his mark for the very first time was something akin to finally meeting a friend of a friend. Even more profoundly, as a person making just a little over minimum wage and who considered himself lucky to be sleeping on someone else's back porch (see Chapter 2), I could identify with Quake and other graffiti writers' right, even their prerogative, to affirm their place within the city.

The impact of urban gentrification on the character and culture of turn-of-the-century San Francisco is well documented (see Hartman 2002; Hwang 2000). These changes were particularly noticed by underground hip hoppers who, along with members of other musical and artisan communities (and many marginalized racial and ethnic groups), saw tech-based professionals as a principal threat to their ability to live in the city (Glasner and Dean 2000). In a 2001 interview, deejay/skateboarder Satva Leung reflected on some of these changes:

> SL: The whole dot.com craze obviously had a big effect on the city. In the last couple of years there's just all these loft spaces being built up South of Market [Street]. Rents going up a lot. . . . I've heard a lot of stories [about] illegal evictions, landlords just being scandalous. . . . I think there's a lot more money in the city. You know, Haight Street is a big mall. . . . I mean everyone comes here. It's crazy here on the weekends. It wasn't like that before. At least I don't think so. It was more squatter-punks. . . . I think they're definitely trying to clean it up.

In 2000, a GAP clothing store opened on the corner of Haight and Ashbury Streets. The significance of having this corporate franchise (as well as a more tolerable Ben and Jerry's ice cream shop) at what many people consider the most important countercultural intersection in America (Perry 2005) did not go unnoticed. In what was unmistakably a political act aimed at addressing the paradox of the store's placement, during its first summer on "the Haight," the GAP had its front windows smashed seemingly every other week.

Quake's tagging the Haight was neither this spectacular nor this criminal. However, in a city where during a four-year period (1995–1999) rents had more than doubled, and it was estimated (then) that an annual income of $100,000 was needed to afford an average two-bedroom apartment (Hartman 2002, 325), battle lines were being drawn; graffiti writers, mostly young people with limited financial resources, were responding with a resounding declaration that the streets were theirs. As a service-sector employee, I shared an affinity with graffiti writers. Furthermore, as someone involved in the local hip hop community, I felt an increased sense of pride seeing that hip hop was the medium through which this resistance was being expressed.

Intellectually, I understood how graffiti functioned as a political act long before ever setting foot in the Bay. Moreover, through spending time with Devorah, Destined, and others, I had the (empirically verifiable) knowledge to name both prominent Bay Area graffiti crews and individual writers.

Nevertheless, the sudden intrinsic understanding which came to me on that barren, early Sunday morning streetscape amounted to more than just the sum of these parts. It issued from the interplay of structural awareness and situated investment, and as such had the effect of transforming the way I conceived of my position within my surroundings. Destined's earlier admonishment—that I educate myself about graffiti because it is "the language of the streets" (see Chapter 2)—suddenly made sense. Had I shared this moment with him (and I don't believe I did), it would not have surprised me if his response had been a definitive "that's what's up."

I stress that this ideological dimension of subcultural capital is *thought to be* expressed through politics and social sensibilities to draw attention to the fact that its inferential nature allows for the possibility that it might be feigned. For example, through a good reading of Rose's *Black Noise* (1994) and some knowledge regarding the identity of Devorah's brother—and, of course, a convincing performance—it would be possible to fabricate my preceding testimony. Minus any political sentiment or sense of communalism, I might have simply noticed Quake's tag and recognized it as an act of graffiti. Such is the difficulty with ideological capital of any sort. Even if we arrive at a suitable definition of exactly what it entails—and I would caution that ideological dimensions of subcultural capital like all dimensions are both relative and constantly changing—we can never be completely certain that it is genuine.

For this reason, social scientists have tended to focus on subcultural capital's more observable dimensions. However, within underground music scenes and similar subcultural spaces, worldviews, principles, and sensibilities are often more important than specific tastes in confirming social allegiances. Where shared tastes bring people together, it is the recognition of ideological affinities that actually connect them. It is here where the benefits of ethnography, particularly the critically situated variety that informs this work, offer the most promise of capturing and conveying something of the tenor of underground hip hoppers' views and understandings of their world.

Authenticity and Sincerity

Authenticity, as an essential or constructed quality of both music and musicians, has long been regarded as a standard mode of valuation within many genres (Peterson 1997, 2005). At the start of this chapter, I explained that debates surrounding authenticity within hip hop music, particularly with regards to race, are as robust as any to be found. Within the contexts of music scenes, most notably underground hip hop music scenes, authenticity is not only an attribute of the music and the people who make it, it is also ascribed (or denied) to any social actor who vies for acceptance. Considerations of authenticity, however, are not limited to music scenes and subcultures alone; they are also commonly applied to collective social groups, particularly those who lack the power to define themselves as "normal," and are therefore objectified or essentialized within the societies in which they reside. For African Americans, arguably the most depersonalized American group, issues of authenticity—delineations between who is "real" and who is a "sellout"—have a long history (see, for example, Binder 1999; Frazier 1957; Hare 1965). In the early 1960s, poet-activist Amiri Baraka spoke of an entire class of black people having formed "exclusively around the proposition that it was better not to be black in a country where being black is a liability" (Jones 1963, 123–124). In a similar vein a quarter century later, Public Enemy's Chuck D decried that "every brother ain't a brother" (Public Enemy 1990). Indeed, the precarious position of black people within America's social, political, and economic structures has fostered longstanding tensions between collective loyalties and fractured individual ambitions. Although some have argued that the class dimension of these tensions has been overblown (Dawson 1994; Pattillo-McCoy 1999), among communities of black youth particularly such identity politics are enforced through the demands and expectations associated with the concept of racial authenticity (Clay 2003).

Before going any further, I should make clear that the notion of authenticity I am grappling with here is never an actual property or attribute that is embodied in music, subcultures, or racial identities; it is rather what ethnomusicologist Martin Stokes calls "a discursive trope of great persuasive power" (1994, 7). Any claim to authenticity is by nature constructed, contingent, and potentially deceptive (Bendix 1997). That being said, it is nevertheless well acknowledged that at twenty-first–centuryAmerica's most potent intersection of music, subculture, and race (i.e., hip hop), the impacts of authenticity's demands have been extraordinarily pervasive in creating definitive narratives of young, urban (particularly male) blackness (see, for example, Clay 2003; Gordon 2005; Watkins 2005). At best, the most prominent of these can be viewed as expressions of "artful fantasy and badman style that reflect the competitive spirit of hip hop unorthodoxy" (Ogbar 2007; see also Neal 1999; Neff 2008; Quinn 2006); at worst, they are what journalist Bakari Kitwana has described as unadulterated accounts of a world of "crime, guns, drug-selling and drug using, sexual exploitation, irresponsible parenthood, Black-on-Black homicide, women as inferiors and objects, gang-life, 40oz drinking as routine, and extreme materialism" (1994, 50–51). Regardless of which of these perspectives one ascribes to, it seems clear enough that to young, urban African Americans living in close proximity to the worlds in which these narratives are set, there remains a "spectacularly symbiotic relationship" between such authentic hip hop representations and the pressures to conform to them which saturate their everyday realities (Watts 2004, 601; see also Pattillo-McCoy 1999).

To help make sense of all this, I draw on philosopher Kwame Appiah's (1994) notion of "scripts," which he describes as the restrictive social demands and ideas about appropriate behavior that accompany collective forms of identity such as race, gender, ethnicity, and sexuality. "Scripts," according to anthropologist John L. Jackson Jr., "provide guidelines for proper and improper behavior, for legitimate and illegitimate group membership, [and] for social inclusion and ostracism" (2005, 13). They tell us, for instance, that there are correct ways of being black, or gay, or female, or Filipino. Where the normative nature of whiteness in America has traditionally concealed any notion of a distinct white racial script, within the field of hip hop the status of whites as "other" has served to expose a range of activities and social outlooks specifically associated with white identity.[30] Given the stringent scrutiny placed on underground hip hop authenticity and boundary maintenance, I think it is valid to also frame the above discussion of subcultural capital in terms of a specific sort of underground hip hop script.[31]

In an important essay dealing with developments in the politics of black representation, cultural theorist Stuart Hall (1996) proposed that the lens of critical focus was undergoing a progressive shift from particular concerns over portrayals of blackness to broader questions regarding the very act of its representation. In doing so, Hall called for a greater "recognition of the extraordinary diversity of subjective positions, social experiences and cultural identities which compose the category 'black'" (1996, 443). If Appiah is correct in viewing the insistence on authentic identities (i.e., scripts) as a form of tyranny over the individual (1994, 162–163), then Hall's insights suggest that new analytic tools for assessing subcultural and racial subjectivities are needed. By offering up the concept of "sincerity" as a counter to "authenticity's hegemony," Jackson (2005, 175) answers this call.

Whereas *scripts* orient around preset notions of what is thought to be authentic, *sincerity* breaks from this dynamic by prioritizing qualities of character and integrity. In the words of author Lionel Trilling, sincerity demands "that we actually are what we want our communities to know we are" (quoted in Jackson 2005, 14). In terms of underground hip hop, this distinction is crucial in that it subverts the standard checklist of subcultural capital in favor of a personal code of underground hip hop ethics and integrity. Assessments of sincerity, then, are significant in distinguishing between those who know and those who do not "know what's up." Jackson clarifies this further by explaining that authenticity "presupposed a relationship between an independent, thinking subject and a dependent, unthinking thing" (2005, 14); sincerity, on the other hand, "presumes a liaison *between subjects*" (15 [emphasis in original]). This dividing line between objectified and subjectified subjectivities is precisely what Hall is getting at when he announces that we have reached "the end of innocence" (1996, 443).

Young people are increasingly attuned to the standard scripts surrounding their various identities. For many, music provides an opportunity to experiment with these scripts through the enactment of new, self-constructed identity forms (Frith 1996). Hip hop, in particular, being a music/culture that foregrounds the enactment of identity as a key element of its performance (Smith 1997), is saturated with racial symbolism. Rather than feeling confined by their racial and ethnic identities, constituents of multiracial hip hop scenes regularly engage in social performances that are done in dialogue with their understandings of existing scripts. While this provides a good deal of latitude in terms of remixing (Maira 2002) various racialized symbols into new forms of situational identity construction, what matters most is the perceived sincerity of these racial performances.

Jackson insists that "sincerity is never just another way to pass other people's authenticity tests. Instead, it provides justification for redrafting— and maybe even eliminating—the tests themselves" (2005, 175). Thus, for the underground hip hopper, the issue is not how well someone knows the facts of Bay Area graffiti history, but rather if their relationship to graffiti's politics is genuine and invested. Similarly, for the non-black hip hopper, an overzealous display of urban African American racial posturing, no matter how authentic, is under most circumstances suspected as insincere.

In summary, I have presented three different tiers on which considerations of the connection between hip hop and racial identity are made. The first of these concerns a fundamental understanding of hip hop as (or not as) a black music/cultural form. Based on the range of hip hop scholarship on this issue, I would suggest that ultimately recognizing the situational deployment of any of these positions is just as—if not more—important as trying to determine which one is correct. A person might speak of hip hop's definitive blackness at one moment and discuss it as the music of an entire generation the next, all the while citing well-rehearsed folk knowledge about its origins and evolution that is documented in the existing literature. The second tier organizes the various racial and ethnic groups found within the Bay Area underground scene according to what is thought to be their predisposed connection to hip hop. Here I peremptorily reject any notion of color-blindness, instead insisting that the opportunity for hip hoppers of all shades and colors to legitimately participate does not occur on equal terms. In the third and final tier, I explain how underground hip hop subcultural capital, manifested via authenticity and sincerity, becomes a means through which situated individuals negotiate hip hop's racial landscape.

Together these three spheres of dialogue and deliberation form the framework for underground hip hop's participatory ethics. In considering them in conjunction, they are perhaps best thought of as a series of overlaid grids. We begin with the various declarations of hip hop understanding, which take on an added dimension when factoring in the racial identities of those who enlist them, and finally become three dimensional when paired with the personal attributes and integrities of individual underground hip hoppers.

In closing this chapter, I offer another, equally appropriate, metaphor for making sense of this. I have discussed the relationship between race and hip hop through the imagery of a landscape a number of times; in this light, the varied conceptions of hip hop reflected in the scholarship serve as something akin to the terrain or footing. Is it solid in affirming hip hop as black culture? Or is it treacherous and slippery? Perhaps both, depending on the situation. Furthermore, my Preliminary Map of Hip Hop Racialism sets the slope. For African Americans, the view is good from above; however, for those on the lower rungs of the hierarchy, there is a steep and potentially ominous incline ahead. Lastly, the self-presentations and ideologically informed sensibilities—the moves of the underground hip hopper—that are grouped under the heading of subcultural capital reflect the actual traversing of the landscape. The specifics of these practices and their outcomes are detailed in the next chapter.

4

The Re-vision and
Continued Salience of Race

The San Francisco hip hop group Universal Figures probably never made anyone's shortlist of "artists most likely to carry the mantle of Bay Area underground hip hop into the twenty-first century." In fact, between my first learning of them—from DJ Baxsmackwards, who dropped their name as an example of "real" emcees who attended the Rockin' Java open-mic—and writing this, they appear to have disbanded. A recent online search for the group yielded only one member's 2006 solo album; it was by Japanese American emcee Bucc Rogerz, whose album, ironically enough, is titled *Music for the 21st Century*. Still, on the late September 2000 evening when Devorah, Satva, and I ventured out to the Velvet Lounge to attend the group's (first and only) CD release party, I could not help but feel that somehow, amid the blend of inebriation and exuberance, what we were witnessing epitomized the leading edge of the scene's folk-music evolution.

When we entered the club, nothing seemed particularly remarkable. A few "flossed out" doormen—as Satva described them—all African American, sporting logos like Mecca, Timberland, and Tommy Hilfiger, messed with us a little at the door. Nothing too dramatic: just the usual "hold up"— "let's have these five people I know cut in front of you"—"I'll just have you stand here for another few minutes,"—"okay you can go in now"—"and there better not be any trouble tonight" kind of posturing that reminds you of who is in charge. For all the security at the gate, the scene inside seemed anything but controlled. Just after walking in, Devorah nudged me and pointed to the floor beneath one of the tables where a smattering of broken beer glasses lay. Within minutes we had all commented on the "touchy-feely" spirit of the crowd. In addition to flirtatious elbow-touches and "arm around the waist slide-bys" from members of the opposite sex, I received a few drunken bumps from members of my own. As summer-long veterans of the San Francisco nightlife this was not what we had expected but seemed familiar enough.

Like many of the underground hip hop shows Devorah and I had been to that summer, the crowd at the Velvet Lounge was typically diverse. I would not have expected anything less from the Figures, a crew whose eight emcees included young men of African, European, Asian, and Latin descent, with several showing a combination of racial signifiers suggesting mixed parentage. "So are they eclectic enough for you?" Devorah leaned over and asked me at one point during the show. Of course our trio— including Satva, a part-Asian/part-European American deejay and professional skateboarder—fit the mix.

It was when the Figures first started their performance that things got interesting. Beginning with a few adventurous souls but soon reaching an "open-floodgate" of sorts, dozens of (mostly male) audience members proceeded to make their way onto the stage with the group. I had seen this type of thing before as part of a show's finale. For instance, I recall a Foreign Legion performance at Storyville where seemingly half the audience jumped on stage for the final song. My lasting memory of that night was of six-foot four, three-hundred pound African American emcee Marc Stretch rocking the mic with a white girl in a red Kangol hat riding piggy back! But what was different about this show was that the crowd's taking to the stage seemed to commence the moment the first beat dropped. And it remained constant—well over thirty people on a small stage standing shoulder-to-shoulder and sometimes arm-in-arm—for the entire duration of their set.

While the Figures seemed to relish the infectious energy that being outnumbered by so many close friends and zealous supporters created, the anthropologist in attendance was left trying to sort things out. One consequence of all this folly was that it became increasingly difficult to distinguish between actual group members and fans.[1] "Has that guy rapped yet?" I leaned over and asked Devorah at one point, gesturing toward a short, stout Asian American dressed in a Hawaiian shirt and white-fur driving cap. "No," she replied without breaking her gaze, "he's part of the scenery."

The very next afternoon, while working at Amoeba Music, the individual I had asked about, who wound up being on stage with his arm draped over one of the lead rapper's shoulders for what seemed like the better part of the evening, suddenly appeared at my register. When he realized that I recognized him from the night before, he called over his shopping companions and presented me as a witness to what had gone down.

For the last twenty years at least, hip hop (or rap) has been one of the most popular music forms among young Americans of all racial and ethnic backgrounds. It is also a genre which owing to its unique production practices—the art of turning music consumption into music production (Rose 1994)—is particularly well poised to engage what I call a fan-to-artist migration. Journalist S. H. Fernando Jr. once remarked that "conceivably, anyone with a knowledge of music and a good ear could produce a rap song" (1994, 241). His point was that the practice of sampling—hip hop's primary mode of music making (Schloss 2004)—is a form of music production that prioritizes technological mastery over traditional notions of musical virtuosity (see Ryan and Peterson 1993). Hip hop producer Sean Julian of the Vinyl Monkeys, who for a short stint worked alongside me behind the Amoeba cash registers, once told me that most Akai MPC[2] owners needed to spend more time reading their manuals. Rasta Cue Tip disagreed, insisting that most of his knowledge about how to "freak" equipment beyond the perimeters of its intended use came from experimentation and mentorship: "The thing with this equipment [is] you can read the book . . . but if you don't have anybody that shows you some hands on stuff, and tips, and tricks, it's just not even worth it."[3]

The allure of this fan-to-artist migration was confirmed for me one morning when another Amoeba co-worker, who had no previous musical aspirations or training that I knew of, suggested to me that she was going to start making beats because she had seen how easy it was on a television program the previous evening. Although she had no beat-making equipment of her own, she reasoned that she could fulfill her newly found ambition by using her friends' equipment. I believe similar, perhaps less explicit, avenues from audience to artist appear with rapping. Their existence might be in part explained through hip hop's mandate of personal (often autobiographical) rhyme writing. Freestyle Fellowship member Micah Nine once asserted that "every high school [in America], every junior high school, every elementary school's got a rapper in it."[4] Whether this is correct or not, I would venture to say that there are significantly more rhyme-writers in our nation's public schools than non-hip hop songwriters. For adolescent males in particular, the idea of chanting self-directed and usually self-aggrandizing rhymes (sometimes sprinkled with profanities) is far more attractive than the prospect of potentially exposing their vulnerability and opening themselves up to ridicule by trying to carry a tune.[5]

It is here where underground hip hop—and most notably its Bay Area manifestation—forms a crucial nexus between the traditional and the new. In the years just prior to the widespread popularity of music production software like GarageBand, music promotion sites like MySpace, and digital music files more generally, underground hip hoppers initiated a sizable fan-to-artist migration through the use of bedroom studios, underground cassette tapes, and supportive local retail outlets (see Chapter 1). In 2003, Berkeley emcee/producer Ayentee estimated that since he started recording music in the mid-1990s, the number of underground hip hop artists in the Bay had grown from twenty or thirty to two or three thousand. Thus, the multiracial independent hip hop movement (i.e., underground hip hop) in the Bay Area was a few years ahead of a curve that has taken shape at the national (not to mention global) level throughout the last decade.

The evolution of the Bay Area scene, however, differs from the world of virtual hip hop in that its multiraciality grew out of and has continued to be nourished through face-to-face interactions. Collective music-making activities are unquestionably sites of aesthetic experimentation and pleasure (Kelley 1997). In such communal social spaces, negotiated commitments to "the music" and to one another are often experienced as shared struggles against the conventions set forth by society (Cohen 1991; Fornäs, Lindberg, and Sernhade 1995). The friendships that form through these activities and the shared experiences of music making can be powerful. As with team sports and other racially integrated group activities, commitments to the crew, to the team, and in the case of music even to the greater scene, can come to supersede other forms of collective identity that vie for one's allegiance.

Even though the jumble of hands in the air, fist pumps, drunken stumbles, and jostling over who needed the mic next at times resembled a brawl, this power of fellowship was evident among the Universal Figures and their fans. At one point a "drunk off his ass" white guy somehow got hold of one of the mics and started to shout "Universal Figures!" and "Say Ho!" to the dismay of both the crowd and the emcee who was in the middle of his verse. But even this could not sour the energy of the evening. The crew simply let him have his moment, then took the microphone away from him and moved on.

Cultural critic Benjamin DeMott warns that the trouble with America's captivation with the black-white friendship—think *Lethal Weapon* (Danny

Glover and Mel Gibson), *Pardon the Interruption* (Michael Wilbon and Tony Kornheiser), *Clueless* (Stacey Dash and Alicia Silverstone), and even "Ebony and Ivory" (Stevie Wonder and Paul McCartney)—is that it "strip[s] experience from its social context, by delet[ing] history and politics" (1998, 24). In this regard, my Velvet Lounge symbolism may falter, for I am not prepared to make any explicit claims about the political depths of the Figures' relationships with their drunken friends. However, I can say something more substantial about the interracial relationships that formed among regular Rockin' Java open-mic attendees, Forest Fires Collective members, and other friendship circles with which I was associated. Without taking too much away from the important points that DeMott raises, within the dynamics of camaraderie and allegiance that pervade underground hip hop, historical and political situatedness is central to informing the ideology of "knowing what's up."

In the remainder of this chapter I examine the personal backgrounds, social dispositions, and interpersonal dynamics that encapsulate underground hip hop's interracial friendships. Attention to the negotiation and management of racial difference is crucial to understanding the formation and maintenance of these relationships. Drawing on the model of underground hip hop participation proposed in the previous chapter, I outline the ways in which assessments of subcultural capital, both empirical and ideological, shape the quality and character of Bay Area hip hop relations. Revisiting the book's subtitle, ultimately I argue that where sincere integrity regarding racial differences and an ethics of social equality govern these relationships something quite meaningful is taking place. In the book's final chapter, I "flip-the-script" so to speak and discuss where these dynamics of race and power fall short.

Colorblind Hip Hop

In both the book's Introduction and Chapter 1, I discussed Bay Area underground hip hop as a purported color-blind social arena. Any suggestion of underground hip hop's color blindness is at best situational. By this I mean that few Bay Area hip hoppers I know of—and none that I can recall meeting—would be naïve enough to believe that a person's racial identity has no impact on the opportunities and life-chances that become available to them as they grow up in, and move through, American society. However, in specifically addressing the question of whether racial identity has any bearing on an individual's ability or right to engage in hip hop, the situation is more complex. It is simple enough to disregard the question of ability.

Any notion that non-black people are unable to rap teeters precariously close to classic racial essentialism (Taylor 2005). Furthermore, such opinions can be easily dismissed as little more than subjective evaluations of an aesthetic field (e.g., Paulo thinks Disflex.6 emcee Lazerus Jackson is one of the best rappers in the Bay, Karl thinks he stinks). In this regard, I can hardly imagine anyone squarely situated within a multiracial underground hip hop community claiming that non-black people cannot rap. However, as I shall demonstrate, the astonishment with which many great white performances were received (even within professed underground hip hop circles) suggests that lingering residuals of such ideas exist. If nothing else, the notable reputations and successes of many non-black emcees in both mainstream rap music and underground hip hop stand as strong evidence that rapping ability is neither biologically hardwired nor exclusively culturally determined through the social constructs that we refer to as race and black culture. The question of right, however, requires greater explication.

The varied understandings of hip hop culture through which many underground enthusiasts establish the traction for making authenticity claims are diffused around the issue of whether what is imagined (Anderson 1991) as a "hip hop nation" is at its essence *primordial* or *civic* in nature. Identity theorist Sasja Tempelman[6] (1999) describes primordial identities as those that are conceived of as natural and homogenous and thus fixed and unchanging; in contrast, civic identities are developed through a system of rules, customary practices, and social arrangements that allow outsiders gradual membership. "What matters from a civic point of view is not that the community keeps its specific 'authentic identities' but rather that it maintains a sufficient degree of coherence and consistency of traditions and institutions to survive as a collectivity" (Tempelman 1999, 23).

It should come as little surprise that many non-black hip hoppers articulate an understanding of hip hop as a fundamentally civic arena. Take, for example, the following statement, given to me by white hip hop retailer Kegs One: "There's kids that are incredible that are from the coast side that have lived on the beach their whole life that are some of the dopest [best] rappers . . . and there's kids from the suburbs that are equally as good as people that are getting paid millions . . . I think that anyone that wants to rap that has the know-how and can write good rhymes, so be it. You know? Anyone. Any color or creed." Similar testimonies were offered to me by other non-black hip hop enthusiasts; for instance, Ricky, a Korean American explained to me that "here in the Bay, ethnicity does not play a strong factor in determining acceptance into the culture."

I was initially far more surprised to find that many of the most inclusive articulations of hip hop's civic character were given to me by African Americans. When compared to African American sentiments I have encountered outside of underground hip hop's social arenas, which more typically locate hip hop squarely within a black music and cultural tradition (see Chapter 3, n. 4), these apparent forfeits of cultural ownership warrant attention. Below I quote two representative positions at length, the first coming from Rasta Cue Tip:

> RCT: If anything stays around for a while and grows out of an area, then of course you're going to have all different types of people coming into it, and all different people liking it, all different people understanding it. I think with hip hop, it has such a generational relation that, just us as youth, we have a connection with each other. Maybe back in the day you had the black youth, and they were like in this part of town doing this thing, you know? You had your white youth, in this part of town, doing this sort of thing. So I think, our generation is one of the first or second generations where you can put twenty different types of people [together], and they can be all in the same age [range], all doing, living, and experiencing the same thing. So I think hip hop is something that anybody can entertain and enjoy and understand.
>
> We are a generation that's together, that are not separated. You can't separate black, white, Asian, Chinese in this generation cause we're into a lot of the same things, we're living next to each other, we live in the same neighborhoods, you know? We're doing a lot of the same things, so of course we're gonna like some of the same things. We're gonna be into the same things. We're gonna have the abilities and then tend to do a lot of the same things.
>
> AKH: Are you speaking nationally or locally?
>
> RCT: I'm speaking worldwide man. You know, cause I've been all over the world. I've been with cats, we don't even speak the same language, but yet we speak hip hop, you know what I'm sayin'? That's gotta be a generation thing. I couldn't do that thing with their parents, you know? They couldn't do that with my parents. But yet, I can do it with them. And it's just a music thing. Music crosses all bounds.

With Kirby Dominant, the articulation of hip hop's civic character shifted slightly to a discussion of whether or not specific social experiences translate well into the ability to emcee:

KD: It's all good. People can do whatever they want to do. All you have to do is be true to yourself. [Say for instance] you're in Montana. I need to listen to [your music] and be like, "this cat's from Montana. He just said he be doin' this. We don't be doin' that." You know what I'm sayin'?

AKH: So in terms of hip hop right now, you don't think there's anything essential in like, the experience of being in Oakland or being in L.A. or being in San Francisco, or being in New York, or being in Atlanta, that . . .

KD: That gives it an authenticness?

AKH: Yeah.

KD: No. I just think that there's more shit going on here so there's more to talk about. But then again, that's not really true either. Cause I can be in the middle of the desert rappin' about how hot it is and how lonely I am, and as long as I can convey that, it's all gravy. You can be in the epicenter of civilization, in New York, New York and not be talking about shit. And then what's the joy in that? . . . So it's just all about how you relate it. And it's yourself, how you really feel. So he can be in Montana, as long as he's keeping it real in Montana. And makes me either want to come to Montana and look around and be like, "that's what you were talkin' about! That mailbox!" or be like "ah man, I don't want to go to Montana."

For someone intent on retaining hip hop as black music, such comments, coming from an African American, might seem like examples of misguided racial infidelity. Yet how can Kirby's preceding declaration of hip hop multiculturalism be reconciled with the fact that his primary group at the time, the Kemetic Suns, espoused one of the most Afrocentric doctrines within the Bay Area scene? Consider the content of the following lyrics, authored by Kirby, against the backdrop of his previous comments:

My feet was once callused on this invalid shore
My hands were paralyzed because of cotton
Rice and tobacco shackles laced me like jewels did in my past life
But now I'm labeled a sinner oppressed by my friend Christ
He said, "God doesn't blame you,
But you're still a beast, nigga let me tame you"
He read me scriptures out the Bible,
I couldn't speak of Shango, my new name was Michael
And I was not to panic,

For these were Puritanic, Chistianic, satanic
God fearing white children, but still
I was raised around skill, and these new metaphors about pain I
    couldn't feel
But I could feel the impact of the lash to my back and felt my ass
    always cramped
From sleeping in a dirt shack right next to where I worked at
I mean where I slaved at, didn't get paid at
But now you will be paid back, cause I created rap
In order to dilute all the damage
Wake up sleepy minds and redefine the true fuckin' savage.
                                                                    (Konceptual Dominance 2000)[7]

For Kirby, acknowledging hip hop's African diasporic origins—"cause I created rap"—is not fundamentally at odds with the idea that it exists as a
medium that can be engaged within an infinite number of social contexts
and positioned perspectives. Furthermore, his decision to utilize hip hop
to express an Afrocentric revisionist history that seeks to challenge prevailing American structures of privilege does not result in his assigning a
fundamental (hip hop) invalidity to different, and potentially even contrary,
usages.

These views on multiracial and ethnic participation within hip hop,
which are expressed with a good deal more certainty than part-Asian/
part-white DJ Mizzo's concerns over his place in hip hop (see Chapter 3),
conform to what political theorist Amy Gutmann (2004) describes as a
liberal democratic position on social diversity. According to Gutmann,
liberal democracies are societies—or in this case subcultural fields—in
which the rights of individuals to be unique and self-creating are re-
spected and protected against both the collective values of the majority
and the weight of traditional institutions: "[This] creative conception of
human beings is not to be confused with a picture of 'atomistic' individuals creating their identities *de novo* and pursuing their ends independent
of each other. Part of the uniqueness of individuals results from the ways
in which they integrate, reflect upon, and modify their own cultural heritage and that of other people with whom they come into contact" (1994,
7). From this perspective, hip hop music and culture are regarded as powerful vehicles through which to convey experiences and create dialogues
across social boundaries. That there is no single correct way of "being hip
hop"—no identifiable hip hop script that trumps all others—does not

jeopardize the basic principles of communication, voiced perspective, and understanding which a secure hip hop community holds most dear.

Biographies of Participation

Writers who have attempted to place hip hop at an "interracial crossroads" (for example, Chideya 1999; Givhan 1993; Stephens 1991) have often been criticized for equating consumption with participation and for failing to account for the production of culture (Peterson 1976) machinations that mediate the relationship between hip hop and its audience. Ewan Allinson, for example, in discussing the "pathologies of white listening" (1994, 439), characterizes white consumption of hip hop as a form of eavesdropping and cultural tourism (see also Samuels 1991). Allinson's point reminds me of a white friend who once confessed to growing scared while sitting at home alone (high on marijuana and in the dark) listening to a CD by Bay Area conscious/militant rapper Paris (he remedied the situation by pressing stop).

Twenty-first–century underground hip hoppers differ from Allinson's early nineties cultural tourists in several important ways. To begin with, rather than being oblivious to the processes through which the Music Industry has promoted specific images of black life in the interest of selling rap records, underground hip hoppers, if anything, are acutely critical of these. Such anticorporate skepticism is fundamental to the subgenre's self definition (see Chapter 1). Additionally, as constituents of a music scene that not only blurs distinctions between producers and consumers but also recognizes rapping as only one of hip hop's principal expressive forms, many Bay Area underground hip hop enthusiasts could recount stories of longtime involvement in one or more of hip hop's artistic realms. In reflecting on his own quite intentional decision to "get involved," DJ Gammaray described the internal deliberations which surrounded his first turntable purchase: "I wanted to get turntables. The main reason was, to be involved in hip hop. To be part of the culture, ya know wha' I mean? And I went through and I was like, emcee? I don't think so. Breakdancin'? Nah. Okay, I have a little money saved up. So I'm gonna get a turntable." Civic understandings of hip hop privilege activity within at least one of its original four elements—emceeing, deejaying, breaking, and graffiti (I would also add beat-making and perhaps beat-boxing)—over any strong sense of primordial racial ownership or right via socioeconomic position. This is not to say that matters of race and social class are inconsequential. In fact, although he did not explicitly say so, I got the impression that Gammaray's general aversion to the idea of getting involved via emceeing was connected to his (white) racial identity, although this certainly wouldn't be true of all white hip hoppers. Nevertheless, what is clear is that Gammaray, and many others like him, saw taking up specific established hip hop artistic practices as a means to membership within hip hop culture.

By narrating personal histories complete with relevant backgrounds, experiences, and stories of enculturation, underground hip hop enthusiasts are attempting to re-inscribe the scripts typically associated with their racial identities by adding new subculturally valued personal dimensions. Destined's recollection of his path to participation in each of hip hop's four elements while growing up in San Diego, is an excellent example:

> D: The San Diego hip hop scene during the early nineties was dope. Like, so much graf, so much b-boying going on. . . . Emceeing was strong as fuck! Like the Impov, Orko, Masters of the Universe, Tony the Skitzo, all those fools. And this is just when I was a young kid, so I didn't even know what was going on. Hip hop in San Diego, like the core of it, was very concentrated. You know? People lovin' it. Like, cause we were from the streets. I mean, I don't know, it was how it was in New York when it started in San Diego. Like, Zulu Nation, you know wha' I mean? Everyone was just a community.
>
> AKH: So you were just a young kid and this was what was around you?
>
> D: Yeah. At school, during lunchtime we'd break . . . I can't really think back and pinpoint the time when I first started b-boying. . . . I mean, when I was probably like real young, I could have done it, like my brother told me to do it and I wouldn't have known. But to my memory, I'd say [I started in] about, sixth or seventh grade.

On his history with graffiti, which he recalls as starting in fifth grade when he and a friend began going around during the daytime with markers, Destined remarks:

> I remember like eighth grade or seventh grade, I was a diehard. I used to like sneak out late at night, like two in the morning. . . . Just for graffiti dude. I would just like, jump off my roof, you know wha' I mean? Cut the window, just jump out, meet my homeboy someplace, sneaking around, hit up the freeway, do throw-ups. That's when I started to get into bombing. I was never too good at burners and pieces, and stuff.[8]

You know? The more intricate art. I was just kinda more out there for the adrenaline. Gettin' up. . . .

I used to write poetry when I was in like eighth grade. It wasn't really rhyming, it was just poetry . . . in ninth grade me and my homeboy were just fuckin' around, I remember the night too. We were just walkin' from *Blockbuster* of all times, and we just started freestylin'. Like "the cat in the hat," like some simple ABC type rhymes, and we just kept doin' it. And as I got more into writing rhymes, I just kept practicing. . . . When I was younger I used to write a lot of rhymes just to shape up to where I'm at right now. . . .

See all of this has been around me, but when I make these points in time, it's when I really started practicing at [something]. I'd say the middle of ninth grade to tenth grade I started really getting into [deejaying]. Getting my own equipment. Like some cheap-ass home turntables. Like thrift shop turntables. Like a fuckin' wackass mixer . . . for forty bucks, I got some janky-ass shit, and a wackass mixer and started collecting records and stuff. But it's always been around me, like my brother was deejaying and all that. But I just never got my hands on it.

The extent to which Destined, described as a true "renaissance" hip hopper by others in the scene (see Chapter 2), sees the different elements of hip hop as part of his normal existence is expressed in this closing statement: "At the time, I didn't even recognize any of this as hip hop. . . . Just in the last couple of years I've been like, damn! I've been into hip hop for quite a while now, and not even knowing." Among the hip hoppers that I got to know, Destined's personal history was somewhat rare in that he could recount years of participation in each of the four principle elements. However, in terms of the length of time and extent of "felt" connection, his history was quite typical.

Inscribing Filipino Hip Hop

Claims to hip hop legitimacy cannot be separated from the historical and political contexts of the groups with which individual claimants identify. Notably, Destined's articulations of his early hip hop memories include little to no premeditation or racial boundary crossing. As a Filipino American growing up on the streets of Southern California, his racial identity and sociogeographic background intersect at a point that is in relative proximity to the racial and socioeconomic experiences that denote hip hop's (at times primordial) association with young urban African Americans. In a moment of originalist lobbying, Destined even compares growing up in San Diego during the early nineties to how things must have been for hip hop's pioneers in 1970s New York (see his comments in the previous section). There were no special circumstances surrounding his budding relationship with hip hop. Destined's friends, classmates, older brother, and the features of his everyday surroundings were all part of this journey. At one point during our interview, when I paused to confirm that he, in fact, had not been the first among his circle of friends to start doing any of these things, his response was, "of course not."

Fast forward to 2008. A group of us are speeding down Highway 101 on a brilliant Saturday afternoon, trying to get to the UC Santa Cruz Social Documentary Program's "Master's Thesis Exhibition" before our friend Eric Tandoc's documentary, *Sounds of the New Hope (Mga Tinig Ng Bagong Pag-Asa)*, is shown. *Sounds of the New Hope* tells the story of Kiwi, one of the premiere Filipino emcees currently residing in the Bay. The film documents his early involvement with hip hop (while growing up in Los Angeles), his ongoing work with San Francisco's Filipino youth, and a recent trip back to the Philippines. I first saw Kiwi rock the mic at a 2002 San Francisco State Ethnic Studies conference. At one point during that noontime set, T. Root, who was standing just in front of me, suddenly turned around and gave me a "What? This guy's good!" look. Kiwi is good. He has both a great sense of rhyme cadence and a keen understanding of how to engage a crowd. But what particularly stood out for me that first time was the extent to which his hip hop performance was so consciously Filipino.

Kiwi is one of the forerunners in a rising generation of politically conscious Filipino American emcees.[9] The scenes from Tandoc's film which document his trip to the Philippines powerfully illustrate the love and respect that young Filipinos in the 'hoods of Metro Manila show him. The struggles they speak of are the struggles Kiwi raps about. Destined also appears in the documentary. Quite characteristically, the brief cameo features him freestyling at a hip hop workshop for local youth. For several years now, Kiwi and Destined have been active in facilitating a conscious and conscientious regard for hip hop as a medium of expression and a tool of communication within the Bay Area's Filipino communities.

Destined's 2000 CD, *Port of San Diego*, is one of the truly hidden gems in the history of Filipino hip hop. It tells the story of a young man's emerging sense of social and political justice, and how his longstanding relationship with hip hop helped him to channel it. Yet the most striking difference between *Port of San Diego* and the assortment of rhymes—including re-corded songs, performed shows, and causal freestyles—that I have heard Destined author more recently, is the distinctly Filipino accent and per-spectives that saturate the latter. There is no question that *Port of San Diego* is both political and conscious, but as a southern Californian teen-ager growing up in the late nineties, Destined had not yet acquired the knowledge, vocabulary, or foresight to engage hip hop, and particularly em-ceeing, from a specifically Filipino point of orientation.[10] It is this more re-cently discovered "voice"—which in the current West Coast underground context does more to legitimize Filipino Americans' embrace of hip hop than to section their efforts off as a marginalized subvariety (i.e., "Filipino hip hop")—that I am calling an emergent Filipino hip hop script.

Despite being the second largest Asian/Pacific Island ancestry group in the United States, Filipinos have historically lacked visibility within virtu-ally all aspects of American popular culture (Pisares 2006). This hidden status has been exacerbated for first and second generation Americans through a condition that has been described as a state of "cultural limbo":

> Filipino immigrant children . . . live with paradoxes. They feel strong symbolic loyalty to the Philippines, but they know very little about it and have little contact with their parents or other adults who might educate them. They feel pressured to become like "Americans," but their experi-ences as racialized subjects leave them with an uneasy relationship with both Filipino and U.S. culture. They display the visible markers of as-similation yet remain ferociously nationalist. (Espiritu 2003, 204)

Even with their gradual rise to middle-class status, Filipinos Americans have had to deal with steady bigotry and intolerance (Tiongson 2006). In a 1995 survey of eight hundred Filipino students attending high school in San Diego—Destined's hometown—close to two-thirds reported experi-encing racial or ethnic discrimination (Espiritu 2003, 180). Outside of areas (and cultural fields) with sizable Pacific Island populations, Filipinos are often misrecognized as Chinese or (more generally) Asian Americans,[11] and sometimes Latinos as a consequence of their colonial Spanish surnames (Pisares 2006).

In response to such dilemmas and difficulties, many Filipino American youths have turned to urban subcultures as a conduit for fashioning their self-identities through a more American frame of reference (de Leon 2004).

Destined's older brother joined the Crips; Destined opted to put his energies into hip hop. While this decision can be looked at as a personal choice, I think it is just as important to emphasize it as one of several paths available to Destined given the confluence of his ethnoracialized identity, sociogeographic location, and gender. In looking back on his early adolescence, Destined emphasized this connection between hip hop and his Filipino upbringing: "Growing up in San Diego there was a Filipino community and a Filipino hip hop scene and then there was the overall San Diego scene. . . . Do you think it's like that for like Mexicans? See I'm not too sure if it's like that with other groups, but it's strongly in the Filipinos. If you grew up in the culture, in a Filipino family, you'd know."

Through skills honed at local dance parties, talent shows, Pilipino Cultural Nights, and other community events, during the 1990s young Filipino American deejays and breakers became focal figures in hip hop scenes throughout the West Coast.[12] For many first- and second-generation Filipino American youth, the oppositional thrust of hip hop has figured centrally in galvanizing efforts that call for a reawakening of Filipino consciousness—or what cultural communications scholar Lily Mendoza describes as a "born-again Filipino" movement (2002)—through a historical recognition of their struggles against white supremacy, centuries of Spanish and American cultural imperialism, and global capitalism. Thomas, a Filipino, explains that "[it's] because our own cultural practices have been dissolved [that] Filipinos have turned to hip hop to fill a void."[13] Similarly, Filipina emcee/poet Shortyrocwell refers to the embrace of hip hop in the interest of recapturing this cultural history and asserting a political voice as a "Filipino Renaissance" (Barrientos 2000).

Even before seeing Kiwi that day at SF State, the signs of this emerging consciousness were apparent to me through hip hop inflected poetry being authored by young Filipinos participating in San Francisco's *Youth Speaks* teen writing workshops and performances, as well as through spoken-word groups like Eighth Wonder. Writer Elizabeth Pisares argues that in their efforts to resolve issues of racial ambiguity and become more visible in the American (popular) cultural landscape, young Filipino Americans have turned to cultural practices that assert "fixed and definitive signs of Filipino identity" as a way to "announce themselves to non-Filipinos and each other" (2006: 187). For the last decade at least, Filipino hip hoppers have moved beyond deejaying (de Leon 2004), breaking, and graffiti to publicly engage the medium of emceeing as a means to explicitly articulate experiences surrounding their marginalized place in America; the messages of marginalization and discontent expressed in their lyrics have further affirmed their legitimate place within underground hip hop.[14]

Special White Boy Status

In contrast to African Americans, Latinos, and Filipino Americans, people whose social identities resided at the bottom end of hip hop's racial hierarchy—most notably white hip hoppers—used narratives of racial boundary crossing to situate themselves within what was often a precarious balance between primordial and civic hip hop understandings. Reminiscent of Bennett's (1999a) discussion of Jim and his record store companions in Newcastle upon the Tyne (see Chapter 3), several of the white hip hoppers I spent time among were forthright in stating that there could be no true understanding of hip hop that did not begin by acknowledging its essential blackness. Such positions were often paired with racially atypical self-biographies which served to resolve the contradictions of their own place within hip hop. These frequently included experiences as a minority within socially black environments. For instance, in addition to having a renowned b-boy as his babysitter when he was young, Top R spoke of having spent several months as an adolescent in St. Thomas and how that experience—as one of the only white people around—opened his eyes, at multiple levels, to the realities of what black people had to endure. Indeed, I heard several such stories about trips to "the Islands" as life-changing experiences.

Feller Quentin, who began writing rhymes at the age of eleven—"whenever I had nothing to do"—and recording them in a group called the Doctors of Rap (DOR) at thirteen, had a personal history marked by his decision to attend a predominantly black high school in Richmond, Virginia. One of his more prominent memories from that time was of the daily lunchroom freestyle sessions by his African American classmates. Even though he frequently sat close to these lunch-table cyphers—sporting a "fade" haircut and assorted hip hop accessories—Feller recalled there being an unspoken understanding that he would not be allowed to join in. "I never tried" he said, reflecting on the sense of isolation that this cause him. At the same time, when he would visit his white friends who were in the suburban school system he remembers his attitude and demeanor would change: "They'd be like 'oh man, you probably get beat up a lot. There's probably a lot of gun shots at your school. It's probably real violent and scary.' And I'd come back like, 'what am I a gangster now cause I go to high school at an inner-city school?' Then all of a sudden I got this attitude like, 'yeah! That's right motherfucker,' you know? It was all an act." Feller's recollections illustrate how identities are never fixed, but are dialogically constructed and adjusted in accordance with one's social surroundings. Through processes of modification and revision, young people who find themselves regularly crossing racial boundaries or inhabiting multiracial worlds develop sensibilities and dispositions that encourage them to break from (and recast) predefined scripts in accordance with the different social situations in which they find themselves.

Personal histories of racial boundary crossing can be found throughout the literature on white hip hoppers. For example, in her travels to Delphi, Indiana, journalist Farai Chideya (1999) met a white teenager named B.J. who immediately pulled out his yearbook to prove that he had attended middle school in Southern California among blacks, Latinos, and Asians. Even writer William "Upski" Wimsatt—who made his fame as an "expert on wiggers"[15] (Wimsatt 1994, 22)—"persuaded his parents to transfer him" from a mostly white Chicago private school to a largely black public one (Kleinfield 2000, A18), which then became his inroad into hip hop culture. The "special white boy" trope, as Wimsatt (1994) calls it, is the basis for the authentically hip hop biographies of both Eminem and MC Serch (of the early nineties white hip hop duo 3rd Bass and more recently the host of VH1's *White Rapper Show*); it was also unsuccessfully plagiarized by Vanilla Ice (Hess 2005).

In theory, this special white boy (or white girl) syndrome does not have to be limited to people of European descent. It does, however, seem to be commensurate with the distance between a person's self-perceived racial identity and the social location where they place hip hop's organic core. For aspiring hip hoppers needing to reconcile this distance, claiming special status is perhaps the most fundamental means of upholding hip hop's qualities as a black music, while simultaneously claiming a legitimate connection to it.[16] Such claims to special white status are not confined to hip hop alone. Surely the hipsters of Norman Mailer's (1957) era sought a similar existential connection to authentic black culture as a way to define themselves as distinct from their "square" white contemporaries. Regardless of whether these biographical narratives are shared with others or merely told to ourselves, they form the essential building blocks of our identities and become germane to the way we interact with our everyday surroundings. Of course, each person's story aspires to a level of narrative unity that is reflexively monitored by foregrounding some experiences and discounting others (Appiah 1994; Giddens 1991).

For European American hip hoppers in particular, such experiences are remembered as engendering a keen awareness of their previously unmarked whiteness (Perry 2002, 181). Philosopher Linda Alcoff suggests that this propensity to consciously "feel white" is a relatively recent phenomenon (2001, 272). Thus, in a manner quite distinct from both the white Negroes (Mailer 1957) of decades past and the more recent wiggers whom Wimsatt (1993) classically commented on, white underground hip hoppers like Top R and Feller Quentin seem to be proposing a different kind of consciously white racial script. And in doing so they are—consciously or unconsciously—challenging the very integrity on which the binary logic of race in America rests (Ingram 2005).

One Saturday night while sitting at Bimbo's waiting for the biracial Los Angeles hip hop duo People Under the Stairs to perform, Devorah shared with me her growing distaste for deejays who play the same songs yet insist on calling them "rare grooves." "It's not rare if everyone's playing it," she said with a frown. The notion of a "special white boy script" is "special" in much the same way that Devorah's "rare grooves" are "rare." Critical racial self-consciousness and the willingness to embrace non-majority white sociality run counter to the traditional expectations that (predominantly non-white) people associate with normative whiteness. White people *are supposed to be* blind to both their racial identity and privilege; they also tend to steer clear of communities and social settings in which too many non-whites reside. Yet as Wimsatt, in commenting on "white boys like [him]" (1994, 30), realized a decade and half ago, special white boys are no longer all that special. To both Top R and Feller's credit, neither seemed all that interested in foregrounding their non-white credentials. Overambitious efforts by white hip hoppers to wear their special status on their sleeves have always left me with an unsavory taste in my mouth. As their numbers increase, questions of racial sincerity become all the more crucial in determining who among them are genuine or really "know what's up."

It is important to recognize how this diversification of scripts surrounding white identity is meaningfully different from what I previously suggested was an emerging Filipino American (hip hop) script. Obviously both can be used to acknowledge that a range of racial and ethnic identities have a legitimate place within underground hip hop; however, where one appears natural the other is presented as exceptional. The absence of prominent Filipino representations within popular culture on the whole makes participation in hip hop an avenue for identity affirmation. Although stereotypes of Filipinos have existed (Espiritu 2003), they have more often been invisible or misrecognized. Thus, where hip hop is being used as a means to constructing a new Filipino American youth identity,[17] European American hip hoppers are more actively seeking to deconstruct normative representations of whiteness. This returns us to the more fundamental question of what becomes of the color line within a context in which the integrities of racial groupings are being simultaneously established and dismantled. I shall return to these issues shortly; for now, I want to shift my focus to the manner in which artistic competencies (or hip hop skills) serve as vehicles of identity transformation, which can provide those who possess them with fast access to hip hop credibility.

Color Conscious Competencies

Narratives of racial border crossing into black communities often carry an implied enculturation into the arts, aesthetics, and music of that community. For example, much has been made of Elvis Presley's coming of age just a few blocks away from Beale St.—"the Main Street of Negro America" (Whitmer 1996, 93)—where his fascination with black people and their music led him to hang around local black musicians during their daytime rehearsals. Similarly, the story of Eminem's having "come up" in Detroit's— American's "blackest" city (Hartigan 1999, 4)—fabled emcee battle circuit is commonly referenced when discussing his lyrical ability and hip hop acumen.

Displays of artistic competency—that is, the ability to give an artistic performance that comes somewhere close to matching the objective measure of authentic practice within a given genre[18]—can compensate for a lack of subcultural capital within many evaluative fields. While the manner in which hip hop racialism is mapped predisposes some individuals, through their racial identities and the particular social experiences which are thought to follow from them, to a more ingrained sense of hip hop belonging, demonstrated "skills" can quickly eclipse these image-based credentials. For example, a switch from *primordial illegitimacy* caused by race/self-presentation to *civic legitimacy* via hip hop musical proficiency was captured in a three minute segment of an interview in which James (of the group Lyrics And Beats [LAB]) discussed his first time meeting Audio Visual (one of the producers for his group):

> JAMES: The first time I met him, my friend was like, "yeah. I know this fool who makes beats. He's super sick [good]. You know? Blah, blah,

blah, blah, blah." And I was like, "aright. Cool. Whatever." you know? And like, he introduced me to some little, skinny, skinny, like, dorky, dorky, dorky looking white dude and I was like, "who's this dude?" (laughs) I totally didn't think that was him, you know? I was just so like, "what? You made those beats on that tape?" This fool looks like, I don't even know, like he goes to opera shows or something dude.

Less than two minutes later in the interview, James spoke of Audio Visual in an entirely different light: "Yeah, that dude Audio Visual, he's just like an old school, you know, true fuckin' b-boy, you understand? You know, he dances and all that shit. Like he makes dope ass hip hop beats! You know what I'm sayin'?" Through the quality of his beat making, and the fact that he b-boys (break dances), Audio Visual, for James, is transformed from the antithesis of hip hop coolness—a three-times "dorky white dude"—to the epitome of hip hop authenticity—a "true fuckin' b-boy."

Another, more spectacular transformation, which occurred during a September 2000 Mos Def show at the Maritime Hall, was relayed to me by Top R and three independent witnesses. According to Top R, the protagonist of this story, at some point during the show they started bringing audience members onto the stage to freestyle. Somehow, either owing to his house connections (for he had worked at the Maritime) or his overbearing personality, Top R found himself on stage. By his account, at first neither the audience nor the person in charge of deciding who would rhyme next took him very seriously; his own self-description was "a bummy white guy in a dirty shirt." But soon enough, "his people"—a group of Maritime regulars in the front section of the audience—started calling for him.[19] "Really? You want this guy?" the master of ceremonies asked. To which Top R said he gave a leaning back, arms extended outward, palms open, curling of the fingers, "bring it on" gesture. When he started to rhyme, a lot of the audience booed Top R. However, when he responded with the line "go ahead and boo me; by the time I'm done you'll all be groupies" the two-thousand person capacity crowd erupted in cheers. He explained the rest of his performance as "hitting every punch line," and "completely turning the crowd." He concluded by describing the episode as the single greatest feeling he had ever had as an emcee.

Without any prompting, this same story was relayed to me by three other people. One Amoeba co-worker, while making a few general comments about the show told me, "Top Ramen got on stage and freestyled. At first they were booing him but then he said a couple tight lines and everyone started cheering." The two other testimonies referred to him as some "white guy." Interestingly, one of these came from a woman who knew Top R but had not actually been at the show to witness his performance. "I heard this white guy was up there and the crowd was booing but by the end he was rockin' it," she explained to me about the show. When I told her it was Top R, I could (figuratively) see the light go on in her head. For her, the story had a sudden clarity to it.

There are two important points to this story. The first, which I have alluded to already and will only speak about briefly here, regards different levels of underground hip hop stratification. While many people refer to Mos Def as an underground hip hop artist, the fact that a great freestyle by a white emcee—perhaps notably someone as "bummy" looking as Top R— was so remarkable to his audience that it reached a level of folkloric circulation (and perhaps surpassed any other aspect of the show), is an indication of just how distinct Mos Def's underground hip hop scene is from the one in which I was immersed (see Introduction).[20]

The second point, which draws a connection to the first, is just how essential Top R's white identity is to the entire narrative. Had Top R not been a *sincere* white guy, and by this I mean that he could have just as easily been an authentically hip hop white guy (cloaked in baggy pants, backwards cap, and a throwback jersey á la Eminem, who by this date had already released two multiplatinum albums), the entire story might have played out differently: no boos, no surprises, no turning of the crowd; perhaps just a great freestyle, which is hardly the kind of thing that gets talked about to any great extent days after the show.

Music performances, particularly those that surround hip hop, offer opportunities for the enactment of new forms of reflexive identity construction. In response to music scholars' extensive focus on the ways in which social identities are reflected through music (see, for example, Fox 2004; Jones 1963; Willis 1978), Simon Frith (1996) has challenged researchers to pay greater attention to how identities are produced through musical activity. Racialization (both its expression and reception) takes place within specific social contexts, of which musical performances provide a particularly pungent instance. The examples of Audio Visual and Top R are both dramatic in that the distance between the performers' sincere whiteness—attending operas, dorky looks, and dirty-shirt bums—and the performances' hip hop legitimacy is striking. For hip hoppers like Bucc Rogerz and Da Golden Ray (both Asian American), Logic (Arab American), or Know Expressions and Phame the Funky Bolivian (both Latino), the identity-work needed to narrow the gap between social expectations and authentic hip hop performance might be less cumbersome if they can display credible competency.

For African American underground hip hoppers, the de facto legitimacy associated with their racial identity can at times become a double-edged sword, particularly in instances where competency is missing or appears to fall short. In narrating my own personal history in Chapter 2, I discussed my traumatic adolescent experience of nearly being singled out as the only black person at an event who couldn't break dance. For me that occasion was certainly extreme. However, to the extent that there are residual expectations that African Americans are able to rap well, such scripts can work to discredit good performances (i.e., the great black freestyler is seen as natural where the great white freestyler—á la Top R—is regarded as exceptional) and cause disillusioned reactions to below average ones. Simply put, in the pursuit of hip hop legitimacy, which is by no means the only motivating factor for performing, a *just* average black freestyler at the Rockin' Java open-mic might be better served to keep his mouth shut (let us not forget that I became a relatively well accepted insider among the regular crowd of emcees before ever setting foot on the stage).

Hip hop is inherently performative; its "vigorous enactment" of identity "remains the most fertile source of artistic creativity" (Smith 1997, 345). Underground hip hop's articulated rejection of exclusively race-based hip hop criteria results in the racialization of artistic performances being simultaneously overstated and unassumed. Despite its claim to be an inclusive social arena, both the significance attached to "special white boys" narratives of racial boundary crossing and the racial dynamics surrounding expected and performed competencies demonstrate that race is still very much a factor, particularly for those who see themselves, and are seen, as having the most to prove.

Suspect Sensibilities: The Case of the Backpacker

Before turning directly to issues of racial integrity and ethics, I think it is helpful to say something about the specific clustering of fashions and subcultural sensibilities that (stereo)typically get ascribed to underground hip hoppers, often by those outside the core of the scene. These clichéd images are important in that they identify an (imagined) *internal other* that "true (underground hip hop) heads" must perpetually be on the lookout for and weary of, not only in the social spaces they both cohabit but also as a dishonorable character tendency within themselves.

The manipulation and management of appearance is unquestionably an important means of self-identity construction (Giddens 1991). Through the visual signals we transmit to others about ourselves, initial terms of social interaction—for instance, what assumptions are made about a person—are set. As a musical subgenre, or music scene, underground hip hop has developed a range of visual codes and symbols that are understood as indexing insider status. At their nexus, they combine to form a quintessential underground hip hop persona, which carries with it a prescribed set of expected behaviors or what we might think of as an underground hip hop script.

If a single underground hip hop fashion type prevails, it is the "backpacker." In a 2000 *SF Bay Guardian* commentary on "the state of West Coast hip hop," Eric Arnold (2000) used the label "post-backpack" as a subheading for the section of his article that featured the Living Legends' Sunspot Jonz (within the scene, the Legends are widely regarded as the collective from which "all these [underground hip hop] kids have taken a page" [see chapter 1]). Similarly, Kegs One, owner of the Below the Surface hip hop shop—a retail outlet specifically catering to the underground community in which I was immersed (see Chapter 1)—referred to his shop as "the epicenter of the backpackers." In our interview, Kirby Dominant elaborated on both the accessories and social characteristics that are associated with the backpacker persona.

> **KD:** It's kinda fucked up cause all a backpacker is is a fuckin' hip hop head. I don't know what the mentality is when people say "backpacker." Is it a close minded hip hop head who only goes to Legends' shows? Or is it just a hip hop head? Is it the cats who really love the music? And the other cats who are not backpackers are just comin' to the club to get drunk and whoride [act crazy] and see Xzibit? Because if that's the case then I'm a fuckin' backpacker.
>
> I got my backpack right now. I got a hoodie on, I got jeans and I got fuckin' skate shoes on. So I mean, I'm a fuckin' backpacker right? We're all backpackers. It's part of the culture . . . I mean, what we do calls for it. You're walking right? You got your bag cause you got your tapes in there, your CDs, maybe your book, maybe your pen cause you're writing rhymes, maybe your pen cause you're graffin'. Maybe your fuckin' records. You have a bag. I don't know a hip hopper who don't walk around with no headphones. I mean, what kinda shit is that? You got your jeans on because you're wearing them probably every day. And you got your shoes on cause you're urban. And you got your hoodie on cause its just, I mean, what do they expect a motherfucker to wear? Most of the time

you're a student, you know I'm sayin'? You don't have a job maybe. So our life calls for it. Just like those conservative dudes wear fuckin' Dockers and whatever cause that's the norm for their jobs, you know what I'm sayin'?

It's like fools who get high all the time don't want to be called a stoner. That's what a fuckin' stoner is, a person who gets high. I'm a hip hop head and a backpacker, unless they come up with a different name or can explain to me what a backpacker is, then that's what the fuck I am!

The richness of Kirby's explanation lies not only in his thorough description of the key wardrobe features that mark backpackers, but also in his discussion of the functions, mentalities, and subcultural tensions that are linked to this identity. Functionally, for a student or anyone who does not own a car, having a bag is an important way of carrying around the various things that are needed in your daily routine. As I mentioned in Chapter 3, prior to my arrival in the Bay I had no idea just how much of an identifying accessory my Ecko messenger bag would be.

Yet Kirby's explanation also alluded to the important tension between underground music fans (who are alleged to "really love the music") and commercial fans (who are viewed as "coming to the club to get drunk and whoride and see Xzibit"). For underground hip hoppers, this division frequently placed them in a curious position between open-minded inclusive principles and narrow-minded exclusive attitudes. On one side of this divide, there are the color-blind, anticorporate, neo-bohemian ethics that—in much the same manner as the college radio stations which support underground music—articulate a progressive, cosmopolitan liberal democratic outlook. On the other side, there is the ardent interest in policing underground hip hop's borders and securing the scene from mainstream and corporate cooptation. Cultural theorist George McKay points out that many underground subcultures are perpetually caught in a tension between recruitment and avoidance lifestyles (1998; see also Maffesoli 1996). The cores of most music scenes tend to organize around artists, promoters, and other culture brokers who covet an expanding fan base. At the same time, fans who are "in the know" (not necessarily who "know what's up") wish to guard their privileged knowledge and guarantee that "their music" remains meaningful and salient to them (Frith 1987). Such frictions are characteristic of the cyclical relationships of mutual appropriation in which underground scenes and dominant cultural industries find themselves continually locked (Stokes 1994). They also create a condition of almost inevitable hypocrisy and some pretension as underground constituents attempt to safeguard their music and community while simultaneously keeping an open-mind.

Big Ant, an Amoeba employee and hip hop deejay/producer who, although liking a good bit of underground hip hop, did not consider himself an insider within the scene, was quite critical of the sectarian mentality he noticed among backpackers.

> BA: They try to be the most open-minded people as far as hip hop music. But they're really closed minded. Like, "okay . . . this is the only shit that's tight [good]. I don't like that because it's got diamonds on the cover . . . or computer graphics." Without hearing it they don't like it . . . when I say "backpacker," it's usually those people that . . . they got a lot of backpacks. That's why I say "backpacker."

Even Gammaray, who often attended the Rockin' Java open-mic nights and had recently completed a well heralded underground hip hop mixtape featuring original songs with several of the Rockin' Java regulars, spoke with considerable aggravation about the underground elitism he witnessed.

> G: It's kinda frustrating dude cause there's this whole kinda underground mentality . . . [where] a person can choose like, I'm kinda interested in hip hop so maybe I'll look at this underground stuff. And what tends to happen, I think is, they catch on to stuff like, "oh, this is underground, and this is underground. I'm going to get that, I'm going to listen to that and I'm going to bump it twenty-four seven." Like, "I'm underground now."
>
> And that's how I was for a little bit, and there's this certain mentality dude. I can't put my finger on it, but it's like very exclusive and almost putting yourself on a pedestal like you're down with the underground. . . . It's empowering listening to this shit that's real and identifying with it, being a part of it. . . . At the same time, I don't like the exclusiveness. I do not like it at all.

According to Gammaray, this type of attitude is most prominent among "the younger kids" he frequently encountered at shows. His comment on age draws attention to the dynamic of turnover within any music scene. Since there will always be a certain number of people who gradually become less involved with a given scene, survival is dependent on recruiting new generations of artists, fans, and other participants. Big Ant echoed Gammaray in explaining that a lot of younger shoppers he observed seemed more interested in building their immediate underground hip hop capital than in getting any sort of holistic understanding of hip hop and its history.

> BA: [A lot of these people] aren't really as into music as much as they think they are. Like, they're into that because their friends told them that that was a cool thing to get, and not because they went out and searched. . . . And they don't bother to know the history of what they're into.
>   Like people that are into rock 'n' roll, they know about Elvis, and they know about the Beatles. And maybe they listen to [more recent stuff], but they know about that and that it existed and what it sounds like. But kids nowadays, they'll hear an Eligh album or the Grouch, or the new Common or Mos Def's new CD, and they're not knowing about other things.

At the heart of these critiques is a fundamental distinction between the intrinsic and extrinsic value of hip hop music. Where the former *implies* a genuine appreciation and commitment to understanding hip hop within a larger context, the latter suggests a derivative worth that is connected to another source of value. In other words, it *applies* to people who seek to use their association with hip hop as a means to attaining other things. In the world of music making, this criticism is commonly expressed through accusations of "selling out." When pertaining to the micro-social exchanges taking place among a music scene's constituents, however, such concerns target more personal questions of honesty and integrity.

Although I do not recall hearing a definition of *backpacker* that explicitly associated the term with white hip hoppers, and a few people even told me that its origins trace back to early 1990s New York City groups like Black Moon and the Diggin' in the Crates (D.I.T.C.) crew (both of which were predominantly black[21]), the criticism leveled at backpackers and the avoidance of the label more generally, for me, necessitates an unpacking of its white racial symbolism. I begin with a simple binary. If one acknowledges that the style of Bay Area hip hop, which some underground hip hoppers referred to as "thug rap" but today people more commonly call "hyphy," is overwhelmingly marked by African American artists and aesthetics, and is most closely associated with predominantly black localities (like East Oakland, Hunters Point, and East Palo Alto),[22] then it seems reasonable to accept that its underground, sometimes conscious, college-student–oriented hip hop corollary would be most readily connected with whiteness. Relatively speaking, there certainly were enough white artists and predominantly white hip hop enclaves (see Chapter 5) to justify this reading. Additionally, as mentioned in the book's Introduction, many people vaguely familiar with the Bay Area underground scene—perhaps not the core arenas that I was most involved with—commonly (mis)recognize underground hip hop's audience as entirely white. One Amoeba co-worker of mine, who had a preference for "thug rap" artists like Killa Tay, Messy Marv, and Cellski, even made a regular practice of sneaking up behind me while I searched through the used underground hip hop CDs in the store, and announcing his presence in the form of a question as to why I listened to "all that white boy rap."

Linking the backpacker persona to white racial identity makes even more sense if we consider the specific position that the backpacker holds within the world of underground hip hop. By this I mean that the backpacker can be thought of as akin to both Run DMC's "Sucker MC" and Wimsatt's "wigger" (1993), in that everyone has seen a backpacker but rarely, if ever, do you meet a person claiming to be one. With the exception of (African American) Kirby Dominant's largely defiant pronouncement,[23] I do not recall anyone definitively embracing the "backpacker" label or any meaningful connection to it. When the article linking Sunspot Jonz with backpack rap came out, for instance, I was told that he was quite upset about the association.

Beneath the veneer of backpacks, hoodies, headphones, and skate shoes there is an unmistakably racialized body associated with the backpacker identity. If we remove yet another layer, now looking beneath the skin color to get a better sense of how the backpacker views and aspires to interact with *his* (the backpacker persona is also highly gendered) world, what we see is a person limited in *his* ability to accept or tolerate difference, and who extrinsically values underground hip hop as a means of claiming to be above the more pedestrian hip hop enthusiasts. Through this ideology of elitism and exclusion, the backpacker—racialized as white—becomes the embodiment of the damaging social sensibilities that more genuinely civic-minded underground hip hoppers (those who "know what's up") must perpetually guard against. Ultimately, the backpacker functions as an entity of recognition and misrecognition. It is at once a style through which underground hip hoppers identify one another and an imagined other that they define themselves in opposition to.

Racial Integrities, Political Ethics, and Social Sensibilities

Just what do the racial dynamics taking place within Bay Area underground hip hop suggest about the future of race in the United States? From much of what I have outlined in the previous pages—with regards to racially diverse constituents of a multiracial scene—it should be clear that the relational and situational aspects of racial identification are becoming more pronounced than ever. Yet we are still left to ponder a number of important questions regarding standards of conduct and the integrity of racial categories more generally. For instance, is the predominance of the black-white binary in American race relations waning and giving way to a greater recognition of people who fall outside this dichotomy?[24] Is the black-white binary equally threatened by the increased recognition of fluidity between and cultural variety within race categories?

Certainly many people who identify (and are identified) as black in America, particularly within cosmopolitan locales like the Bay Area, are only a generation or two removed from homelands in the Caribbean, Latin America, or on the African continent. A *New York Times* article suggested that since 1990 more Africans have immigrated to the United States than were forcibly brought here during the Atlantic slave trade (Roberts 2005). Such intraracial variability was plainly evident within Bay Area underground hip hop circles. It was not uncommon to hear emcees, in the course of freestyled rhymes, referencing themselves as Haitian, Ethiopian, or Liberian. T. Root, for instance, in quite a few rhyming performances mentioned not only his Guyanese heritage but also the fact that he spent some of his childhood in England. Indeed, two of the three black members of the Forest Fires Collective, namely Sim(ile) and Mad Squirrel (myself), drew their first breaths in Kenya and Ghana, respectively.

The safeguarding of white racial purity and social privilege throughout history has at various times facilitated a white versus collective people of color dynamic. For example, the Black Panther Party for Self-Defense, which formed in Oakland in 1966, succeeded in galvanizing a multicolored Left which brought together the collective interests of Arab American, Chinese American, Japanese American, Native American, and Chicano organizations and causes in addition to black ones (Prashad 2001). Alternately, the ability of different racial and ethnic groups to move up the social hierarchy, and in some cases even win their way to whiteness, has always been a compelling draw in encouraging groups to aspire to distance themselves from blackness. The best examples of this include the Irish, Italians, and Jews (Brodkin 1994; Warren and Twine 1997) who, during the late nineteenth and early twentieth century, transformed themselves from a status of racial other to part of a collective white bloc.

In a remarkable reversal of this typical trajectory of Americanization, several of the young "white" people I interacted with in the Bay Area made conscious decisions to identify with distinctly ethnic, and sometimes nonwhite, elements of their ancestry. This was probably most evident during the course of freestyles and other self-referential lyrical performances where testimonies to the effect of "I'm not white, I'm part-Cherokee (or Mexican)" were surprisingly common. Outside of this, mostly in casual conversations, a few people made a point of calling attention to the fact that their family surnames had been de-ethnicized while passing through Ellis Island. One young white woman, with only the slightest degree of shame, recalled a period when she and some of her white girlfriends encouraged the perception that they were Puerto Rican. According to her, this fabricated racial identity was enacted through particular fashions, hairstyles, and the fact that they all had dreadlocked African American boyfriends.

Acts of racial boundary crossing continue to foreground questions of sincerity over authenticity. In commenting specifically on the phenomenon of racial passing, Appiah (1990b) notes that when a person does not readily divulge pertinent aspects of their ethnic identity they are often viewed as inauthentic; however, when the aspects of one's identity that are not freely disclosed are racial, this inauthenticity turns to insincerity. In speaking of racial integrity, I am not only talking about the integrity of race categories as units of identity that maintain their form even in the face of unprecedented challenges to their biological and sociological bases, but also integrity in the sense of being honest, principled, and not necessarily bounded by scripted authenticity in going about fashioning one's racial self-presentation.

On a Monday night following the Rockin' Java open-mic, a group of "folks," including Destined, Devorah, Teddy (a white graffiti writer originally from Australia), Top R, and I, got together at Destined's sister's apartment to watch a video I had of an East Coast emcee battle. Top R, who tended to dominate conversations anyway, sometimes took the opportunity of having this kind of downtime with me—the anthropologist/em-cee studying hip hop and race—to quite deliberately offer his views on various topics pertaining to my research. As a white hip hopper "I can't af-ford to slip up," he explained that night as a rationalization for what he described as his sometimes peaked racial awareness. He went on to say that he did not believe in reverse racism, particularly of the sort that was based on the mere recognition of race, "I call that prejudice." When Teddy, who as a younger graffiti writer held Top R (and perhaps me also) in a cer-tain level of esteem, jumped in with a comment about trying to treat each person he meets as an individual, Top R dismissed it as "idealistic and impossible."

On the whole, I believe Top R genuinely held these views. Spending a good deal of time around not only him but also several of his friends (and some people who did not particularly care for him), I was privy to opinions on him, stories about him, and observations of him, none of which dis-suaded my view that he meant every word he said that night. "Top R's a misunderstood genius," Devorah once told me. Certainly his keen under-standing of racism as a structural force in society which individuals can navigate but never fully escape, would sit well with my old UMass professor Enoch Page (see Page 1999). Writer Jason Tanz has coined the term "Wegro" (a word that strikes some discord in me) to describe a more sophisticated and committed type of wigger who involve themselves with hip hop not "to bolster their self-image . . . [but] in a sincere, if often flawed, attempt to ac-knowledge, and hopefully move beyond the historic responsibilities of their race" (2007, 102). Whereas the wigger's interest is extrinsic—"what can hip hop do for me," the Wegro, according to Tanz, has an intrinsic appreciation in how hip hop can function to improve race relations. While I have defi-nitely met some "Wegroes" in my life, despite Top R's occasional critical race rants, I would not apply that term to him or, for that matter, to most of the white hip hoppers I got to know in the Bay Area.

If he had not made so many direct statements to the contrary, it would be tempting to simply describe Top R as not caring enough (about what black people thought of him) to be a Wegro, although his testimonies of heightened white consciousness (see Chapter 3) and his concerns about "slipping up" suggest otherwise. To fully appreciate the ethics guiding Top R's racialized disposition—and here I mean the confluence of ideologies and sensibilities that both informed and constrained his white racial per-formance—we must consider several interrelated factors. The first of these, which has already been discussed at some length, is Top R's awareness and concern regarding his position within the two racial hierarchies that he perpetually and simultaneously had to navigate. His privileged status as a white person in America was immediately inverted within one of the social fields most central to his everyday satisfaction and feeling of self-worth. This duality contributed to a condition of political stasis, at least as far as race was concerned, which was made all the more pertinent through Top R's sophisticated understanding of the authentic scripts associated with his white hip hop identity.

Once again I return to the matter of sincerity. For the most prominent script of hip hop whiteness, which Top R and other white emcees perpetually had to contend with, was that of the peculiarly insincere wigger of the early nineties who became most noticed through the image that *he* was attempting to pass *himself* off as something *he* could never truly be. As a twenty-first century white hip hopper, Top R was cognizant of his wigger ancestry and in some ways fashioned his efforts at racial sincerity in dialogue with it. For instance, the ostentatious ornamentation which once marked wigger apparel (think "It's a black thing you wouldn't understand" t-shirts and backwards, upside-down visors), for Top R, had been replaced by the sincerely humble "bummy shirt." It is this disposition that I believe would lead Top R and others like him to cast a critical eye toward what they would regard as Wegro pretensions. In sum, Top R did not seem interested in changing who he was in an effort to demonstrate that he "knew what's up" to somebody else; perhaps because he realized that for him, any claim to empathizing with the black experience or allegiance with a politics explicitly aimed at dismantling white privilege would be at best a partial truth.

Of course, Top R's views on, and latent investment in, issues of race and racism are not representative of all underground hip hop enthusiasts, not even all white ones. Many people held views similar to Teddy's: that if everyone treated one another with respect and dignity, racial matters would take care of themselves. However, quite a few—and here I am speaking of those white hip hoppers who were most inclined to participate in interracial social and musical circles—fell somewhere close to Top R in their understanding of racism as a historically and socially pervasive organizing principle in society, yet were reluctant to construct an identity (performance or otherwise) exclusively around this awareness. This sincere sensibility was unquestionably informed by observations of other white hip hoppers who seemed to focus too heavily on achieving authenticity through a convincing social performance.

Feller Quentin, who carried a general cynicism with him much of the time, was certainly not alone in receiving the majority of his fellow white hip hoppers with deep suspicion. For example, he described an early incidence of this while attending a summer high school program for gifted students in the arts and humanities.

> FQ: I met a number of friends and we were all involved in hip hop and a couple of the guys, you know a couple of the dudes that were white, I could see they had a bit of an identity crisis, you know what I mean? But with me I think it was a little bit different because with them they were around all white people and trying to separate themselves by virtue of that . . . with me for some reason, I felt that [going to a black high school] I had the right to be like this b-boy . . . and I've had this complex since then just thinking about shit like that.

This final statement, considered in conjunction with Feller's earlier comments about his assumed inner-city—"That's right motherfucker"—persona being "all an act" designed to meet the expectations of his suburban high school friends illustrates how for him, it was not only the lack of continuity he saw in other white hip hoppers racialized performances but also the fact that he recognized this as part of his own past. Indeed, the extent to which the special white boy narrative appeared consistently in so many personal histories suggests that, for a lot of white hip hop enthusiasts, efforts toward racial sincerity were attempts to revise and ultimately resolve the missing integrity they could see in their own hip hop biographies. Thus stripped of its normative status, whiteness, and the specifically hip hop inflected scripts that accompanied it—the wigger, the wannabe, the "more underground than thou" backpacker—served as both abstractions and targets of personal reflection with which new efforts at a more genuine hip hop whiteness could be constructed. For Bay Area underground hip hoppers in particular, participation in a multiracial scene helped to cultivate a nuanced understanding of how to engage the black-white polemic they were consistently performing identity work within.

While the position of European Americans like Feller Quentin and Top R —simultaneously at the top and bottom of intersecting social and subcultural hierarchies prompted a certain political ambivalence, on the whole their situation appeared to be far less ambiguous than, for instance, second-generation Korean Americans who found themselves caught between the dual pressures of assimilation and ethnicization (Kim 2004). One of the appealing aspects of underground hip hop, as a scene and subgenre that prioritizes racial sincerity as much as if not more than racialized hip hop authenticity, is that it offers young people an opportunity to do both. As with the Filipino hip hoppers discussed earlier in this chapter, participation in hip hop becomes a means of expressing one's Americanness *and* a way of articulating distinct elements of one's ethnic and racial identity in America.

Until recently, unresolved questions regarding the hip hop merits of individuals who do not fit neatly within the black-white paradigm were further obscured by the fact that, in the realm of emceeing, many groups had very few role models with which to identify. Of course, much of this has changed with regard to Filipinos, and seems to be changing for other groups occupying the "collective people of color" strata (see Chapter 3) as well. In examining the history of Asian American rappers, Oliver Wang (2007) highlighted the different strategies used to navigate or evade the symbolic landscape of blackness and whiteness that both guides hip hop's Music Industry decision making and steers its consumer market (see also Ogbar 2007). Whereas Wang concludes that "hip hop has its own power as a locus of cultural identity [that] at least provides an alternative" (p. 61) to racial and ethnic allegiances, I wish to emphasize the extent to which these identification processes involve actively balancing the demands of situational hip hop racialization against an ethics of racial and ethnic sincerity.

Although Wang mentions the "sometimes hostile differences in history, language, culture, and class" (p. 40) found between different Asian American groups, the artists he surveys inevitably spend more time presenting themselves as, or not as, Asian American than as any specific Asian nationality. It is here again where I believe that, by forwarding perspectives and experiences which resonate intimately with young people of Philippine descent, the Filipino hip hop music movement has been remarkably successful in generating scripts of hip hop legitimacy. Admittedly, there is always a danger that such ethnic specificity, in conjunction with the aforementioned hostilities, can be more divisive than productive. To the contrary, I would argue that in this case of Filipino participation within a wider multiracial hip hop scene, the emergence of a distinctly Filipino hip hop script has done more to foster political dialogue and ethical sensibilities which translate across racial and ethnic lines than to delineate a specific "Filipinos only" hip hop realm. I should be clear in stating that the majority of Filipino hip hoppers I have met, through both their music and social dispositions, seem more inclined to explore aspects of common subjectivity particularly with peoples of African descent[25] and other historically marginalized groups than to mark their struggles as exclusive. Thus, where the hip hop accent is distinct, it is not inaccessible; in fact, I would argue that it aspires to create multiracial and multiethnic (although perhaps non-white) coalitions.

In cases of people identifying as of mixed racial backgrounds, the nuances of these situational identifications appear to be even more elusive. Take, for example, Bored Stiff's Professor Whaley, who simultaneously identified as Ethiopian, Choctaw Indian, French, and English (Way 2000). Whaley's willingness to acknowledge the varied ethnic and racial strands of his identity, to paraphrase Appiah, gave him greater choices from the "tool kit of options" made available to each of us by our culture and society (1994, 155). From my own experiences (several times in fact) with people inquiring about the possibility of my partial Asian ancestry, not to mention the many occasions when I witnessed similar inquiries being made of others, it appears that strands of partial descent offer individuals more situational flexibility and further opportunities to connect (along racial lines) with others.[26]

In multiracial social spheres especially, mixed-race individuals regularly leveraged their multiple identifications to test racial boundaries and experiment with ethnoracial malleability. One young hip hop enthusiast, who described herself as of Puerto Rican/Japanese/Filipino/Chinese/Spanish descent, explained how having grown up in Hawaii caused her to "identify as a Hawaiian" even though she technically had no Polynesian ancestry. "I find it incredibly difficult to pick just one ethnicity," she explained. Indeed, in this context as much as any other, multiracial identification serves to lessen the imperative demands of racial scripts. A recognition of mixed-race identities, then, has transformed the question of "what are you?" from an imposition of a strict racial designation into an opportunity to narrate one's own racial and ethnic biography, and to seek out mutual lines of ancestry with others. Whereas Americans have traditionally avoided identifying themselves as too much of a "mishmash" (Waters 1990), within the situations and social instances that characterize many underground hip hop scenes the opposite seems to hold true.

Despite all that I have said here about the complex and multifaceted racial dynamics that characterize Bay Area underground hip hop, there are still indications that America's black-white racial paradigm remains remarkably resilient. For example, when listening to music featuring emcees whose voices and styles seemed racially ambiguous, the common question that hip hop enthusiasts of all races asked was, "Is he [it was almost always male] black or white?" This occurred despite the fact that virtually all underground hip hoppers were aware of numerous emcees who were neither one nor the other. Such inquiries seemed to take place as frequently among Asian American, Latino, and mixed-race hip hoppers as they did among African Americans and European Americans.

The salience of race has always been most profoundly felt as a binary opposition. People align themselves with who they believe they are, but fortify this position largely through awareness of who they are not and with whom they most wish not to be associated.[27] It is thus critical to recognize that for both people living within multiracial social environments and the researchers who work among them, there are situations and circumstances in which continuing to look at things through a binary racial lens makes sense. The key for the latter group is to better understand where, when, and under what conditions this is so.

Whereas identity implies a quality or characteristic that is specifically assigned to people—either you are black or you are not black—identification more accurately targets the processes through which individuals and groups negotiate how they wish to be perceived in dialogue with their understandings of how they are perceived. Mica Pollock has coined the term "race wrestling" in reference to people's everyday self-conscious struggles with "normalized ideas about 'racial' difference and about how racial inequality is produced" (2006, 9; see also 2004b). In the ongoing deliberations over hip hop authenticity and racial sincerity taking place within the Bay Area underground, this notion of *wrestling*—with both the meanings and implications of race—effectively captures an important ethical imperative that guides people's desires to be truthful about who they are and upfront about the kinds of communities they wish to be a part of. The integrity and ethics of racial identification hold these, at times competing, interests in a productive tension that in my optimistic view (I will save my pessimism for Chapter 5) encapsulates the future of interpersonal race relations in this country.

From all that has been discussed in this chapter, one can gather that Stuart Hall was quite correct in describing the late twentieth century as the "end of innocence" (see Chapter 3). What has been lost is the naivety with which authentic identities, both racial and subcultural, were once accepted and even embraced (see Bennett 1999b; Jackson 2005). Within racially diverse youth social arenas like underground hip hop, the processes that Hall described apply not only to representations of blackness but also to scripts of racial whiteness, as well as to other emerging groups. As the critical focus shifts from questions regarding the accuracy of what is represented toward a scrutinization of the fact of representation itself (Hall 1996), authenticity becomes less important to the dialogue and sincerity emerges as its logical replacement.

5

(Re)Mixed Messages

It is hard to forget the night that Megabusive showed up at the Anticon eviction party[1] carrying a twelve-pack of Budweiser that he refused to share. The members of Anticon at one time seemed interested in having Megabusive join their ranks. Adding a black emcee would have helped alleviate the air of suspicion that perpetually surrounded the group's all-white image. Doseone—perhaps the only Anticon member whose appearance could allow him to claim some non-white racial ancestry—was once quoted in a *SF Bay Guardian* article as saying, "the white thing has become so fucking dead to us." To which Sole, his fellow (European American) Anticon emcee, added: "It wasn't like we planned it. It's just a really weird coincidence" (Wang 2000, 63). The week this article ran, a few people I knew made a point of showing me this quote, and usually laughed hardily while doing so. Part of the animosity toward Anticon was probably just sour grapes. They were, and continue to be, one of the foremost (and I would say more innovative) underground hip hop collectives in the Bay Area. However, many in the scene, understandably, did not take too well to this all-white crew choosing to entitle their debut album *Music for the Advancement of Hip Hop*.

At least once, I have seen Megabusive express some regret about not pursuing the Anticon offer. On the night of their eviction party, however, he seemed to be more interested in starting trouble. At first he was pleasant enough, chatting with people he knew and drinking cans of Budweiser. But things changed when two of the Anticon members decided to liven up the party by doing a short performance. At this point in the evening I was admittedly a bit sour on at least one of them who, after claiming to be "completely moved out," told me that anything I found lying around the empty apartment I could have; then, minutes later, when I showed him my newly found Willie D *Controversy* cassette tape, he immediately claimed it was a "classic" and demanded it back. The Anticon performance was done by the duo Sole and the Pedestrian. They had a project together going by the name "Da Babylonians" where they satirically rapped (or "drunkenly freestyled" as the liner notes on the CD claim) in exaggerated black vernacular emcee style about typically sensationalized commercial rap music topics, and used the names Blazefest and Whitefolks.[2] According to underground hip hop folklore, the CD had made its way into the stereo of at least one major record label executive who, mistaking them for "real black rappers," immediately wanted to sign them.

The night of their eviction party, when Da Babylonians ended their hypermasculine ghetto-inspired freestyle set with a call out to "any emcee [in da house] who dared to step to dem," Megabusive's ears must have perked up. He immediately took the microphone and, after getting the deejay to stop the music, began explaining in a fabricated southern accent that he was not even into rap. When this short diatribe had finished, he gave an unusual performance that he described as a mixture of punk and country. In all honesty, I found the style, which included several yodel-like outbursts, more insane than impressive. But throughout his performance Megabusive's demeanor stayed steady and serious. When he finished, there was a stunned silence in the crowd as well as from the Da Babylonians. They knew Megabusive was a formidable battle emcee but seemed a bit unsure of whether he was actually serious about trying to battle them at their own party. In an effort to hold strong and save face, Blazefest and Whitefolks looked at one another and mutually asked "should I take him out or should you?" It was decided that Whitefolks would handle it, and from there he got up in Megabusive's face and began confronting him with a series of hard-hitting "dis is what you get for tryin to battle Da Babylonians" rhymes.

Upon reclaiming the mic, Megabusive's energy had completely changed. It was as if he had set a trap and Da Babylonians had taken the bait. His style was bold and extraordinarily confident. Although I cannot recall any of his exact lyrics, as he stood there staring down Blazefest and Whitefolks, alternating between pointing and waving his finger at them, his attitude conveyed a "how dare you step to me like you're hard!" and "this is about to get ugly" message. His assault was relentless, although interestingly enough, he made little to no mention of the racial politics which were at work in the room: two white boys aping blackness as a comedic performance for a majority white audience. Nevertheless, mid-way through the freestyle, both Babylonians stood there looking disappointed and dejected as they realized that the night—or at least their good natured minstrel show—had been ruined.

By the time Megabusive had finished, neither Blazefest nor Whitefolks was in much of a mood to respond. Rather, Whitefolks pulled Megabusive aside and, in a hushed whisper, tried to explain to him that they were just kidding around with their performance. A minute later, Megabusive was on the mic again, this time apologizing for ruining the party. His explanation was that he had somehow made the mistake of thinking they were trying to start a battle with him and had not realized it was only a joke. I have always wondered whether he was being sincere.[3]

For reasons that should be apparent, I choose to characterize Da Babylonians' performance that night—and perhaps every performance they have ever done—as a form of contemporary minstrelsy. Even with the absence of black cork on their faces, it is hard to look at their lampooning of African American hip hop stereotypes as a means to getting an easy laugh from a mostly white audience as anything else. Yet if you probe a little more deeply into the Anticon biography (or discography), this depiction is a bit more problematic than it initially appears.

Shortly after my arrival in the Bay Area, one of the first hip hop shows I attended was an Anticon-hosted "cover night" at Rico's Loft in San Francisco featuring members of Anticon (Dose, Alias, Sole, and the Pedestrian), Kirby Dominant, members of L.A.'s Shape Shifter crew (Circus, Radioinactive, and Awol One), and perhaps others. The evening's set-list included classic hits like O.C.'s "Time's Up," Mobb Deep's "Shook Ones," Brand Nubian's "Steal Ya 'Ho," and Digital Underground's "Humpty Dance" (the last performed by Dose dressed in a raccoon hat, green blazer, and pink shirt). Toward the end of their set, the members of Anticon did a song that Sole described as "an ode to [their] forefathers." It was the Young Black Teenagers' "Tap the Bottle" (see Wang 2000).

Of the assorted white emcees who suddenly (if only briefly) appeared at the start of the early 1990s, a case could be made for the Young Black Teenagers (YBT) being the most notorious of the bunch. Vanilla Ice is easily the most famous; his manufactured biography of growing up on the mean streets of Miami and attending the same high school as 2 Live Crew's Luther Campbell (Tannenbaum 1990) probably makes him the most infamous as well. But the idea of five white guys (in truth one was Puerto Rican) from Long Island referring to themselves as black, justifiably got the attention of a number of critics. Whereas a few people hailed the group for recognizing something along the lines of what critical theorists call the social construction of race, far more took issue with what they saw as the naivety of statements like "being black is a state of mind, a lifestyle, a cultural identity—not a skin color" (to which former-Public Enemy "media assassin" Harry Allen retorted "millions of my people line the bottom of the Atlantic Ocean. They don't do that because of their habits" [Koen 1990]). Even with the somewhat perplexing endorsement and support of Public Enemy—at the time the hip hop nation's undisputed barometer of correct racial politics—YBT failed to make any significant impact on the music's landscape. In fact, the group's name, which journalist Armond White (1996) described as the only artistic thing about them, seems to have garnered far more attention than any of their music. By identifying their direct line of descent from YBT, the members of Anticon were acknowledging a level of racial awareness that was linked to the controversial history of white artists in hip hop. And this, perhaps to a more manifest degree than anything else I witnessed, illustrated how contemporary hip hop artists perform race in dialogue with racialized hip hop scripts from the past. Bravo Anticon!

As one of my own hip hop side projects, after several engaged readings of Barbara Tuchman's *The Guns of August* (1962), I got it into my mind to do a rap song about World War I. Though committed to the concept, for several weeks I struggled with finding the appropriate voice. Then one day while working at Amoeba it came to me in the form of an opening line: "I am the 1914 lyricist." The idea was to do the song through the voice of Kaiser Wilhelm II—one of the stars of Tuchman's book. I must have been aware of the reverse racial symbolism surrounding a dreadlocked African American pretending to be a German emperor, but that certainly was not my driving purpose. In order to really embrace the Kaiser persona, I even took on what could only be described as a pathetically fabricated German accent, which amounted to little more than substituting a "Z" for any "Th" and a "V" for any "W": "Ve are driving in Ze car." Certainly borderline cultural insensitivity, but no worse, I would argue, than Da Babylonians' substituted "D," the Young Black Teenagers' song "Daddy Kalled Me Niga Cause I Likeded to Rhyme," or the countless other European American attempts to season their linguistic repertoire with African American vernacular: "Where you at, Yo!"

Through the luck of fate (and an anthropology student/filmmaker named Will Holloway from Colorado College), both the Kaiser and Anticon's Doseone were featured in a West Coast hip hop documentary entitled *Incantations.*[4] Shortly after viewing the film, Sole and Dose approached me at an all-female hip hop show in Oakland asking a lot of questions about whether I was "for real" or "just kidding around" about the Kaiser. I assured them I was dead serious.[5] "That's some crazy shit!" Sole said. Months later when the first Forest Fires Collective CD was released, Sole's only interest in the album seemed to be in whether or not "the Kaiser [was] on it."

Part of what the Anticon guys, and I believe many others, found so fascinating about the Kaiser persona was the way in which I played with racial symbolism, boundary crossing, and performance. In much the same manner as I assume Megabusive had intended with his punk/country skit— although from an Anticon perspective far more digestible since it was not directed as a challenge to them—this was one of the rare instances when hip hop's racial boundary line was crossed from the opposite direction. Although I maintain that my purpose all along was first and foremost to make a rap song about World War I, and (given my source of inspiration) the Kaiser persona was merely a sensibly artistic way of doing this, my experimentation with performed race and identity was received by many as a commentary on white appropriation of black music and culture.

The fact that Sole and Dose both recognized this and seemed to appreciate it so greatly confirmed my own thinking that, for them, Da Babylonian project was intended more as a sophisticated racial commentary than as a simple attempt at adolescent humor. I think it is quite likely that the members of Anticon, in enacting the racialized performances that were Da Babylonians, were not even immediately focused on stereotypes of blackness. Rather, I would contend that Sole and the Pedestrian saw themselves as crafting a tremendously ironic satire of the racial insincerity embodied by the Young Black Teenagers and other wigger icons of the past.[6] Arguably, if we accept that this group of white hip hoppers was engaged in a theatrical performance of past white hip hoppers' exaggerated performances of blackness, this could be viewed as about as profound an expression of white

racial sincerity as one might find. However, somewhere within this caul-
dron of sincerity, satire, and racial symbolism, for me, the circumstantial
logic breaks down.

Unlike some people I met (more on that below), I am certainly not suggesting any malicious intent on the part of Sole or the Pedestrian. To the
contrary, I believe that as white artists operating in what continues to be a
normative black music field, they, like Top R, wished to avoid "slipping up"
at all costs (see Chapter 4). But sometimes in being too focused on sophisticated sarcasm and irony—that is, the intentions and modes of depiction
that underlie given representations—one can lose sight of the content of
the representations themselves.[7] In other words, despite the symbolic motivations which might have preceded the conception of Da Babylonians, or
for that matter the degree to which their audiences recognized these, when
all is said and done we are still left with two white boys giving an over-
embellished performance of an aesthetic and poetic style modeled after
blackness in order to get a few cheap laughs from a mostly white audience.
They slipped up.

What is perhaps most disappointing is that the members of Anticon
were (and I would argue still are) at or near the forefront of advancing hip
hop performance styles that were quite sincere in their performed whiteness. So sincere that many people who defined hip hop in terms of more
African American aesthetic conventions had difficulty appreciating Anticon, and thus described their music as "avant-garde hip-hop," "emo-rap," or
"goth-hop." Out of the entire Anticon catalogue of music, which even at this
early point in their careers amounted to well over a dozen releases, Da
Babylonians project was probably the farthest from where any of the crew
members normally hung their artistic hats. It was a minor side project that
(at the time I write this) is not even among the eighty-plus albums currently
listed on the group's website (www.anticon.com). The question remains,
why did the members of Anticon choose to bring out Da Babylonians in
this particular context.

The German writer Johann Wolfgang von Goethe once remarked that
"men show their character most clearly by what they find amusing" (Watkins 1999, 24). In previous chapters, I have mentioned that young people
are drawn to hip hop not solely as a voice of expression and social commentary, but also because the activities involved with producing and consuming
hip hop music can be a lot of fun. Both Kelley (1997) and Krims (2000) see
this point as a necessary correction to the historical overemphasis on politics

within hip hop scholarship. Yet one of the things that has struck me in the course of collecting personal biographies as part of my research, and talking with people about hip hop more generally, is just how many white hip hop enthusiasts can recall early, and often admittedly imitative, forays into rapping that involve adolescent drinking and/or smoking pot. To hear such stories from Top R, Dope Cigars, or Gammaray would be one thing; each of these individual's early involvements in hip hop amounted to much more than just a joke. What concerns me more are all those people who do not identify with hip hop in any meaningful way yet at one time or another have gotten drunk and done a "rap song."[8]

What I am proposing here is a triangular relationship between white male juvenility, intoxication, and buffoonery through imitated blackness. This is common enough at many college house parties, sometimes through specified "ghetto" themes, and sometimes simply because a rap song comes on and people are drinking. In this play of racial impersonation, hip hop is merely the fashionable style of the times. However, the advent of music videos and the fact that hip hop has maintained its black face through its mainstreaming have only amplified these dynamics. In this regard, it is hard to imagine the Anticon guys choosing anything other than Da Babylonians for their performance that evening. Most of us had been drinking, and this was a hip hop party. One troubling aspect of the way contemporary identities are constructions, particularly racialized ones, is that they tend to be much more experimental, temporary, and fleeting than an invested racial politics insists upon. I will return to this.

"I feel that there is a big difference between groups that are mostly black with a few white members and all white groups," a European American friend once said to me as he listened to my *Deep Puddle Dynamics* (one of the Anticon collective's first releases of note) CD with a frown on his face. By developing a hip hop sound that was so sincere and self-assured in its whiteness, Anticon, I believe, began a steady process of forfeiting its non-white audience. The appearance of almost exclusively white Bay Area underground hip hop enclaves—white groups with mostly white audiences—certainly warrants attention. Beyond just the members of Anticon, there are several other examples of white artists with nearly entirely white followings. In fact, I will go so far as to say that having an all white crew almost assures such a fan base. Attributing this development to mere "coincidence" fails to appreciate what it can tell us. For me, the issue is not white hip hop fans' attraction to white artists, but rather the degree to which people of all races and ethnicities view the appearance of all-white hip hop enclaves with suspicion.

An African American Amoeba co-worker of mine who happened to stumble on an Anticon show, one in which Da Babylonians skits were left at home, still came away with the impression that this was a "minstrel." A European American emcee, who was familiar with these groups and their all-white followings, suggested that their mere existence demonstrated that white hip hoppers had been acting irresponsibly. He even went so far as to point to a number of specific incidents surrounding all white groups—including Anticon—where he felt that an unconscious degree of racism was at work.

For instance, someone relayed to me a story about the Overheard Voices (a pseudonym), an all-white crew who, as a promotional effort, had a bunch of fortune cookies made that read "I'm nobody's white man." This Anglicized reversal of the expression "I'm nobody's nigger" outraged a few African Americans who happened to catch word of it. Within entirely white hip hop circles, this ironic twist, much like Anticon's Babylonians performance, might have been celebrated as an antiracist statement of common humanity, or even a Foucauldian comment on how the demands of conforming to social scripts weigh as heavily on the powerful as on the powerless. For many African Americans who recognize how their ancestors (and perhaps they themselves) had to endure the weight of the word "nigger," and whose kinfolk line the bottom of the Atlantic, there was nothing funny about the joke, particularly if you do not trust the racial politics that motivated it. All-white racial discourses have tendencies to fall back on what philosopher David Ingram (2005, 261) calls the liberal racial symmetry thesis. This thesis states that because racial identifications are immoral, it is best that all people be treated in the exact same way. Although a belief in racial symmetry does not prescribe the cross-pollination involved in appropriating an adage which speaks to a particularly painful aspect of the black experience through an Asian medium to comment on whiteness, it does endorse such artistic license. I do not know if anything ever came out of the fortune cookie incident, but I can assume that if the objections to it were never brought to the attention of the Overheard Voices, nothing would have stopped them from doing the same thing (or something even "funnier") again.

The lack of accountability fostered through all-white hip hop enclaves has the potential to cause "special" white hip hoppers' (see Chapter 4) heightened racial consciousnesses to revert back to a more conventional white "double-unconsciousness" (Aaron 1999). Ingram explains:

> [c]omplementary to the "double consciousness" informing blacks' self understanding is the "false consciousness" of persons who do not have to worry about being discriminated against because of their skin color, who can view the world around them as a sea of open opportunity and, because of their privileged position, can universalize this "color-blind" experience as normative for all social relations (2005, 274).

Although some people felt this fortune cookie incident was an example of the true racism that lurks behind the mask of pretending to "know what's up," I take a more constructionist approach which emphasizes how identities are produced through social interaction. As philosopher Judith Butler has notably explained, "there need not be a 'doer behind the deed' [since] the 'doer' is variably constructed in and through the deed" (1990, 142). Thus, the question is not whether the Overheard Voices are or are not racist, but rather the extent to which their situationally specific actions express a "reality" skewed by racism or a lack thereof (Trepagnier 2006).

While people took issue with Anticon and other predominantly white groups' (including Disflex.6, the English League, Manifest Destiny, and the Moonies) lack of melanin, no one seemed all that concerned that the groups were all male. Perhaps someone should have been. The dearth of female voices and actions throughout the preceding pages says a great deal about underground hip hop, as well as some things about my relation to it. Despite my close friendship and frequent outings with Devorah, the majority of my Bay Area underground hip hop experiences took place in male-dominated social spaces. This is especially notable considering that several underground hip hoppers from other locales commented on the high numbers of women in attendance at Bay Area shows, particularly compared to cities like Chicago or Washington, DC. One of these female showgoers, Amelia, who was from San Francisco but attended college in New York City, commented on the feeling of inclusiveness she could hear in the musical aesthetics of the Bay Area sound: "If you listen to some of the Bay Area underground, it's not happy, [but] it's so much more beautiful in my opinion. You know, you listen to it and you're like, 'oh my god. That's amazing.' In New York, I listen to music and I'll be like, 'I wanna go beat someone up.'"

The fact that women are not featured more prominently in *Hip Hop Underground* is certainly in some ways connected to my male identity. Ethnographers have long recognized that the gender of a researcher impacts the relationships he or she forms in the community in which they work (see, for example, Golde 1986; Whitehead and Conway 1986). Such dynamics can be even more pronounced within heterosexual nightlife-oriented youth music scenes where events have a tendency to drift precariously close to becoming "meat markets" (see Chapter 2). For example, in both building rapport and attempting to arrange interviews with young women, there were times when I felt that my claims to being a researcher were being received as attempted pickup lines.[9] Even my friendship with Devorah was at first mistaken for a romantic partnership by my fellow Forest Fires Collective members and others. In addition, my decision to immerse myself in the role of an emcee participant—that is, to make the stage my home rather than the audience—further contributed to the predominantly male tenor of my research; for even if women do attend shows in relatively high numbers, there are not large numbers of female performers. The sad fact of the matter is that gender norms—the scripts outlining appropriate female behavior—in underground hip hop are not a whole lot more participatory[10] than those that are found in its commercial rap counterpart. This is somewhat striking considering the progressive and inclusive ideals of both underground hip hop's anticorporate production practices and its antimaterialistic music messages.

As both a structural basis of social inequality and a means to "understanding the organization and interpretation of human relationships" (Nayak and Kehily 2008, 4), the power exerted through categories of gender is as pervasive as that which is wielded through race. Accordingly, I believe that many male underground hip hoppers, when articulating their version of "knowing what's up" (see Chapter 3), would invariably include an acknowledgment of gender equality as part of their enlightened view of the world, all of which makes the scene's decidedly male character even more disturbing.

Several researchers have highlighted a history of struggle on the part of women to gain equal access and recognition within commercial hip hop spheres (see, for example, Guevara 1996; Keyes 1993; Perry 2004). Removed from the patriarchal structures and asymmetrical power relations that characterize the Music Industry, one might expect underground hip hop to be different. During my time in the Bay Area, I saw several women hip hop artists perform, many times through an all-female concert series (highlighting the four elements of hip hop) called "Sisterz of the Underground" (see P 2004). And at the usual underground hip hop shows, I would estimate the proportion of women performers as compared to men was somewhat equivalent to what you would find in commercial rap music. For instance, I would approximate that one in every eight acts that I saw during my time in the Bay Area included at least one female.[11]

Women's appearances on stage at hip hop open-mics were far less frequent. For example, on a typical evening at Rockin' Java approximately twenty emcees would appear on stage. Although many women regularly attended these performances, including recognized female artists that I had seen give paid performances at other venues, on many evenings no female emcees would get on the mic, and I do not recall seeing more than two women get on stage on any given night. The only journalistic coverage of the Day One open-mic that I have ever come across is an article entitled, "A Hip-Hop Coffeegoer's Heaven in the Haight," which appeared in the *Golden Gate [X]Press Online*. In the article, which details one visit to the Rockin' Java open-mic, author Michael Austin states, "female emcees usually bless the mic but tonight it's a testosterone fest" (2001). Having attended at least forty of these weekly open-mics, I would say that Austin's testosterone-filled experience was not unusual. However, I can sympathize with his mischaracterization. What it signals to me is the disjuncture between the underground hip hop ideal and the actual nature of the scene.

So many things about Rockin' Java's "mellow atmosphere" and "cool vibe" (M. Austin 2001) suggest female inclusion. Could Common's quintessential "coffee shop chick" experience (see Introduction) be captured any better than through the image of a young lady sitting in a Haight Street café, sipping "lattes with a shot of caramel" and "nodding [her] head to Pete Rock and CL Smooth's old school hit, T.R.O.Y." (M. Austin 2001)? Prior to the open–mic event, one of the young women Austin interviewed even joked about "going up there and flowing for a minute" (2001).

Almost without exception, on the occasions when female emcees would get on stage, they were well received. Although debates regarding good versus bad open-mic performances are subjective, I feel comfortable saying that part of this favorable reception was due to the fact that most of these young women were (by consensus judgment) quite good. However, attributing these successful performances to this element alone overlooks an important contradiction between ideology and social climate. Although the prevalent sensibilities of most open-mic attendees desired female participation, and therefore welcomed it on the rare instances when it occurred, it seems to me that the social character of the space and specific activities surrounding the open-mic fostered a lack of awareness of gender politics and worked to discourage women from participating.

This male predominance was supported by a reigning atmosphere within open-mic settings into which newcomers were quickly socialized. After her first night out at the Rockin' Java, Renée, a close friend who had no qualms about claiming center stage within dancing circles, told me very casually that she had considered "getting up there." However, during her several subsequent visits to the open-mic, she seemed more than resigned to stay in the audience. The parallels between this and Austin's interviewee suggest to me that his experience was more typical than he realized.

Near the end of one of the first Sisterz of the Underground events ever held (P 2004), they opened up the microphone to audience members to get on stage and rhyme. While two or three women immediately approached the stage, they were soon outnumbered by at least ten men. I never did get the chance to rock the microphone that night. Just moments before the microphone was going to be passed to me, an adamant young woman decisively closed the open-mic on the grounds of testosterone overload. To paraphrase DJ Mizzo (see Chapter 3): I was part of the problem.[12]

The final and seemingly most democratic arena of rhyming public performance is the curbside[13] freestyle rhyme cypher. Out of the hundreds of cyphers that I witnessed or took part in, I do not recall ever seeing a woman participate. In reflecting on a discussion I had with T. Root regarding the energy surrounding cyphers, I came to realize that within these tight-knit circles (which T. Root tellingly compared to fighting circles), gender became the key axis of exclusion. For instance, on the night when I first cyphered with T. Root, Destined, Top Ramen, and others in Golden Gate Park (see Introduction), despite the fact that we had traveled to the park in the interest of celebrating two black Swedish women's last night in San Francisco, the commencing of a freestyle cypher immediately on our arrival in the park instantly created a dynamic of separate male and female space. Looking back on the situation, I vaguely remember that the four women spent the time sitting at a picnic table a few feet away from us listening and having their own conversation. These spaces were so separate that weeks later, when I was first introduced to Devorah (see Chapter 2), I did not recall that she had been among us that evening.[14]

There seems to be an inverse correlation between degrees of performance formality and the exclusion of women as performers. In stark contrast to race and ethnicity, where the less formalized contexts of music performance facilitate greater diversity, the same absence of an official performance event (and defined performers) appears to generate overwhelmingly male-dominated hip hop settings. In this regard, underground hip hop is no different from many subcultural spaces which, by and large, tend to become definitively masculine and are juxtaposed to what has been described as the "feminization of the mainstream" (Thornton 1995).

"Don't let Devorah fool you," a friend of hers said to me a few weeks after she left town to return to Tahoe, "the only reason she got into hip hop is because all the hot guys in high school were into it." With the exception of (at Top R's urging) contemplating making a mixtape out of her impressive collection of underground cassettes (see Chapter 2 n. 21), for Devorah the idea of participating beyond being an audience member (i.e., trying to dee-jay, emcee, b-girl, or graffiti write) never really surfaced.[15] But, as my Chapter 2 discussion of online posts about "white girls wearing hair kerchiefs" attests to, even this role was at times resented. From my observations, nothing seemed to irritate male hip hop enthusiasts who tended toward underground elitism more than the sight of an attractive woman (who *presumably* would not give *them* the time of day) wearing their favorite group's t-shirt or attending their favorite group's show. This hostility toward "groupies in the underground" is linked to the earlier discussion about how surpassing a certain "girl quota" ultimately marks the deterioration of a scene (see Chapter 2). Subcultural theorists Angela McRobbie and Jenny Garber suggest that within male-dominated social spaces young women may negotiate their roles by taking on a posture of reticence (1997 [1975], 113). Even without an awareness of any animosities directed toward them, a few women I spoke with felt some uncertainty about how to carry themselves within these resolutely underground hip hop spaces.[16] The following admission by Leigh Ann, who was an avid hip hop consumer and show-goer, stands as a case and point: "When I go to a show, I feel, not out of place, but I feel almost nervous in a way. It's not that I care what other people think. It's just like . . . I'm unsure about how to handle myself."

When making assessments of subcultural capital, factors of gender are second only to age (Thornton 1995). Within underground hip hop, although progressive ideals are commonly upheld, women continue to struggle for access to its more participatory roles. Furthermore, on the whole, issues of gender are conspicuously absent from the subcultural discourse. This is somewhat surprising, if only because the subjugation of women and objectification of female sexuality has been so prevalent within the commercial rap music industry that underground hip hop has defined itself against. It would seem that an ideology of hip hop anticorporatism could seemingly translate into an active critique of major-label Music Industry gender inequality. Disappointingly, this hasn't seemed to have been the case.

Despite all that Destined shared with me and taught me, he was not the person most responsible for alerting me to the strength and magnitude of the Bay Area's (and the entire West Coast's) burgeoning Filipino American hip hop community.[17] Nor was it Kiwi, although he absolutely blew me away that day at San Francisco State (see Chapter 4). If I was to credit any one person it might very well be Lily—a.k.a. Dirtydot—of the hip hop/spoken-word group Lady Wonders,[18] or her partner Shortyrocwell, both of whom I bumped into with casual regularity.

The two Lady Wonders' performances that I managed to attend had some of the best collective energy and spirit of all the shows I went to during that first year in the Bay. Much of this, I am quite sure, was due to their very deliberate efforts to disrupt the usual male hegemony. "No disrespect to the men," Shortyrocwell announced at the same show where Sole and Dose had grilled me so thoroughly about my Kaiser persona, "but could I have all my ladies in the front . . . I want to smell the estrogen." While it was disappointing for me to have to give up the front row spot I had so diligently secured, I could certainly understand the gesture. Dirtydot was one of those female emcees who attended the Rockin' Java open-mic but never got on stage. I would surmise that she and the rest of the Lady Wonders well understood the tendency for the gravity within most hip hop settings to settle toward masculinity. But this was their show and, as one of six female acts who took the stage that night, they were very conscious in defining the femininity of the space.

Identifying the thrust of any hip hop community through its female involvement would seem to run counter to the prevailing subcultural "wisdom" regarding feminized mainstreams and girl quotas, yet the role of the Lady Wonders and a host of other young Filipina Americans within the hip hop-inflected arts, as well as their activism in their communities, suggests something altogether different. Even with their at times sensual and sexy performing styles, it would be hard for anyone to walk away from a Lady Wonders show feeling as if they had just left a "meat market."[19] Some of this virtuous self-presentation is likely connected to what ethnic studies scholar Yen Le Espiritu describes as the way in which Filipina morality has been constructed in relation to the immorality of the dominant group—or as one of her interviewees explains, "we don't sleep around like white girls do" (Espiritu 2003, 157). However, where Espiritu locates the source of such ethics in young Filipina's orientations toward home and family, within the nondomestic, nonfamilial spaces of music scenes, I see it issuing through their investment in and allegiance to the politics of their communities: first and foremost to the Filipino American community but easily extending to other groups and individuals who espouse similar political agendas and sensibilities (see Chapter 4).[20]

The example of Filipina involvement within Bay Area hip hop (in addition to the Lady Wonders I should also mention artists like Rhapsodistas and Hopie Spitshard) underscores an important link between the Anticon party episode that introduced this chapter and the broader questions of race and ethnicity that this book aims to explore. In the preceding chapter, I asked what becomes of the color line within contexts in which the salience of racial integrities is being simultaneously fortified and dismantled. The mutual participation of young Filipinos and Filipinas is motivated by a proactive politics of recognition and representation that manifests in the specific terms through which these new Filipino American (hip hop) identities are being scripted. Starting from a "Black Atlantic"-inspired understanding of hip hop as a postcolonial voice for the politically, culturally, and economically disenfranchised and dispossessed, Filipino American artists draw attention to similarities between their experiences and, most notably, those of African Americans, but also those of Native Americans and other oppressed groups in U.S. history, in order to leverage a posture of hip hop entitlement (see Chapter 4). European American hip hoppers are also active in identity work that seeks to create new forms of white racial scripting. However, where Filipinos' "born again" (Mendoza 2002) consciousnesses are inspired by sentiments regarding the need to redress their historical invisibility, political marginalization,[21] and experiences with discrimination (all of which serve as points of reference in negotiating hip hop's racial landscape), European Americans, on the whole, appear to be in a state of racial and cultural limbo situated between the irreconcilable demands of an authentically underground hip hop politics and their own white racial sincerity.

This is certainly no reason to feel sorry for white hip hoppers—they are doing just fine. However, as European American emcees continue to indulge in the late modern art of experimenting with, and at times ironically inverting, conventional white identity—that is, as they engage in the performative dismantling of the symbolic structures on which U. S. racial inequality has been reified—the potential of unwittingly continuing the same racially privileged dispositions they imagine themselves critiquing remains.

The refusal of many male hip hoppers to cultivate a space that facilitates female inclusion within hip hop's participatory domains should be viewed as cause for concern. Taken in conjunction with episodes like Da Babylonians's minstrel show and the white man fortune cookie incident, it suggests to me that rather than a truly emancipatory identity politics, what we are witnessing with this generational embrace of underground hip hop might very well be a particular form of what my British colleagues call *laddism*, which they define as a cluster of attitudes and behaviors around shared interests in sport, alcohol, and sex associated with young men (see Attwood 2005). In this hip hop version of laddism, music replaces sports and, in underground circles in particular, direct allusions to sex might be more subdued. Yet, like the more general form, hip hop laddism remains rooted in the male prerogative to gather socially and to engage in certain distinctly masculine ways of having fun. Male friendships and visceral pleasure are paramount.

Of course, there is nothing wrong with young people (or anyone for that matter) having fun. And, as many of the activist friends I have made over the years can attest to, being involved in initiatives aimed at bringing about social change can be a lot of fun. It can also be a lot of work. The key distinction is initiative. Inclinations toward having fun that do not issue from a politically inspired sense of traction, rarely produce any measurable social difference; they are more likely to reproduce the same old social order. Even those African American (and Hispanic) youths growing up in 1970s New York who fashioned the cultural materials for a billion-dollar industry largely around the project of having fun were responding to social and economic circumstances which gave their gestures toward pleasure an unmistakably political tone. I am less optimistic about the potential for a meaningful political thrust to organically emerge out of the fun activities of groups of people, who—in terms of both standard quality-of-life measures[22] and their everyday experiences with issues of race, class, and gender—are among the most privileged on the planet. I do not say this to discount the genuineness of individuals or the (still under-theorized) influence of music on sociality. However, regardless of the genre, the political functions of music alone are never inherent. As Kirby Dominant well understood (see Chapter 4), music can be recruited in the service of multiple agendas.

This ethnographic project formed around questions of how time spent within racially diverse and integrated social environments affects the way young people conceive of and assign meaning to racial differences. Whereas the various places that make up the Bay Area can be thought of as the local context for these social interactions, the subcultural spaces where underground hip hoppers of all races and ethnicities converge are their most immediate and intimate settings. To what extent do the new negotiations of identity discussed in the preceding pages, in and of themselves, constitute a meaningful social change? I am referring here to the type of change that begins at the everyday level and concerns how people reflect on their own racial identity and those of others around them, as well as how such understandings influence dynamics of social interaction; most notably, who people choose to interact with and how they construct their identities when doing so.

In their daily interactions and affiliations with hip hoppers of various racial and ethnic identities, participants in the Bay Area underground hip hop scene are exploring the contradictions and implications of essentialized racial authenticity. The interests and experiences that shape their social dispositions emerge from the recognition that racial identities are never as stable as their "invented histories, biologies, and cultural affinities" would lead us to believe (Appiah 1992, 174; also see Taylor 2005). Yet the paradox here rests on the observation that there seems to be more confluence, self-assuredness, and possibly even sincerity in the firm scripting of racial identities than in the erosion of such scripts. Such affirming scripts must not be thought of as unyielding sets of authentic demands to which every member of a designated racial group is expected to conform, but rather as constellations of principles that give shape to the politics and sensibilities associated with various racial identifications. This moves me toward a somewhat ambivalent prognosis since, as Appiah reminds us, we only have so much power in determining the identity toolkit options from among which we choose (1994, 155). The destabilization of race in America—its revision, remixing, and reformation (Omi and Winant 1986)—is most potentially consequential precisely because its outcomes are so uncertain. Within multiracial social arenas like the world of Bay Area underground hip hop, young people are engaging in creative and substantive efforts to re-draw the color line through their own understandings of integrity and ethics. But historically precedented conceptions of race and racism are never out of earshot. Like Megabusive at the Anticon party, they lurk just outside the room with a twelve pack of beer, waiting for the opportune moment to grab center stage and "ruin" someone's feel-good occasion.

Notes

INTRODUCTION

1. As a subgenre, West Coast underground hip hop can be identified through the prominence of specific regional artists and aesthetic sensibilities. Its core geographic area spans from Vancouver to San Diego, and eastward through the Rockies. My decision to place Bay Area underground hip hop within this broader "West Coast underground" subgenre is in no small part influenced by the fact that this label was frequently used by people I did research among when discussing their music.

2. *Beat-boxing* is a form of vocalized percussion that within hip hop is often done in the absence of any other musical source.

3. In fact, days later while walking down Haight Street, T. Root beckoned me from the window of a passing Number 33 bus, yelling, "Hey! Do you have the tape from that night?"

4. This notion of racial and ethnic performativity is borrowed from gender theorist Judith Butler's (1990) insights on the ways in which gender identities are produced and reproduced through locally situated discursive practices (see also Smith 1997).

5. Beacon Hill is a southeast Seattle neighborhood that is home to the city's most diverse racial and ethnic populations.

6. All of this sounds remarkably similar to what Schloss (2004) describes, which makes me wonder if there are even stronger tendencies for these types of relationships within hip hop–oriented popular music studies.

7. T. Root once explained to me that The Roots *had* to be considered an underground group because "roots *are* underground."

8. Bizzaro (a.k.a. Bicasso) is far better known for his membership in the Living Legends (see Chapter 1). Yet even this relative fame pales in comparison to artists like Common and The Roots. Lyrics courtesy of J. Whitaker.

9. Of course, this model allows for the existence of both lesser-known all-white hip hop enclaves (see Chapter 5) and underground hip hop acts who achieve commercial success and again begin to attract considerable numbers of non-white fans.

10. There is plenty to suggest that as the fan base becomes more overwhelmingly white, nonwhite fandom subsides (see Chapter 5).

11. Amoeba has since opened a larger store in Hollywood.

12. Despite the fact that I had several unprompted inquiries about my mixed-race heritage in staying consistent with the way that I have been perceived for most of my life in America, I choose to describe my social identity as African American.

CHAPTER 1. RACE IN AMERICA AND UNDERGROUND HIP HOP IN THE BAY

1. For more critical perspectives on these issues, see Grant-Thomas and Orfield 2008.

2. The term *Hispanic* officially came about as a government designation. For this reason, many people, particularly on the West Coast, prefer Latino/a. Another distinction between the two terms is that Hispanic technically implies native Spanish-speaking, where Latino/a (referring to Latin America) includes other languages—most notably Portuguese-speaking Brazilians (Dávila 2001).

3. Percentages of other groups also correspond with the projected 2050 trajectory.

4. As critical race scholars Jonathan W. Warren and Francis Winddance Twine explain, during the late nineteenth and early twentieth centuries when immigrants from Ireland and southern and eastern Europe began arriving in America in great numbers "they found themselves being defined as a 'race apart,' as non-White (1997, 204; see also Brodkin 1994).

5. Anthropologist Mica Pollock describes race as a "mind-boggling oversimplification of human diversity" (2004a, 43).

6. *Hernandez v. Texas*, 347 U.S. 475 (1954).

7. Directive No. 15's specific definitions of the five groups are as follows: "*American Indian or Alaskan Native*—A person having origins in any of the original peoples of North America, and who maintains cultural identification through tribal affiliations or community recognition; *Asian or Pacific Islander*—A person having origins in any of the original peoples of the Far East, Southeast Asia, the Indian subcontinent, or the Pacific Islands. This area includes, for example, China, India, Japan, Korea, the Philippine Islands, and Samoa; *Black*—A person having origins in any of the black racial groups of Africa; *Hispanic*—a person of Mexican, Puerto Rican, Cuban, Central or South American, or other Spanish culture or origin, regardless of race; *White*—a person having origins in any of the original peoples of Europe, North Africa, or the Middle East" (Office of Management and Budget 1995). Note that black

is the only category for which a specific racial designation is mentioned. A much more common designation is "original peoples."

8. In an effort to eliminate confusion and misreporting, the U.S. Commission on Civil Rights considered adding "Hispanic" to the main list of racial categories on the 2010 Census (Lewis 2006).

9. Even this is more complicated than it initially appears. For one, the correlation between Hispanic identity and speaking Spanish is not absolute; furthermore, while *Hispanic* and *Latino* are often used interchangeably, the two terms have different linguistic implications (see note 2 above).

10. Further distinctions are sometimes made by region of origin as well as by age and time of immigration (Cha 1999).

11. Following Raquel Rivera, I adopt the term *ethnoracial* as an acknowledgment of the "constitutional racialization of ethnic categories" (2001, 255 n. 2).

12. Many people falling under these broad racial groupings hail from societies in which greater degrees of racial mixing have historically been acknowledged.

13. Democratic Senator Jim Webb is married to Vietnamese American Hong Le Webb.

14. In a study of multiracial births in California, Sonya Tafoya (2002) demonstrated how treating Hispanic as an ethnic designation as opposed to a racial category on the census decreases the number of multiracial births.

15. I use the uppercase "Music Industry" to indicate any of the vast collection of companies releasing music under (what was at the time) the Big Five (now the Big Four) entertainment conglomerates; namely, Universal Music Group (UMG), Sony Music, Electric and Musical Industries Ltd (EMI), Warner Music Group (WMG), and Bertelsmann Music Group (BMG).

16. For an excellent discussion of the motivations and contradictions surrounding DiY cultures, see McKay 1998.

17. This avoidance of convention is also apparent in the packaging of underground hip hop albums (see Harrison 2006).

18. On this last point, a student in one of my classes once made the astute observation that within much of the rap music she preferred, even without knowing a particular song she could anticipate when and how the rhyme was going to be delivered (a quality that for her enhanced a song's danceability); however, in most of the West Coast underground hip hop I was playing for her, this was not the case.

19. Two particularly striking examples from the Bay Area are Hieroglyphic's Del the Funky Homosapien, whose artist image fuses Japanese video game connoisseurship and language studies as well as hallucinogenic drug use (Fox 1999), not to mention rumors of dating Jerry Garcia's daughter; and the Mystik Journeymen, a duo who rose to underground hip hop prominence as two emcees going by the names Brother From Another Planet (or BFAP) and the Psychedelic Step Child (PSC) (Ducker 2004a).

20. Extreme displays of wealth have always been a part of hip hop. However, as with other aspects of hip hop's corporatization, what is most significant here is the

degree to which this "ghetto fabulous," "bling bling" self-presentation style became one of the only recognized modes of rap music authenticity.

21. By this I mean that those who had at one time made the deliberate decision to embrace hip hop, not as the most obvious choice of music to follow but as one that they perceived as saying something distinctive about themselves, were best positioned to recognize how the oppositional stance that had originally appealed to them was now functioning as "a camouflaged means of negotiation" with mainstream sensibilities (Smith 1997, 348).

22. For instance, by 2000 it was not uncommon to find music stores with separate sections for "rap music" and "underground/independent hip hop music."

23. For two excellent (and provocative) discussions of the dynamics and concerns surrounding these processes, see Hall 1997 and Farrow 2004.

24. Company Flow was an early (multiracial) underground hip hop group hailing from Brooklyn. Although the group disbanded in 2000, their 1997 *Funcrusher Plus* album—released on the (pseudo independent) *Rawkus Records* label—is widely regarded as one of the most important albums in the emergence of the underground hip hop subgenre.

25. An Akai MPC 2000 is a prominent hip hop sampler/production station usually costing around $1,500.

26. Discussion Forum Post: Lotta BRIGADE DJ StillDope. 1999. "How easy is it to be accepted as an underground artist??" *Legends' Labyrinth* (May 2): http://disc .server.com/discussion.cgi?id=11608&article=14614 (accessed May 27, 1999).

27. Too $hort's DiY music activities are credited with inspiring other aspiring hip hop artists "within a 50 mile radius of Oakland" to adopt similar practices (Arnold 2006, 73).

28. By 2006, Too $hort had "accumulated more gold and platinum recordings than any other rap artist in history" (Arnold 2006, 73).

29. Prior to returning to New Orleans and starting No Limit, Master P spent several years pursuing his independent hip hop ambitions while living in the Bay Area city of Richmond.

30. Hunters Point, again, is a largely African American neighborhood in San Francisco (see above). Similarly, sections of Oakland, most specifically the neighborhoods being alluded to in this comment, are well regarded as predominantly black.

31. Others early Bay Area underground hip hop music artists include: Elements of Change, Various Blends, Kemetic Suns, Derelicts, Twisted Mind Kids, Subcontents, Most Desh, Charisma, Cytoplasmz, Mixed Practice, Homeless Derelix, Sacred Hoop, Ninety-ninth Dimension, Third Sight, Insomniac, and Tape Master Steph.

32. Their affinity with New York City–based conscious rappers is demonstrated by the appearance of Del, the Souls of Mischief, Casual, and the Pharcyde on A Tribe Called Quest's *Midnight Marauders* album cover.

33. For a complimentary observation on how the Bay Area's "isolation" nurtured innovations in deejaying see Wang n.d.

34. Bay Area rap and a variety of deejay mix CDs are included in this number.

35. Discussion Forum Post: chip. 2001. "selfless posting..respect is due . . . (cont'd) read this." *Legends' Labyrinth* (June 13): http://disc.server.com/discussion.cgi ?id=11608&article=104065&date_query=992459673 (accessed June 14, 2001).

36. I would also add influential West Coast underground hip hop groups from Los Angeles like the Pharcyde, Freestyle Fellowship, Abstract Tribe Unique, and others hailing from the Project Blowed camp.

CHAPTER 2. EXPERIENCING THE BAY

1. For a far more favorable reading of the diary's content see Raymond Firth's "Second Introduction" (1989).

2. Both feminist researchers and native anthropologists have claimed their embedded position with members of the communities in which they work as a basis for a commitment to an "ethics of representation" and the "emancipatory ends of research" (Brown and Dobrin 2004, 4; see also Flax 1987). This idea of common politics on the basis of common womanhood or common nationality has been found to be problematic by several scholars, including Strathern 1987 and Stacey 1988 with regards to feminism and anthropology, and Narayan 1993 and Sahlins 1995 on anthropological nativeness.

3. I should also note Derek Freeman's (1983) attack on Margaret Mead's observations in *Coming of Age in Samoa,* a highly visible controversy that furthered the debate on ethnographic interpretation and authority.

4. High profile hilltown residents include singer-songwriter Sonya Kitchell, playwright Jean-Claude van Itallie, and actor/comedian Bill Cosby.

5. In October 1986 (two years prior to my arrival on campus), following a disappointing Boston Red Sox loss in the seventh game of the World Series, a series-long rivalry between (Bostonian) Red Sox fans and (New Yorker) Mets fans on a particular dormitory floor erupted into a campus incident. With a large proportion of the UMass African American population coming from the New York area, as the confrontation escalated, race became its key signifier. According to reports, a mob of intoxicated angry white males set out on a crusade for revenge which to them could best be achieved by inflicting punishment on any black person they could get their hands on. During my freshman year at UMass I heard several firsthand accounts from Red Sox loving African American Bostonians who had had to run for their lives to escape groups of several dozen "pissed off white boys." Needless to say, a generation of on-campus racial tension resulted, which included the aforementioned black community's strong criticisms of any black person who appeared to venture too far into the white world.

6. This is not to undermine the significance of a handful of specific racist incidents directed at us. However, being in such a small minority, racial tension was generally low, if for no other reason than simply because there were not enough nonwhite students to make the white majority feel threatened.

7. Probably "Fresh Air" kids, a program that each summer sent inner-city kids, mostly from New York City, to stay with families in our area for a few weeks. I

suspect this because I had never seen these kids before and this tended to be the most common explanation for the sudden presence of African American adolescents during the summer months.

8. See Ignatieff's account of his childhood expedition against the "Frenchies" hiding in the neighborhood cemetery (1993, 143–144).

9. In the sociogeography of Massachusetts, East equals urban as opposed to the West which is considered rural.

10. Including the aforementioned five colleges and Williams, and the prep schools Northfield Mount Hermon, Stoneleigh Burnham, and Deerfield Academy.

11. Only years later did I recognize the connection between this topic and the fact that Jake's ex-girlfriend had recently started dating another guy.

12. The term describes the common housing crisis phenomenon of sleeping on different friends' couches, which involves making sure you do not stay in one place so long that you terminate your welcome in the probable event that you will need to return.

13. "Living in San Francisco —Guide for Newcomers." Available online at http://msp.sfsu.edu/International/newcomers/welcome.html.

14. My staying there was a violation of the lease. Furthermore, as a resident of the apartment for many years, Maggie's rent was regulated by rent control laws. It was no secret that if new tenants were to move in, the rent of that apartment would at least double. Therefore, as Maggie explained it, the landlord did not like her and had a vested interest in getting rid of her.

15. Generally speaking, cool hunters are consultants/fieldworkers hired by large companies to identify cutting-edge fashions and trends. Cool hunters typically move through subculturally pungent zones (like Haight Street and Amoeba Music) in the interest of documenting "what the cool kids in major American cities are thinking and doing and buying" (Gladwell 1997).

16. A 1998 *Rolling Stone* article suggested that Amoeba San Francisco might be "the world's greatest record store" (Hermes 1998, 19).

17. For a similar ethnographic example, see Tsuda 1998.

18. There were two reasons why I could be relatively sure of this: (1) what I had already gathered about Destined's rhyming style and subject matter from having seen him freestyle several times; and (2) the fact that he was one of only a few artists thus far to approach me with their product. In the early stages of my field stay, I was definitely interested in having the music of, and supporting, any such artist.

19. Tagging is the quickest, most elementary form of graffiti writing. It typically involves scrawling one's name or crew affiliation (i.e. "tag"), and is valued within graffiti scenes on the basis of the overall quantity and placement of tags rather than the quality of any particular piece.

20. Sometimes referred to as the "little Philippines," almost a third of Daly City's population is Filipino and over half the population is of Asian descent. As one of the Bay Area's most recent destinations for newly arriving immigrant groups, Daly City is made up of rolling hills of unattractive tract housing built on what was once a Pacific Gas & Electric toxic waste dump (see Vergara Jr. 2008).

21. On several occasions Top R mentioned to me that he thought Devorah should compile a mixtape (to be sold) from her vast collection of underground tapes.

22. "Her brother's the leader of my crew," was one of the more common examples of this.

23. For Anderson, "decent" families have a firm commitment to middle-class values involving sacrificing for the future, whereas the "street" lifestyle involves the pursuit of immediate respect by any means available (1994).

24. The only other place he specifically mentioned was Kegs One's Below the Surface record store (see Introduction).

25. I use professional manufacturing as the criterion to distinguish between official and unofficial releases. If I were to factor in unofficial (homemade) releases with circulations of at least 50 units (again to weed out the randomly circulated CD-Rs), this catalogue would include an additional CD-R, a CD single, two underground cassette tapes, and several solo project/permutations.

26. Obviously some of this can be attributed to the fact that two FFC members were Amoeba employees, although not every employee album makes the "pick of the year" list.

27. Dr. Lester was yet another white, East Coast transplant who had attended Wesleyan with Feller and Eddie Vic.

28. Dr. Lester ended up contributing only one track (out of 17 total [skits not included]) to the original Forest Fires Collective CD; Simile, who eventually shortened his name to "Sim," also appeared on just one of that first CD's songs.

29. For the last several years, Feller has concentrated more on (what could best be described as) psychedelic folk rock than hip hop, and continues to make and release songs as the "musical genius" behind the San Francisco bands Hattattak, Black Fiction (Strachota 2006), and his most recent musical incarnation, The Fresh & Onlys. Prego hosts an online hip hop radio show (the Al Dro Show) and continues to record and release music, although recently more as a guest on other artist's albums. Eddie Vic has moved back East, started a family, and earned a master's degree from Johns Hopkins.

CHAPTER 3. CLAIMING HIP HOP

1. Slug is widely regarded as a white rapper although his father's racial identity is black.

2. Not to mention the largely white hip hop scenes that can be found throughout Europe and Australia (see, for example, Bennett 1999a; Maxwell 2001) as well as the handful of white emcees currently operating in the commercial hip hop realm.

3. BET's daily top ten video countdown.

4. Perhaps not surprisingly, many who support this position come out of the field of Black Studies (see, for example, Baldwin 1999, Henderson 1996, Salaam 1995)

5. Aside from her title (and the continual references to "Black Cultural Production," "Black Cultural Practice," and "Black Cultural Expression" in the subheadings of chapters), an additional reason why Rose's work was received as a testimonial to

hip hop's essential blackness may have to do with the time period in which it was written and published (1994). At that time, hip hop (or rap music specifically) was in the midst of its most rapid thrust into the American mainstream. Much of this meteoric rise in popularity among middle-class white youth had been engineered through Afrocentric and ghettocentric images of hip hop as "terra incognita" (Potter 1995, 65), which capitalized on America's longstanding vilification/romanticization of African Americans, not to mention its difficulty in understanding urban America's ethnic hybridity (Rivera 2001). To me this would seem to be an important point to consider in reflecting on the general tenor and reception of many of the works that fall within this early wave of hip hop scholarship.

6. For differing perspectives on hip hop scholarship's consistency, or lack thereof, in doing this see De Genova 1995 and Perry 2004.

7. It is notable that Charlie's justification—that "he grew up with black people" and that his best friend ("he's like a brother to me") is black (Flores 1996, 89)—sound acceptable coming from someone with a Puerto Rican identity, yet, I believe, would be greeted with much more skepticism coming from a white person.

8. Colon's perspectives (via personal interview) are also featured heavily in *Black Noise* (Rose 1994).

9. For a compelling discussion of how distinctions between Latinos and blacks are perceived differently in dissimilar contexts, see Ogbar 2007 (particularly p. 189, n. 9).

10. Forman's (2002) insights regarding the importance space and place to processes of hip hop identity formation are arguably the most substantive of these.

11. The Last Poets is a group of black nationalist poets and musicians that formed in New York City during the late 1960s. The group, which has retrospectively been hailed as forerunners to hip hop's emcee tradition, has recently been featured on hip hop albums by artists such as Common and Nas.

12. Perhaps the most resounding end point would be 1979, when the Music Industry first became involved in hip hop. Toop explains that prior to 1979, the "lack of industry connections in the Bronx, the young age group involved in hip hop and the radical primitivism of the music itself conspired to produce an island of relatively undisturbed invention in a sea of go-getter commerce" (2000, 78). As compelling as this point may be, ultimately, I believe that such an emphasis on the Music Industry's corruptive influence does more to legitimize independent underground hip hop than to delegitimize it due to its multiraciality.

13. For other excellent discussions of this history see the work of Keyes (1993, 2002), Perkins (1996), and Szwed (1999).

14. For a fascinating firsthand account of an incident where pioneering DJs Afrika Bambaataa and Jazzy Jay attempted to "sound battle" Kool Herc, see Fernando (1994, 8).

15. In fact, Lipsitz only touches on a small bit of Bambaataa's eclectic arsenal here, which also included television theme songs, Beethoven, Led Zeppelin, the Rolling Stones, calypso, Japanese electronic music, and the donning of Native American and Viking headwear (see Chang 2005; Fernando 1999; Toop 2000).

16. Jeff Chang's discussion of "How DJ Kool Herc Lost His Accent and Started Hip-Hop" (2005, 67–85) supports this point.

17. In saying this, I am not disavowing the profound continuities between hip hop music and culture and specific black communities. I am, however, raising questions about the extent to which these relationships should be thought of as exclusive.

18. Ewan Allinson (1994) cleverly twisted this phrase, in his article "It's a Black Thing: Hearing How Whites Can't."

19. And, as Eithne Quinn rightfully points out, rap music's "nihilistic gang-bangers and enterprising hustlers" (2006, 92) are consistent with earlier "badman" forms (Roberts 1989) found throughout the legends and lore of African Americans.

20. For a fascinating twenty-first–century example of the cultural distance between authentic hip hop performers and Music Industry taste makers, see Williams 2004.

21. Other notable articles include James Ledbetter's "Imitation of Life" (1992), which appeared in the premiere issue of *Vibe* magazine; Harry Allen's inflammatory *Source* magazine article "The Unbearable Whiteness of Emceeing" (2003); and N. R. Kleinfield's *New York Times* front page feature entitled "Guarding the Borders of the Hip-Hop Nation"(2000).

22. And despite the longstanding link between rap authenticity and blackness, it is notable that hip hop's three other professed elements (namely graffiti, breaking, and deejaying) have been thoroughly integrated for much of this time.

23. For instance, Forman refers to rap music videos as the "single greatest influence on rap's enhanced exposure" (2002, 240).

24. At the time, a relatively popular mainstream rapper.

25. As with all evaluations of underground status this is a subjective assessment. However, based on my experience of carrying this Ecko bag with me practically everywhere for two years, I feel confident in stating that this is how many underground hip hoppers saw it.

26. For detailed discussions of this history, see Jefferson (1973), Jones (1963), and Tate (2003).

27. This would include the fist-to-fist meeting (or "pound"), the clutching of the fingers (or "dap"), and sometimes the after-dap finger-snap. It is my thinking that although all of these are accepted as subculturally appropriate greetings, interactions between two people who tend toward the same form have a certain synchronicity or rhythm to them which, initially at least, is taken as an indication that the two are probably on the same page with regards to some of the finer nuances of underground hip hop tastes and sensibilities.

28. In all discussions of this episode, pseudonyms will be used for all participating parties. Furthermore, these individuals are in no way connected to hip hop artists having the same or similar names.

29. A tag is a quickly written signature—usually in spray paint or marker—that earns its author status through its ubiquity. It is considered the most basic form of graffiti writing (see Chapter 2 n. 19).

30. In her essay "Representations of Whiteness in the Black Imagination," bell hooks (1992) engages in a similar project.

31. Although exactly what they entail may be highly debated.

CHAPTER 4. THE RE-VISION AND CONTINUED SALIENCE OF RACE

1. This blurred distinction between artists and audience—touched on briefly in both the Introduction and Chapter 1—which since the early nineties has facilitated the racial diversity within the Bay Area underground scene, has reached its greatest proliferation since the appearance of musically mediated social networking websites like MySpace.

2. Akai MPC series digital samplers are among the most popular samplers used by hip hop producers. Both the MPC and E-mu SP1200 samplers are considered legendary "beat making" machines among hip hop aficionados (Schloss 2004; see also Chapter 1 n. 25).

3. See also Tricia Rose's discussion of "Technological Orality and Oral Technology in Hip Hop" (1994, 85–86).

4. This quote comes out of an early version of Kevin Fitzgerald's hip hop documentary, *Freestyle: The Art of Rhyme.* The scene does not appear in the officially released version (Fitzgerald 2005). I was able to gain access to the earlier version through J-Smoove of Project-Blowed/B-Boy Kingdom.

5. I confidently say this from self-experience and a lifetime of observations.

6. Tempelman's work draws from the theories of Shmuel Eisenstadt and Bernhard Giesen (1995).

7. Konceptual Dominance is comprised of Kemetic Suns' members King Koncepts and Kirby Dominant. The duo released one album, *Savage Intelligence,* in 2000. Lyrics courtesy of Kirby Dominick.

8. Graffiti terminology: a "throw-up" is a simple but larger form of a tag (see Chapter 2 n. 19 and Chapter 3 n. 29) typically involving outlined letters that are sometimes filled in; a "piece"—short for masterpiece—is a far more elaborate and highly stylized work that is judged on the basis of its artistic quality as opposed to a writer's quantity of work (see Chapter 2 n. 19); the term "burner" which originally developed in reference to train car pieces, today generally refers to any piece involving bright colors that appears to be "burning" off of its surface (see Macdonald 2001).

9. Including groups like Blue Scholars (featuring a Filipino American emcee and Iranian American deejay/producer) and Power Struggle, and solo artists like Bambu (who along with Kiwi at one time formed the duo Native Guns).

10. I put considerable emphasis on knowledge (and vocabulary) here because, in much the same way that Oliver Wang (2007, 42) discusses Asian American emcees' deciding to become rappers while in college, and gaining social and political knowledge through university classes, there are undeniable parallels between the central critiques (of U.S. racism and imperialism) being made by Filipino emcees and the emerging body of Filipino Studies academic literature (see, for example, Bonus 2000; de Jesús 2005;

Espiritu 1995, 2003; Mendoza 2002; Tiongson, Gutierrez, and Gutierrez 2006). Also note the place of public universities in my narratives of engagement with Kiwi.

11. As postcolonial subjects whose identities have been shaped through the specter of American imperialism and "differential inclusion" (Espiritu 2003), Filipino Americans, Antonio Tiongson Jr. (2006) argues, bear a closer resemblance to Chicanos and Puerto Ricans than to the Asian American groups that they are typically lumped together with.

12. Certainly some of this was accelerated by Filipino American's unparalleled success within the arena of competitive deejaying—sometimes called turntablism (de Leon 2004; Sue 2002; Wang 2004).

13. Thanks to Neil Ordinario for also making this point and for sharing similar ideas regarding how "Hawaiian heads" have turned toward hip hop as a means of filling the space left empty through the ethnocide of American imperialism and the cultural prostitution of Hawaiian tourism (November 8, 1999, email correspondence).

14. Although the unique position of Filipino hip hoppers cannot simply be equated with Asian American hip hoppers more generally (see note 11 above), two recent works on Asian American rappers deserve noting. In contrast to what I am suggesting about a distinct Filipino legitimacy, Oliver Wang (2007) argues that for Asian American emcees, foregrounding ethnicity has been a liability. My position is more in line with Jeffrey Ogbar's claim that "Asian American rappers have chosen to use their racial and ethnic identity as a touchstone for their own articulations of authenticity" (2007, 53). In fact, I would argue that Filipino emcees are engaged in a more pronounced political "raptivism" than any of the examples offered by Ogbar.

15. The term "wigger" is a sometimes derogatory epithet derived from the combination of "white" and "nigger." Wiggers can generally be thought of as a late-twentieth century, hip hop version of Norman Mailer's (1957) white Negro (see below).

16. In Bennett's article, even Jim's story of his brilliant stay with a black family in "Cleveland near New York" is a claim to a special status among white northeast Englanders (Bennett 1999a, 11; see also Chapter 2).

17. To the extent that all "scripts" denote "proper ways of being" X or Y, "there will be expectations to be met [and] demands will be made" (Appiah 1994, 162; see also Chapter 3). In light of this, Melinda L. de Jesús (2005) warns that the "cultural nationalist agenda" alive among many West Coast Filipinos—and actively disseminated via hip hop music—has the potential to put narrow confines on Filipino subjectivity in much the same way as it has historically done with black subjectivity.

18. I do not mean to imply that evaluations of artistic performance are objective. To the contrary, as I have already stated they are extremely subjective. However, when assessing artistic performance relative to a defined subgenre—in this case underground hip hop—there is an objective set of standards, however broad, that mark a performance as hip hop, and not, for instance, opera (Peterson 1997).

19. In more resolutely "underground" Bay Area circles, Top R was a renowned freestyler.

20. I should clarify here that I am making a simplified distinction between two levels of underground strata. In truth these differences exist on more of a continuum

that individual underground hip hop enthusiasts float freely along. Such variability is the principal basis on which many micro-social assessments are made. The example of Dope Cigar's guarded knowledge of Jurassic Five, which was talked about in the previous chapter, is a clear indication of this. Although at the time Jurassic Five was not yet as popular as Mos Def, their rising national prominence (and the fact that they were already signed to Interscope Records), for me, put them nearer to Mos Def than to Top R or any of the other underground hip hoppers who were at the core of my study. However, for Dope, particularly in relation to the downtown San Francisco lunch crowd, Jurassic Five was resoundingly underground.

21. D.I.T.C. includes Fat Joe, who is Puerto Rican.

22. For example, see DJ Mizzo's comments in Chapter 1.

23. I did once see an African American emcee named Subtitle (from the West Coast Workforce) performing a song entitled "Backpackers" while wearing a backpack on stage at San Jose's Cactus Club. Due to the song's curious ending, in which Subtitle and the rest of his crew repeatedly chanted "after backpack's it's all over!" I am uncertain about whether this should be thought of as a pro-backpacker song.

24. As many commentators have suggested (Atkins 1991; Bonilla-Silva 2004; Darder and Torres 2004; Lind 1998).

25. This is abundantly clear by the number of references to Bob Marley and Malcolm X that can be found within the music.

26. I recall usually seeing (or at least sensing an air of) disappointment when I explained to those who asked that I had no Asian background.

27. This extends beyond just matters of black and white to include other binary understandings such as hip hop's white/people of color dynamic.

CHAPTER 5. (RE)MIXED MESSAGES

1. An "eviction party" is a party that is thrown on the occasion of being evicted (or simply moving) from an apartment. It typically takes place after the residents have moved all their things out.

2. Da Babylonians Red Dawn: A Baybridge Epic CD includes song titles like "On da Strength," "Knowledge the Truth," and "Back in da Dayz."

3. Less than six months after this, Megabusive would post a "public apology" on an prominent Bay Area underground hip hop online forum in which he specifically apologized to Sole and the Pedestrian for "slandering [their] character." In all probability this apology was connected to the aforementioned episode. Discussion Forum Post: chip [megabusive]. 2001. "selfless posting . . . respect is due . . ." Legends' Labyrinth (June 13): http//disc.server.com/discussion.cgi?id=11608&article=104036 (accessed June 13, 2001).

4. Will Holloway's 2001 Incantations documentary can be viewed online at http://www.spike.com/video/incantation/1049431.

5. And I was. My extensive getting into character preparations involved not only several engaged readings of Tuchman's book, but also my going out in public cloaked as Ze Kaiser on a handful of occasions.

6. For example, while recently describing Da Babylonians to my friend Owa (see Chapter 2), he mistook my description for the Young Black Teenagers' cover he had seen with me at Rico's that night. "Oh yeah, I've seen them do that," he said.

7. I am making a subtle reference to Hall's "end of innocence" here (see Chapter 4).

8. Perhaps the hip hop archetypes for this were Jim McMahon, Gary Fencik, and Steve Fuller, who (drunken with confidence) in 1985 performed raps on the Chicago Bears' hit song "The Super Bowl Shuffle."

9. This did not seem to be the case the first time I spoke with emcee/b-girl Jun Dax about the possibility of an interview. Yet she was very deliberate in telling me that I could get her number from Destined and that I should tell him that she said it was okay for him to give me her number, which illustrates something about the awkwardness of some of these exchanges.

10. I am specifically speaking of opportunities to participate in cultural production, first and foremost as emcees. I do believe that underground hip hop does much better than commercial rap in its refusal to depict women as exclusively sexual objects to be possessed by men.

11. On many of these occasions, a female emcee would either be part of a predominantly male crew or would appear on stage to perform a specific song that she had recorded with the featured male artist. Although hardly amounting to equal footing, this is a degree of female representation.

12. Earlier in the night an underground hip hop retailer who was there selling his merchandise walked up to me and casually said, "female rap, it's like its own genre."

13. Also occurring publicly in parks, clubs, Bay Area Rapid Transit stations, or any other public social gathering that brings emcees together.

14. I believe the fact that the majority of our time together that evening was spent in the darkness of a nighttime park also played a role.

15. Even though on one night, while accompanying a pair of intoxicated graffiti writers who were recklessly going about "tagging up" the Mission district, I watched as Devorah suddenly took charge of the situation and reprimanded the pair for going about their business completely the wrong way.

16. There were a few select social spaces and roles that seemed to be more inclusive of female involvement. These include more spoken word-oriented open-microphone events, dancing circles, and promoting.

17. Notwithstanding the fact that Filipino Americans have established themselves as world leaders in deejaying/turntabling, I am speaking specifically about the rise of Filipino/Filipina emcees.

18. Lady Wonders also include spoken-word poets HiFive and Supernova.

19. One of the highlights of this particular show was a captivating solo song/piece—complete with a good deal of erotic imagery—about being seduced by one's partner's intellect.

20. This is perhaps nowhere better exemplified than in the example of Lady Wonders, who form the feminine half of the larger Filipino American hip hop/spoken-word crew Eighth Wonder.

21. Which draws heavily on the combination of precolonial ersatz nostalgia (Appadurai 1996, 78) and a contemporary focus on the U.S. occupation of the Philippines.

22. Such things as social class, life chances, health and life expectancy, and lifestyle (Hughes and Kroehler 2008).

References

Aaron, Charles. 1999. "Black Like Them." *Utne Reader* (May/June). Available online at http://www.utne.com/1999-05-01/black-like-them.aspx.

Abrahams, Roger D. 1964. *Deep Down in the Jungle: Negro Narrative Folklore from the Streets of Philadelphia*. Hatboro, PA: Folklore Associates.

Abu-Lughod, Lila. 1988. *Veiled Sentiments: Honor and Poetry in a Bedouin Society*. Berkeley: University of California Press.

Alcoff, Linda Martín. 2001. "Towards a Phenomenology of Racial Embodiment." In *Race*, ed. Robert Bernasconi, pp. 267–283. Malden, MA: Blackwell Publishers.

Allen, Harry. 2003. "The Unbearable Whiteness of Emceeing: What the Eminence of Eminem Says About Race." *The Source* (February): 91–92.

Allinson, Ewan. 1994. "It's a Black Thing: Hearing How Whites Can't." *Cultural Studies* 8, no. 3: 438–456.

Alsup, Janet. 2004. "Protean Subjectivities: Qualitative Research and the Inclusion of the Personal." In *Ethnography Unbound: From Theory Shock to Critical Praxis*, ed. Stephen Gilbert Brown and Sidney I. Dobrin, pp. 219–237. Albany: State University of New York Press.

Anderson, Benedict. 1991. *Imagined Communities: Reflections on the Origin and Spread of Nationalism*. London: Verso.

Anderson, Elijah. 1994. "The Code of the Streets." *Atlantic Monthly* 273: 80-94.

Aponte, Robert. 2000. "Urban Hispanic Poverty: Disaggregation and Explanations." In *Taking Sides: Race and Ethnicity* (3rd ed.), ed. Richard Monk, pp. 163–169. Guilford, CT: Dushkin/McGraw Hill.

Appadurai, Arjun. 1996. *Modernity at Large: Cultural Dimensions of Globalization.* Minneapolis: University of Minnesota Press.

Appiah, Kwame Anthony. 1986. "The Uncompleted Argument: Du Bois and the Illusion of Race." In *Race, Writing, and Difference,* ed. Henry Louis Gates Jr., pp. 21–37. Chicago: University of Chicago Press.

———. 1990a. "Racisms." In *Anatomy of Racism,* ed. David Theo Goldberg, pp. 3–17. Minneapolis: University of Minnesota Press.

———. 1990b. "'But Would That Still Be Me?' Notes on Gender, 'Race,' Ethnicity, as Sources of Identity." *The Journal of Philosophy* 87, no. 10: 493–499.

———. 1992. *In My Father's House: Africa in the Philosophy of Culture.* New York: Oxford University Press.

———. 1994. "Identity, Authenticity, Survival: Multicultural Societies and Social Reproduction." In *Multiculturalisms: Examining the Politics of Recognition* (exp. ed.), by Charles Taylor et al., pp. 149–163. Princeton, NJ: Princeton University Press.

Arnold, Eric K. 2000. "Breaking Down the State of West Coast Hip-Hop." *Sfbg.com.* Available online at http://www.sfbg.com/noise/22/post.html.

———. 2006. "From Azeem to Zion-I: The Evolution of Global Consciousness in Bay Area Hip Hop." In *The Vinyl Ain't Final: Hip Hop and the Globalization of Black Popular Culture,* ed. Dipannita Basu and Sidney J. Lemelle, pp. 71–84. London: Pluto Press.

Atkins, Elizabeth. 1991. "When Life Simply Isn't Black or White." *New York Times,* June 5, C1, C7.

Attwood, Feona. 2005. "'Tits and Ass and Porn and Fighting': Male Heterosexuality in Magazines for Men." *International Journal of Cultural Studies* 8, no. 1: 83–100.

Austin, Joe. 2001. *Taking the Train: How Graffiti Art Became an Urban Crisis in New York City.* New York: Columbia University Press.

Austin, Michael. 2001. "A Hip-Hop Coffeegoer's Heaven in the Haight: Monday Nights at Rockin' Java." *Golden Gate [X]Press Online.* Available online at http://epressarchive.sfsu.edu/storys01.php?storyid=2611.

Babiracki, Carol M. 1997. "What's the Difference: Reflections on Gender and Research in Village India." In *Shadows in the Field: New Perspectives for Fieldwork in Ethnomusicology,* ed. Gregory F. Barz and Timothy J. Cooley, pp. 121–136. New York: Oxford University Press.

Back, Les. 1996. *New Ethnicities and Urban Culture: Racism and Multiculture in Young Lives.* New York: St. Martin's Press.

Balce, Nerissa S. 2006. "Filipino Bodies, Lynching, and the Language of Empire." In *Positively No Filipinos Allowed: Building Communities and Discourse,* ed. Antonio T. Tiongson, Jr., Edgardo V. Gutierrez, and Richardo V. Gutierrez, pp. 41–60. Philadelphia: Temple University Press.

Baldwin, Davarian. L. 1999. "Black Empires, White Desires: The Spatial Politics of Identity in the Age of Hip-Hop." *Black Renaissance Noir* 2: 138–159.

Barrientos, Darleene. 2000. "Students Pour Out Hearts at Open Mic." *The Daily Titan* (California State University Fullerton), October 31. Available online at http://dailytitan.fullerton.edu/issues/fall_00/10_31/news/studentspour.html.

Beaudry, Nicole. 1997. "The Challenges of Human Relations in Ethnographic Inquiry: Examples from Arctic and Subarctic Fieldwork." In *Shadows in the Field: New Perspectives for Fieldwork in Ethnomusicology*, ed. Gregory F. Barz and Timothy J. Cooley, pp. 63–83. New York, NY: Oxford University Press.

Becker, Howard. 1982. *Art Worlds*. Berkeley: University of California Press.

Becker, Howard and Irving Louis Horowitz. 1971. "The Culture of Civility." In *Culture and Civility in San Francisco*, ed. Howard Becker, pp. 4–19. New Brunswick, NJ: Transaction Books.

Bendix, Regina. 1997. *In Search of Authenticity*. Madison: University of Wisconsin Press.

Bennett, Andy. 1999a. "Rappin' on the Tyne: White Hip Hop Culture in Northeast England—An Ethnographic Study." *Sociological Review* 47, no. 1: 1–24.

———. 1999b. "Subcultures or Neo-Tribes? Rethinking the Relationship Between Youth, Style and Musical Taste." *Sociology* 33, no. 3: 599–617.

———. 2000. *Popular Music and Youth Culture: Music, Identity, and Places*. London: Macmillan.

———. 2001. *Cultures of Popular Music*. Philadelphia, PA: Open University Press.

Bennett, Andy and Richard A. Peterson. 2004. *Music Scenes: Local, Translocal, Virtual*. Nashville, TN: Vanderbilt University Press.

Best, Amy L. 2007. "Introduction." In *Representing Youth: Methodological Issues in Critical Youth Studies*, ed. Amy L. Best, pp. 1–36. New York: New York University Press.

Binder, Amy. 1999. "Friend or Foe: Boundary Work and Collective Identity in the Afrocentric and Multicultural Curriculum Movements in American Public Education." In *The Cultural Territories of Race: Black and White Boundaries*, ed. Michèle Lamont, pp. 221–248. Chicago, IL: University of Chicago Press.

Blue Scholars. 2005. "Southside Revival." *The Long March EP*. Seattle, WA: Massline.

Bonilla-Silva, Eduardo. 2004. "From Biracial to Triracial: The Emergence of a New Racial Stratification System in the United States." In *Skin Deep: How Race and Complexion Matter in the "Color-Blind" Era*, ed. Cedric Herring, Verna Keith, and Hayward Derrick Horton, pp. 224–239. Chicago: University of Illinois Press.

Bonus, Rick. 2000. *Locating Filipino Americans: Ethnicity and Cultural Politics of Space*. Philadelphia, PA: Temple University Press.

Borland, Katherine. 1991. "'That's Not What I Said': Interpretive Conflict in Oral Narrative Research." In *Women's Words: The Feminist Practice of Oral History*, ed. Sherna Berger Gluck and Daphne Patai, pp. 63–75. New York: Routledge.

Bourdieu, Pierre. 1984. *Distinctions: A Social Critique of the Judgment of Taste*, trans. by R. Nice. Cambridge: Harvard University Press.

Bowman, Glenn. 1997. "Identifying Versus Identifying with 'the Other': Reflections on the Siting of the Subject in Anthropological Discourse." In *After Writing Culture: Epistemology and Praxis in Contemporary Anthropology*, ed. Allison James, Jenny Hockey, and Andrew Dawson, pp. 34–50. New York: Routledge.

Boxwell, D. A. 1992. "'Sis Cat' as Ethnographer: Self-Presentation and Self-Inscription in Zora Neale Hurston's Mules and Men." *African American Review* 26: 605–617.

Brace, C. Loring. 2005. *Race Is a Four-Letter Word: The Genesis of the Concept.* New York: Oxford University Press.

Braiker, Brian. 2005. "California's Latest Sound: Hyphy." *MSNBC Web Exclusive,* January 14. Available online at http://www.msnbc.msn.com/id/6826555/site/newsweek/.

Brand, Mieka. 2007. "Making Moonshine: Thick Histories in a U.S. Historically Black Community." *Anthropology and Humanism* 32, no. 1: 52–61.

Branigin, William. 1998. "The Myth of the Melting Pot—Part Three: Immigrants Shunning Idea of Assimilation." *Washington Post,* May 25. Available online at http://www.washingtonpost.com/wp-srv/national/longterm/meltingpot/melt0525a.htm.

Brodkin, Karen. 1994. *How Jews Became White Folk and What That Says About Race in America.* New Brunswick, NJ: Rutgers University Press.

Brown, Stephen Gilbert and Sidney I. Dobrin. 2004. "Introduction: New Writers of the Cultural Sage: From Postmodern Theory Shock to Critical Praxis." In *Ethnography Unbound: From Theory Shock to Critical Praxis,* ed. Stephen Gilbert Brown and Sidney I. Dobrin, pp. 1–10. Albany: State University of New York Press.

Butler, Judith. 1990. *Gender Trouble: Feminism and the Subversion of Identity.* New York: Routledge.

Caplin, Pat. 1988. "Engendering Knowledge: The Politics of Ethnography." *Anthropology Today* 4, no. 5: 8–12.

Carroll, Glenn R. 1985. "Concentration and Specialization: The Dynamics of Niche Width in Populations of Organizations." *American Journal of Sociology* 90: 1262–1283.

Carroll, Glenn R. and Anand Swaminathan. 2000. "Why the Microbrew Movement? Organization Dynamics of Resource Partitioning in the U.S. Brewing Industry." *American Journal of Sociology* 106, no. 3: 715–762.

Cha, Ariana Eunjung. 1999. "Sorting Out an Identity." *San Jose Mercury News,* May 11, 47.

Chambers, Iain. 1976. "A Strategy for Living: Black Music and White Subcultures." In *Resistance Through Rituals: Youth Subcultures in Post-War Britain,* ed. Stuart Hall and Tony Jefferson, pp. 157–166. London: Hutchinson.

Chang, Jeff. 2005. *Can't Stop Won't Stop: A History of the Hip-Hop Generation.* New York: St. Martin's Press.

Chavez, Linda. 1991. *Out of the Barrio: Towards a New Politics of Hispanic Assimilation.* New York: Basic Books.

Chideya, Farai. 1999. *The Color of Our Future.* New York: William and Morrow.

Clay, Andreana. 2003. "Keepin' It Real: Black Youth, Hip-Hop Culture, and Black Identity." *American Behavioral Scientist* 46, no. 10: 1346–1358.

Clifford, James. 1986. "Introduction: Partial Truths." In *Writing Culture: The Poetics and Politics of Ethnography,* ed. James Clifford and George Marcus, pp. 1–26. Berkeley: University of California Press.

———. 1988. *The Predicament of Culture: Twentieth-Century Ethnography Literature and Art.* Cambridge: Harvard University Press.

Clifford, James and Marcus, George, eds. 1986. *Writing Culture: The Poetics and Politics of Ethnography.* Berkeley: University of California Press.

Cobb, William Jelani. 2007. *To the Break of Dawn: A Freestyle on the Hip Hop Aesthetic.* New York: New York University Press.

Cohen, Sara. 1991. *Rock Culture in Liverpool: Popular Music in the Making.* Oxford: Clarendon Press.

———. 1993. "Ethnography and Popular Music Studies." *Popular Music* 12, no. 2: 123–138.

Condry, Ian. 2006. *Hip-Hop Japan: Rap and the Paths of Cultural Globalization.* Durham, NC: Duke University Press.

Cooley, Timothy J. 1997. "Casting Shadows in the Field: An Introduction." In *Shadows in the Field: New Perspectives for Fieldwork in Ethnomusicology,* ed. Gregory F. Barz and Timothy J. Cooley, pp. 3–19. New York: Oxford University Press.

D, Davey. 1999. "Respect Those Who Came Before Us." *Davey D's Hip Hop Corner.* Available online at http://www.daveyd.com/fnvcomrespectpioneers.html.

D'Amico-Samuels, Deborah. 1991. "Undoing Fieldwork: Personal, Political, Theoretical and Methodological Implications." In *Decolonizing Anthropology: Moving Further Towards an Anthropology for Liberation,* ed. Faye Harrison, pp. 68–87. Washington, DC: American Anthropological Association.

Darder, Antonia and Rodolfo D. Torres. 2004. *After Race: Racism After Multiculturalism.* New York: New York University Press.

Darity Jr., William A., Jason Dietrich, and Darrick Hamilton. 2005. "Bleach in the Rainbow: Latin Ethnicity and Preference for Whiteness." *Transforming Anthropology* 13, no. 2: 103–109.

Davies, Charlotte Aull. 1999. *Reflexive Ethnography: A Guide to Researching Selves and Others.* New York: Routledge.

Dávila, Arlene. 2001. *Latinos, Inc.: The Marketing and Making of a People.* Berkeley: University of California Press.

Dawson, Michael C. 1994. *Behind the Mule: Race and Class in African Americans Politics.* Princeton, NJ: Princeton University Press.

De Genova, Nick. 1995. "Check Your Head: The Cultural Politics of Rap Music." *Transitions* 67: 123–137.

de Jesús, Melinda L. 2005. *Pinay Power: Theorizing the Filipina/American Experience.* New York: Routledge.

de Leon, Lakandiwa M. 2004. "Filipinotown and the DJ Scene: Expression and Identity Affirmation of Filipino American Youth in Los Angeles." In *Asian American Youth: Culture, Identity, and Ethnicity,* ed. Jennifer Lee and Min Zhou, pp. 191–206. New York: Routledge.

del Barco, Mandalit. 1996. "Rap's Latino Sabor." In *Droppin' Science: Critical Essays on Rap Music and Hip Hop Culture,* ed. William Eric Perkins, pp. 63–84. Philadelphia: Temple University Press.

Delgado, Fernando Pedro. 1998. "Chicano Ideology Revisited: Rap Music and the (Re)articulation of Chicanismo." *Western Journal of Communication* 62, no. 2: 95–113.

DeMott, Benjamin. 1998. *The Trouble with Friendship: Why Americans Can't Think Straight about Race*. New Haven, CT: Yale University Press.

Denzin, Norman K. 1998. "The New Ethnography." *Journal of Contemporary Ethnography* 27, no. 3: 405–415.

Di Stefano, Christine. 1990. "Dilemmas of Difference: Feminism, Modernity, and Postmodernism." In *Feminism/Postmodernism*, ed. Linda Nicholson, pp. 63–82. New York: Routledge.

Domina, Lynn. 1997. "'Protection in My Mouf': Self, Voice, and Community in Zora Neale Hurston's Dust Tracks on a Road and Mules and Men." *African American Review* 31: 197–209.

Domínguez, Virginia R. 1997. *White By Definition: Social Classification in Creole Louisiana*. New Brunswick, NJ: Rutgers University Press.

Du Bois, W.E.B. 1996 [1903]. *The Souls of Black Folk*. New York: Penguin Books.

Ducker, Jesse. 2004a. "Sunspot Jonz." *Shout Magazine* 1. Available online at http://shoutmagazine.blogspot.com/2004/07/sunspot-jonz.html.

———. 2004b. "Tajai on the Spot: The Hieroglyphics Crew Showed that Underground Hip Hop Artists Could Be More than Just "Cool"; They Could Also Be Successful." *Shout Magazine* 1. Available online at http://shoutmagazine.blogspot.com/2004/07/tajai-on-spot.html.

Dunn, James. 2001. "Living Legends: The Gamble Pays Off . . ." *SP Magazine: Subterranean information Periodical* 2, no. 1: 22–25.

Edmonston, Barry, Sharon M. Lee, and Jeffery S. Passel. 2002. "Recent Trends in Intermarriage and Immigration and Their Effects on the Future Racial Composition of the U.S. Population." In *The New Race Question: How the Census Counts Multiracial Individuals*, ed. Joel Perlmann and Mary C. Waters, pp. 227–255. New York: Russell Sage Foundation.

Eisenstadt, Shmuel N. and Bernhard Giesen. 1995. "The Construction of Collective Identity." *Archives of European Sociology* 36: 72–192.

Eljera, Bert. 1996. "Filipinos Find Home in Daly City." *Asian Week*, May 3–9. Available online at http://www.asianweek.com/050396/dalycity.html.

Espiritu, Yen Le. 1992. *Asian American Panethnicity: Bridging Institutions and Identities*. Philadelphia, PA: Temple University Press.

———. 1995. *Filipino American Lives*. Philadelphia, PA: Temple University Press.

———. 2003. *Homebound: Filipino American Lives Across Cultures, Communities, and Countries*. Berkeley: University of California Press.

Fardon, Richard. 1992. "Postmodern Anthropology? Or, An Anthropology of Postmodernity." In *Postmodernism and the Social Sciences*, ed. Joe Doherty, Elspeth Graham, and Mo Malek, pp. 24–38. New York: St. Martin's Press.

Farley, Christopher John. 1999. "Hip-Hop Nation." *Time*, February 8: 54–64.

Farrow, Kenyon. 2004. "We Real Cool?: On Hip-Hop, Asian-Americans, Black Folks, and Appropriation." *Chicken Bones: A Journal for Literary and Artistic African-American Themes*. Available online at http://www.nathanielturner.com/wereal coolkenyon.htm.

Fernando Jr., S. H. 1994. *New Beats: Exploring the Music, Culture, and Attitudes of Hip Hop*. New York: Anchor Books, Doubleday.

———. 1999. "Back in the Day: 1975–79." In *The Vibe History of Hip Hop*, ed. Alan Light, pp. 13–21. New York: Three Rivers Press.

Firth, Raymond. 1983 [1936]. *We the Tikopia: A Sociological Study of Kinship in Primitive Polynesia*. Stanford, CA: Stanford University Press.

———. 1989. "Second Introduction 1988." In *A Diary in the Strict Sense of the Term*, by Bronislaw Malinowski, pp. xxi–xxxi. Stanford, CA: Stanford University Press.

Fitzgerald, Kevin. 2005. *Freestyle: The Art of Rhyme*. New York: Palm Pictures.

Flax, Jane. 1987. "Postmodernism and Gender Relations in Feminist Theory." *Signs: Journal of Women in Culture and Society* 12, no. 4: 621–643.

Fletcher, Michael A. 1998. "The Myth of the Melting Pot —Part Six: Interracial Marriages Eroding Barriers." *Washington Post*, December 28. Available online at http://www.washingtonpost.com/wp-srv/national/daily/dec98/melt29.htm.

Flores, Juan. 1994. "Puerto Rican and Proud, Boyee! Rap, Roots, and Amnesia." In *Microphone Fiends: Youth Music and Youth Culture*, ed. Andrew Ross and Tricia Rose, pp. 89–98. New York: Routledge.

———. 1996. "Puerto Rocks: New York Ricans Stake Their Claim." In *Droppin' Science: Critical Essays on Rap Music and Hip Hop Culture*, ed. William Eric Perkins, pp. 85–105. Philadelphia: Temple University Press.

Folklore. 2004. "Rasco." *Shout Magazine* 1. Available online at http://shoutmagazine.blogspot.com/2004/07/rasco.html.

Forman, Murray. 2002. *The 'Hood Comes First: Race, Space, and Place in Rap and Hip Hop*. Middletown, CT: Wesleyan University Press.

Fornäs, Johan, Ulf Lindberg, and Ove Sernhade. 1995. *In Garageland: Rock, Youth, and Modernity*. London: Routledge.

Fox, Aaron A. 2004. *Real Country: Music and Language in Working Class Culture*. Durham, NC: Duke University Press.

Fox, Luke. 1999. "Del: Off Both Sides of the Dome." *Pound Magazine* (poundmag.com). Available online at http://www.poundmag.com/magazine/features/articles/del/del.html.

Frankenberg, Ruth. 1993. *White Women, Race Matters: The Social Construction of Whiteness*. Minneapolis: University of Minnesota Press.

Frazier, E. Franklin. 1957. *The Black Bourgeoisie*. New York: Free Press.

Freeman, Derek. 1983. *Margaret Mead and Samoa: The Making and Unmaking of an Anthropological Myth*. Cambridge: Harvard University Press.

Frey, William H. 1996. "Immigration, Domestic Migration, and Demographic Balkanization in America: New Evidence for the 1990s." *Population and Development Review* 22: 741–763.

Friedman, Jonathan. 1987. "Beyond Otherness or the Spectacularization of Anthropology." *Telos* 71: 161–170.

———. 1992. "The Past in the Future: History and the Politics of Identity." *American Anthropologist* 94, no. 4: 837–859.

Frith, Simon. 1987. "Towards an Aesthetic of Popular Music." In *Music and Society: The Politics of Composition, Performance and Reception,* ed. Richard Leppert and Susan McClary, pp. 133–149. New York: Cambridge University Press.

———. 1996. "Music and Identity." In *Questions of Cultural Identity,* ed. Stuart Hall and Paul du Gay, pp. 108–127. London: Sage Publication.

Gans, Herbert J. 1999. "The Possibility of a New Racial Hierarchy in the Twenty-First–Century United States." In *The Cultural Territories of Race: Black and White Boundaries,* ed. Michèle Lamont, pp. 371–390. Chicago: University of Chicago Press.

Garofalo, Reebee. 1994. "Culture versus Commerce: The Marketing of Black Popular Music." *Public Culture* 7: 275–287.

Gates Jr., Henry Louis, 1988. *The Signifying Monkey: A Theory of African American Literary Criticism.* New York: Oxford University Press.

Geertz, Clifford. 1973. *Interpretations of Cultures.* New York: Basic Books.

George, Nelson. 1998. *Hip Hop America.* New York: Viking Penguin.

———. 2004. *Post-Soul Nation: The Explosive, Contradictory, Triumphant, and Tragic 1980s As Experienced by African Americans (Previously Known As Blacks and Before That Negroes).* New York: Viking Penguin.

Giddens, Anthony. 1991. *Modernity and Self-Identity.* Cambridge: Polity.

Gilroy, Paul. 1993. *The Black Atlantic: Modernity and Double Consciousness.* London: Verso.

Givhan, Robin D. 1993. "Wiggers See Style a Way into Another Culture." *Detroit Free Press,* June 21, 1-D.

Gladwell, Malcolm. 1997. "The Cool Hunt." *The New Yorker,* March 17. Available online at http://www.gladwell.com/1997/1997_03_17_a_cool.htm.

Glasner, Joanna and Katie Dean. 2000. "Dot-Commers Go Home!" *Wired,* August 26. Available online at http://www.wired.com/print/culture/lifestyle/news/2000/08/38313.

Glassie, Henry. 2003. "Tradition." In *Eight Words for the Study of Expressive Culture,* ed. Burt Feintuch, pp. 176–197. Urbana: University of Illinois Press.

Goffman, Erving. 1959. *The Presentation of Self in Everyday Life.* New York: Doubleday.

Golde, Peggy. 1986. *Women in the Field: Anthropological Experiences.* Berkeley: University of California Press.

Gooding-Williams Jr., Robert. 2001. "Race, Multiculturalism and Democracy." In *Race,* ed. Robert Bernasconi, pp. 237–259. Malden, MA: Blackwell Publishers.

Gordon, Lewis R. 2005. "Grown Folks' Business: The Problem of Maturity in Hip Hop." In *Hip Hop and Philosophy: Rhyme 2 Reason,* ed. Derrick Darby and Tommie Shelby, pp. 150–116. Chicago: Open Court.

Gordon, Milton M. 1964. *Assimilation in American Life: The Role of Race, Religion, and National Origins.* New York: Oxford University Press.

Gracyk, Theodore. 2001. *I Wanna Be Me: Rock Music and the Politics of Identity.* Philadelphia: Temple University Press.

Grant-Thomas, Andrew and Gary Orfield (eds.). 2008. *Twenty-First Century Colorlines: Multiracial Change in Contemporary America.* Philadelphia: Temple University Press.

Grossberg, Lawrence. 1984. "Another Boring Day in Paradise: Rock and Roll and the Empowerment of Everyday Life." *Popular Music* 4: 225–258.

Guevara, Nancy. 1996. "Women Writin' Rappin' Breakin'." In *Droppin' Science: Critical Essays on Rap Music and Hip Hop Culture*, ed. William Eric Perkins, pp. 49–62. Philadelphia: Temple University Press.

Guinier, Lani and Gerald Torres. 2002. *The Miner's Canary: Enlisting Race, Resisting Power, Transforming Democracy*. Cambridge: Harvard University Press.

Gutmann, Amy. 1994. "Introduction." In *Multiculturalism*, by Charles Taylor, pp. 3–24. Princeton: Princeton University Press.

Hall, Perry A. 1997. "African-American Music: Dynamics of Appropriation and Innovation." In *Borrowed Power: Essays on Cultural Appropriation*, ed. Bruce Ziff and Pratima V. Rao, pp. 31–51. New Brunswick, NJ: Rutgers University Press.

Hall, Stuart. 1996. "New Ethnicities." In *Stuart Hall: Critical Dialogues in Cultural Studies*, ed. David Morley and Kuan-Hsing Chen, pp. 441–449. London: Routledge.

Hall, Stuart and Tony Jefferson (eds.). 1976. *Resistance through Rituals: Youth Subcultures in Post-War Britain*. New York: Holmes and Meier.

Hammersley, Martyn and Paul Atkinson. 1995. *Ethnography: Principles in Practice* (2nd ed.). New York: Routledge.

Handler, Richard and Jocelyn Linnekin. 1984. "Tradition, Genuine or Spurious." *Journal of American Folklore* 97: 273–290.

Harding, Sandra. 1987. "Introduction: Is There a Feminist Method?" In *Feminism and Methodology*, ed. Sandra Harding, pp. 1–14. Bloomington: University of Indiana Press.

Hare, Nathan. 1965. *The Black Anglo Saxons*. New York: Marzani and Mansell.

Harrison, Anthony Kwame. 2003. "Real Niggaz, Cracker Rap, and Filipinos with Perms: The Situational Racialization of Identities within a 'Colorblind' Hip Hop World." Paper presented at the Harvard Civil Rights Project's Color Lines Conference: Segregation and Integration in America's Present and Future, Cambridge Massachusetts, August 30, 2003.

———. 2004. *"Every Emcee's a Fan, Every Fan's an Emcee": Authenticity, Identity, and Power within Bay Area Underground Hip Hop*. PhD. diss., Syracuse University.

———. 2006. "'Cheaper Than a CD, Plus We Really Mean It': Bay Area Underground Hip Hop Tapes as Subcultural Artifacts." *Popular Music* 25, no. 2: 283–301.

———. 2008a. "Multiracial Youth Scenes and the Dynamics of Race: New Approaches to Racialization within the Bay Area Hip Hop Underground." In *Twenty-First Century Colorlines: Multiracial Change in Contemporary America*, ed. Andrew Grant Thomas and Gary Orfield, pp. 201–219. Philadelphia: Temple University Press.

———. 2008b. "Racial Authenticity in Rap Music and Hip Hop." *Sociology Compass* 2: 1783–1800.

Harstock, Nancy. 1987. "Rethinking Modernism." *Cultural Critique* 7: 187–206.

Hartigan Jr., John. 1999. *Racial Situations: Class Predicaments of Whiteness in Detroit*. Princeton, NJ: Princeton University Press.

Hartman, Chester. 2002. *City for Sale: The Transformation of San Francisco* (rev. ed.). Berkeley: University of California Press.

Hattam, Victoria. 2007. *In the Shadow of Race: Jews, Latinos, and Immigrant Politics in the United States*. Chicago: University of Chicago Press.

Hebdige, Dick. 1979. *Subculture: The Meaning of Style*. London: Methuen.

———. 1987. *Cut 'n' Mix: Culture, Identity, and Caribbean Music*. London: Methuen.

Henderson, Errol A. 1996. "Black Nationalism and Rap Music." *Journal of Black Studies* 26, no. 3: 308–339.

Hermes, Will. 1998. "The World's Greatest Record Store? San Francisco's Amoeba Music Is a Shoppers' Paradise." *Rolling Stone*, February 19: 19.

Herring, Cedric. 2004. "Skin Deep: Race and Complexion in the 'Color-Blind' Era." In *Skin Deep: How Race and Complexion Matter in the "Color-Blind" Era*, ed. Cedric Herring, Verna Keith, and Hayward Derrick Horton, pp. 1–21. Chicago: University of Illinois Press.

Herskovits, Melville. 1941. *The Myth of the Negro Past*. Boston, MA: Beacon Press.

Hesmondhalgh, David and Casper Melville. 2001. "Urban Breakbeat Culture." In *Global Noise: Rap and Hip Hop Outside the USA*, ed. Tony Mitchell, pp. 86–110. Middletown, CT: Wesleyan University Press.

Hess, Mickey. 2005. "Hip-Hop Realness and the White Performer." *Critical Studies in Media Communication* 22, no. 5: 372–389.

Hill, Mike. 2004. *After Whiteness: Unmaking an American Majority*. New York: New York University Press.

Hix, Lisa. 2006. "Hyphy." *San Francisco Chronicle*. October 22. Available online at http://www.sfgate.com/cgi-bin/article.cgi?file=/c/a/2006/10/22/PKGBKLPE8G1.DTL.

Hobsbawm, Eric. 1983. "Introduction: Inventing Traditions." In *The Invention of Tradition*, ed. Eric Hobsbawm and Terrence Ranger, pp. 1–14. Cambridge: Cambridge University Press.

hooks, bell. 1992. *Black Looks: Race and Representation*. Boston, MA: South End Press.

Hughes, Michael and Carolyn J. Kroehler. 2008. *Sociology: The Core* (8th ed.). New York: McGraw Hill.

Hurston, Zora Neale. 1990 [1935]. *Mules and Men*. New York: Harper Perennial.

———. 1991 [1942]. *Dust Tracks on a Road*. New York: Harper Perennial.

Hutchins, Francis. 2001. "Anthropologists Are Not Tourists." Paper presented at the Annual Meetings of the American Anthropological Associations, Washington, DC, December 1.

Hwang, Suein. 2000. "Real Bands Sing the IPO Blues As 'Dot-Commers' Long for Oldies." *The Wall Street Journal*, March 2. Available online at http://www.mmuldrow.com/bloodroses/wsjblood.htm.

Hymes, Dell. 1969. *Reinventing Anthropology*. New York: Pantheon.

Ignatieff, Michael. 1993. *Blood and Belonging: Journeys into the New Nationalism*. New York: Noonday Press

Independent Sounds. 2001. *Amoeba Music Compilation Vol. III*. Liner Notes. San Francisco: Hip Hop Slam Records/Amoeba Music.

Ingram, David. 2005. "Towards a Cleaner White(ness): New Racial Identities." *The Philosophy Forum* 36, no. 3: 243–277.

Israel. 2002. *The Freshest Kids: A History of the B-boy*. Chatsworth, CA: QD3 Entertainment and Brotherhood Films.

Jackson Jr., John L. 2005. *Real Black: Adventures of Racial Sincerity*. Chicago: University of Chicago Press.

Jackson, Michael. 1998. *Minima Ethnographica: Intersubjectivity and the Anthropological Project*. Chicago: University of Chicago Press.

Jacobson, David. 1991. *Reading Ethnography*. New York: State University of New York Press.

Jam, Billy. 1997. "Dirt Hustlin.'" *San Francisco Bay Guardian*, April 9.

————. 1999. "Too Short." In *The Vibe History of Hip Hop*, ed. Alan Light, pp. 220–221. New York: Three Rivers Press.

Jefferson, Margo. 1973. "Ripping of Black Music: From Thomas 'Daddy' Rice to Jimi Hendrix." *Harpers*, January: 40–45.

Jenkins, Sacha. 1999. "Graffiti: Graphic Scenes, Spray Fiends, and Millionaires." In *The Vibe History of Hip Hop*, ed. Alan Light, pp. 35–41. New York: Three Rivers Press.

Jones, Delmos. 1970. "Towards a Native Anthropology." *Human Organization* 24, no. 4: 251–259.

Jones, Leroi. 1963. *Blues People: Negro Music in America*. New York: William Morrow.

Jones, Simon. 1988. *Black Culture, White Youth: The Reggae Tradition from JA to UK*. London: MacMillan Education.

Kasindorf, Martin and Haya El Nasser. 2001. "Impact of Census' Race Data Debated." *USA Today*, August 13. Available nline at http://www.usatoday.com/news/census/2001-03-12-censusimpact.htm.

Keast, Darren. 1999. "Rhyme Schemes." *SF Weekly*, November 3.

Kelley, Robin D. G. 1994. "Kickin' Reality, Kickin' Ballistics: 'Gangsta Rap' and Postindustrial Los Angeles." In *Race Rebels: Culture, Politics, and the Black Working Class*, pp. 183–227. New York: The Free Press.

————. 1997. *Yo Mama's Disfunktional: Fighting the Culture Wars in Urban America*. Boston: Beacon Press.

Kelly, Raegan. 1993. "Hip Hop Chicano: A Separate but Parallel Story." In *It's Not About a Salary: Rap, Race, and Resistance in Los Angeles*, ed. Brian Cross, pp. 65–76. New York: Verso Press.

Keyes, Cheryl. 1993. "'We're More than a Novelty, Boys': Strategies of Female Rappers in the Rap Music Tradition." In *Feminist Messages: Coding in Women's Folk Culture*, ed. Joan Newlon Radner, pp. 203–220. Urbana: University of Illinois Press.

————. 1996. "At the Crossroads: Rap Music and Its African Nexus." *Ethnomusicology* 40, no. 2: 223–248.

————. 2002. *Rap Music and Street Consciousness*. Chicago: University of Illinois.

Kim, Rebecca Y. 2004. "Made in the U.S.A.: Second Generation Korean American Campus Evangelicals." In *Asian American Youth: Culture, Identity, and Ethnicity*, ed. Jennifer Lee and Min Zhou, pp. 235–250. New York: Routledge.

Kisliuk, Michelle. 1997. "(Un)doing Fieldwork: Sharing Songs, Sharing Lives." In
    Shadows in the Field: New Perspectives for Fieldwork in Ethnomusicology, ed.
    Gregory F. Barz and Timothy J. Cooley, pp. 23–44. New York: Oxford University
    Press.
Kitwana, Bikari. 1994. *The Rap on Gangsta Rap*. Chicago, IL: Third World Press.
Kleinfield, N. R. 2000. "Guarding the Borders of the Hip-Hop Nation: In the 'Hood and
    in the Burbz, White Money Feeds Rap." *The New York Times*, July 6, A1, A18–19.
Koen, David. 1990. "Taking the Rap: Are White Hip-Hoppers Stealing Black Thun-
    der?" *Phoenix New Times*, November 28. Available online at http://search.phoe
    nixnewtimes.com/1990-11-28/music/taking-the-rapare-white-hip-hoppers-stealing-
    black-thunder/full.
Konceptual Dominance. 2000. "Savage Intelligence." *Savage Intelligence*. Oakland:
    Dominant Records, DM 209-2.
Krims, Adam. 2000. *Rap Music and the Poetics of Identity*. Cambridge: Cambridge
    University Press.
Kuper, Adam. 1994. "Culture, Identity, and the Project of a Cosmopolitan Anthropol-
    ogy." *Man* 19: 537–554.
———. 1999 [1973]. *Anthropology and Anthropologists: The Modern British School*.
    New York: Routledge.
Ledbetter, James. 1992. "Imitation of Life." *Vibe*, Fall, 112–114.
Lee, Sharon and Marilyn Fernandez. 1998. "Trends in Asian American Racial-
    Ethnic Intermarriage: A Comparison of 1980 and 1990 Census Data." *Sociologi-
    cal Perspectives* 41, no. 2: 323–342.
Leland, John. 1992. "Rap and Race." *Newsweek*, June 29, 46–52.
Levy, Claire. 2001. "Rap in Bulgaria: Between Fashion and Reality." In *Global Noise:
    Rap and Hip Hop Outside the USA*, ed. Tony Mitchell, pp. 134–148. Middle-
    town, CT: Wesleyan University Press.
Lewis, Tyler. 2006. "Race Categories to Change on 2010 Census Form." *Civilrights.
    org*, April 12. Available online at http://www.civilrights.org/press_room/buzz_
    clips/race-categories-to-change-on-2010-census-form.html.
Light, Alan. 1992. "Ice T." *Rolling Stone*, August 20, 31–32, 60.
Lind, Michael. 1998. "The Beige and the Black." *The New York Times Magazine*,
    August 16, 38–39.
Lionnet-McCumber, Francoise. 1993. "Autoethnography: The An-Archic Style of
    Dust Tracks on a Road." In *Zora Neale Hurston: Critical Perspectives Past and
    Present*, ed. Henry Louis Gates, Jr. and Kwame Anthony Appiah, pp. 241–266.
    New York: Amistad.
Lipsitz, George. 1994. *Dangerous Crossroads: Popular Music, Postmodernism and the
    Poetics of Race*. London: Verso.
———. 1998. *The Possessive Investment in Whiteness: How White People Profit from
    Identity Politics*. Philadelphia: Temple University Press.
Lopate, Carol. 1979. "On Objectivity in Fieldwork." In *The Politics of Anthropology:
    From Colonialism and Sexism Towards a View from Below*, ed. Gerrit Huizer and
    Bruce Mannhiem, pp. 319–323. The Hague: Mouton Press.

Lopez, Ian F. Haney. 2000. "The Social Construction of Race." In *Critical Race Theory: The Cutting Edge* (second edition), ed. Richard Delgado and Jean Steancic, pp. 163–175. Philadelphia, PA: Temple University Press.

Lusane, Clarence. 1993. "Rap, Race, and Politics." *Race and Class* 35: 41–56.

Macdonald, Nancy. 2001. *The Graffiti Subculture: Youth, Masculinity and Identity in London and New York*. New York: Palgrave.

Maffesoli, Michel. 1996. *The Time of Tribes: The Decline of Individualism in Mass Society*. London: Sage.

Mailer, Norman. 1957. "The White Negro." *Dissent* 4: 276–293.

Maira, Sunaina Marr. 2002. *Desis in the House: Indian American Youth Culture in New York City*. Philadelphia: Temple University Press.

Malinowski, Bronislaw. 1989 [1967]. *A Diary in the Strict Sense of the Term*. Stanford: Stanford University Press.

Marcus, George and Dick Cushman. 1982. "Ethnographies as Texts." *Annual Review of Anthropology* 11: 25–69.

Marcus, George E. and Michael M. J. Fischer. 1986. *Anthropology as Cultural Critique: An Experimental Moment in the Human Sciences*. Chicago: University of Chicago Press.

Mascia-Lees, Frances, Patricia Sharpe, and Colleen Ballerino Cohen. 1989. "The Postmodern Turn in Anthropology: Cautions from a Feminist Perspective." *Signs* 15, no. 1: 7–33.

Maxwell, Ian. 2001. "Sydney Style: Hip-Hop Down Under Comin' Up." In *Global Noise: Rap and Hip Hop Outside the USA*, ed. Tony Mitchell, pp. 259–279. Middletown, CT: Wesleyan University Press.

———. 2002. "The Curse of Fandom: Insiders, Outsiders and Ethnography." In *Popular Music Studies*, ed. David Hesmondhalgh and Keith Negus, pp. 103–116. London: Arnold.

McClaurin, Irma. 2001. "Theorizing a Black Feminist Self in Anthropology: Towards an Autoethnographic Approach." In *Black Feminist Anthropology: Theory, Politics, Praxis, and Poetics*, ed. Irma McClaurin, pp. 49–76. New Brunswick, NJ: Rutgers University Press.

McKay, George. 1998. "DiY Culture: Notes Towards an Intro." In *DiY Culture: Party and Protest in Nineties Britain*, ed. George McKay, pp. 1–53. New York: Verso.

McLaren, Peter. 1995. "Gangsta Pedagogy and Ghettoethnicity: The Hip Hop Nation as Counter Public Sphere." *Socialist Review* 25, no. 2: 9–55.

McLeod, Kembrew. 1999. "Authenticity within Hip Hop and Other Cultures Threatened with Assimilation." *Journal of Communication* 49, no. 4: 134–150.

McRobbie, Angela, and Jenny Garber. 1997 [1975]. "Girls and Subcultures." In *The Subculture Reader*, ed. Ken Gelder and Sarah Thornton, pp. 112–120. New York: Routledge.

Mendoza, S. Lily. 2002. *Between Homeland and Diaspora: The Politics of Theorizing Filipino and Filipino American Indentities*. New York: Routledge.

Mills, Charles W. 1998. "Revisionist Ontologies: Theorizing White Supremacy." In *Blackness Visible*, pp. 97–118. Ithaca, NY: Cornell University Press.

Mitchell, Tony. 2001. "Introduction: Another Root—Hip-Hop Outside the USA." In *Global Noise: Rap and Hip Hop Outside the USA*, ed. Tony Mitchell, pp. 1–38. Middletown, CT: Wesleyan University Press.

Moonrocks. 1999. "Walking Fences." *Moonrocks Project, Vol. 1.* Oakland, CA: Dirtworks.

Moore, Alan. 2002. "Authenticity as Authentication." *Popular Music* 21, no. 2: 209–223.

Morelli, Sarah. 2001. "Who Is a Dancing Hero? Rap, Hip-Hop, and Dance in Korean Popular Culture." In *Global Noise: Rap and Hip Hop Outside the USA*, ed. Tony Mitchell, pp. 248–258. Middletown, CT: Wesleyan University Press.

Nakhleh, Khalil. 1979. "On Being a Native Anthropologist." In *The Politics of Anthropology: From Colonialism and Sexism to the View from Below*, ed. Gerrit Huizer and Bruce Mannheim, pp. 343–352. The Hague: Mouton.

Narayan, Kirin. 1993. "How Native Is a 'Native' Anthropologist?" *American Anthropology* 95: 671–686.

Nayak, Anoop and Mary Jane Kehily. 2008. *Gender, Youth and Culture: Young Masculinities and Feminities.* New York: Palgrave Macmillan.

Neal, Mark Anthony. 1999. *What the Music Said: Black Popular Music and Black Public Culture.* New York: Routledge.

Neate, Patrick. 2004. *Where You're At: Notes from the Frontlines of a Hip-Hop Planet.* New York: Riverhead Books.

Neff, Ali Colleen. 2008. "Bigger, Banner, Badman: Conjuring the Trickster in the Church of Crunk." Paper presented at the 2008 International Association for the Study of Popular Music (IASPM) Annual Conference, Iowa City, IA, April 27, 2008.

Negus, Keith. 1997. *Popular Music Theory: An Introduction.* Hanover, NH: Wesleyan University Press.

Nelson, Havelock. 1999. "DJ Kool Herc." In *The Vibe History of Hip Hop*, ed. Alan Light, pp. 16–17. New York: Three Rivers Press.

Nobles, Melissa. 2000. *Shades of Citizenship: Race and the Census in Modern Politics.* Stanford, CA: Stanford University Press.

Office of Management and Budget. 1995. "Statistical Policy." *Federal Register* 60, no. 166 (August 28): 44692–44693.

Ogbar, Jeffrey O. G. 2007. *Hip Hop Revolution: The Culture and Politics of Rap.* Lawrence: University of Kansas Press.

Olivas, Michael A. 2005. "Forward, Hernandez v. Texas Special Issue." *UCLA Chicano-Latino Law Review* 25: 1–8.

Omi, Michael and Howard Winant. 1986. *Racial Formation in the United States: From the 1960s to the 1980s.* New York: Routledge and Kegan Paul.

Orr, Jackie. 1995. "Re/Sounding Race, Re/Signifying Ethnography: Sampling Oaktown Rap." In *Prosthetic Territories: Politics and Hypertechnologies*, ed. Gabriel Brahm Jr. and Mark Driscoll, pp. 441–482. Boulder, CO: Westview Press.

Ortner, Sherry. 1974. "Is Female to Male as Nature is to Culture?" In *Women, Culture, and Society*, ed. Michelle Zimbalist Rosaldo and Louise Lamphere, pp. 67–87. Stanford, CA: Stanford University Press.

Outlaw, Lucius. 1990. "Toward a Critical Theory of 'Race.'" In *Anatomy of Racism*, ed. David Theo Goldberg, pp. 58–83. Minneapolis: University of Minnesota Press.

P, Miz. 2004. "Sisterz of the Underground." *Shout Magazine* 2. Available online at http://shoutmagazine.blogspot.com/2004/10/sisterz-of-underground.html.

Page, Enoch. 1999. "Definition of Racism. Center for the Study of White American Culture." Available online at http://www.euroamerican.org/library/Racismdf.asp.

Pandey, Triloki Nath. 1979. "The Anthropologist—Informant Relationship: The Navajo and Zuni in America and the Tharu in India." In *The Fieldworker and the Field: Problems and Challenges in Sociological Investigation*, ed. M. N. Srinivas, A. M. Shah, and E. A. Ramaswamy, pp. 246–265. Delhi: Oxford University Press.

Pattillo-McCoy, Mary. 1999. *Black Picket Fences: Privilege and Peril Among the Black Middle Class.* Chicago: University of Chicago Press.

Perkins, William Eric. 1996. "The Rap Attack: An Introduction." In *Droppin' Science: Critical Essays on Rap Music and Hip Hop Culture*, ed. William Eric Perkins, pp. 1–45. Philadelphia: Temple University Press.

Perlmann, Joel and Mary C. Waters. 2002. "Introduction." In *The New Race Question: How the Census Counts Multiracial Individuals*, pp. 1–30. New York: Russell Sage Foundation.

Perry, Charles. 2005 [1984]. *The Haight-Ashbury: A History.* New York: Wenner Books.

Perry, Imani. 2004. *Prophets of the Hood: Politics and Poetics in Hip Hop.* Durham, NC: Duke University Press.

Perry, Pamela. 2002. *Shades of White: White Kids and Racial Identities in High School.* Durham, NC: Duke University Press.

Peterson, Richard A. 1976. *The Production of Culture.* Beverly Hills: Sage Publications.

———. 1997. *Creating Country Music: Fabricating Authenticity.* Chicago, IL: University of Chicago Press.

Peterson, Richard A. and Andy Bennett. 2004. "Introducing Music Scenes." In *Music Scenes: Local, Translocal, Virtual*, ed. Andy Bennett and Richard A. Peterson, pp. 1–15. Nashville, TN: Vanderbilt University Press.

Pisares, Elizabeth H. 2006. "Do You Mis(recognize) Me: Filipina Americans in Popular Music and the Problem of Invisibility." In *Positively No Filipinos Allowed: Building Communities and Discourse*, ed. Antonio T. Tiongson, Jr., Edgardo V. Gutierrez, and Richardo V. Gutierrez, pp. 172–198. Philadelphia, PA: Temple University Press.

Pollock, Mica. 2004a. *Colormute: Race Talk Dilemmas in an American School.* Princeton, NJ: Princeton University Press.

———. 2004b. "Race Wrestling: Struggling Strategically with Race in Educational Practice and Research." *American Journal of Education* 111, no. 1: 25–67.

———. 2006. "Everyday Antiracism in Education." *Anthropology News* 47, no. 2 (February): 9–10.

Pool, Robert. 1991. "Postmodern Ethnography?" *Critique of Anthropology* 1, no. 4: 309–331.

Potter, Russell A. 1995. *Spectacular Vernaculars: Hip Hop and the Politics of Postmodernism.* Albany: State University of New York Press.

Prashad, Vijay. 2001. *Everybody was Kung Fu Fighting: Afro-Asian Connections and the Myth of Cultural Purity.* Boston: Beacon Press.

Public Enemy. 1990. "Welcome to the Terror Dome." *Fear of a Black Planet.* New York: Def Jam/Columbia Records, CK-45413.

Quinn, Eithne. 2006. *Nuthin' but a 'G' Thang: The Culture and Commerce of Gangsta Rap.* New York: Columbia University Press.

Quinn, Michael. 1996. "Never Shoulda Been Let Out the Penitentiary: Gangsta Rap and the Struggle over Racial Identity." *Cultural Critique* 24: 65–89.

Rabinow, Paul. 1986. "Representations Are Social Facts: Modernity and Post-Modernity in Anthropology." In *Writing Culture: The Poetics and Politics of Ethnography*, ed. James Clifford and George Marcus, pp. 234–261. Berkeley and Los Angeles: University of California Press.

Reiter, Rayna R. 1975. *Toward an Anthropology of Women.* New York: Monthly Review Press.

Rietveld, Hillegonda. 1998. "Repetitive Beats: Free Parties and the Politics of Contemporary DiY Dance Culture in Britain." In *DiY Culture: Party and Protest in Nineties Britain*, ed. George McKay, pp. 243–267. London: Verso.

Rivera, Raquel Z. 2001. "Hip Hop, Puerto Ricans, and Ethno-Racial Identities in New York." In *Mambo Montage: The Latinization of New York*, ed. Agustín Laó Montes and Arlene Dávilla, pp. 235–261. New York: Columbia University Press.

———. 2003. *New York Ricans from the Hip-Hop Zone.* New York: Palgrave McMillan.

Roberts, John. 1989. *From Trickster to Bad Man: The Black Folk Hero in Slavery and Freedom.* Philadelphia: University of Pennsylvania Press.

Roberts, Sam. 2005. "More Africans Enter U.S. Than in Days of Slavery." *New York Times.* February 21. Available online at http://www.nytimes.com/2005/02/21/nyregion/21africa.html.

Rodriquez, Jason. 2006. "Color-Blind Ideology and Cultural Appropriation in Hip-Hop." *Journal of Contemporary Ethnography* 35, no. 6: 645–668.

Roediger, David. 1998. "What to Make of Wiggers: A Work in Progress." In *Generations of Youth: Youth Cultures and History in Twentieth-Century America*, ed. Joe Austin and Michael Nevin Willard, pp. 358–366. New York: New York University Press.

Roots, The. 1999. "Act Too (Love of My Life)." *Things Fall Apart.* Santa Monica, CA: MCA Records.

Rosaldo, Michelle and Louise Lamphere. 1974. *Woman Culture and Society.* Stanford, CA: Stanford University Press.

Rosaldo, Renato. 1987. "Politics, Patriarchs, and Laughter." *Cultural Critique* 6: 65–86.

———. 1989. *Culture and Truth: The Remaking of Social Analysis.* Boston: Beacon.

Rose, Tricia. 1994. *Black Noise: Rap Music and Black Culture in Contemporary America.* Middletown, CT: Wesleyan University Press.

Rudinow, Joel. 1994. "Race, Ethnicity, Expressive Authenticity: Can White People Sing the Blues?" *The Journal of Aesthetics and Art Criticism* 52, no. 1: 127–137.

Ryan, John and Richard A. Peterson. 1993. "Occupational and Organizational Consequences of the Digital Revolution in Music Making." *Current Research on Occupations and Professions* 8: 173–201.

Sahlins, Marshall. 1995. *How "Natives" Think: About Captain Cook, For Example.* Chicago: University of Chicago Press.

Salaam, Mtume ya. 1995. "The Aesthetics of Rap." *African American Review* 29, no. 2: 303–315.

Samuels, David. 1991. "The Rap on Rap: The Black Music That Isn't Either." *New Republic* 205, no. 20 (November 11): 24–29.

Sangren, P. Steven. 1988. "Rhetoric and the Authority of Ethnography." *Current Anthropology* 29, no. 93: 405–435.

Sanjek, Roger 1996. "Intermarriage and the Future of Races in the United States." In *Race*, ed. Steven Gregory and Roger Sanjek, pp. 103–130. New Brunswick, NJ: Rutgers University Press.

———. 2000. "Color-Full before Color Blind: The Emergence of Multiracial Neighborhood Politics in Queens, New York City." *American Anthropologist* 102, no. 4 (2000): 762–772.

Schloss, Joseph G. 2004. *Making Beats: The Art of Sample-Based Hip-Hop.* Middletown, CT: Wesleyan University Press.

Shanks, Barry. 1994. *Dissonant Identities: The Rock 'n' Roll Scene in Austin, Texas.* Hanover, NH: Wesleyan University Press.

Shelemay, Kay Kaufman. 1997. "The Ethnomusicologist, Ethnographic Method, and the Transmission of Tradition." In *Shadows in the Field: New Perspectives for Fieldwork in Ethnomusicology*, ed. Gregory F. Barz and Timothy J. Cooley, pp. 189–204. New York: Oxford University Press.

Slocum, Sally. 1975. "Women the Gatherer: Male Bias in Anthropology." In *Towards an Anthropology of Women*, ed. Rayna Reiter, pp. 36–50. New York: Monthly Review Press.

Smith, Christopher Holmes. 1997. "Method in the Madness: Exploring the Boundaries of Identity in Hip Hop Performativity." *Social Identities* 3: 345–374.

Srinivas, M. N. 1979. "The Fieldworker and the Field: A Village in Karnataka." In *The Fieldworker and the Field: Problems and Challenges in Sociological Investigation*, ed. M. N. Srinivas, A. M. Shah, and E. A. Ramaswamy, pp. 19–28. Delhi: Oxford University Press.

Srinivas, M. N., A. M. Shah, and E. A. Ramaswamy. 1979. "Introduction." In *The Fieldworker and the Field: Problems and Challenges in Sociological Investigation*, ed. M. N. Srinivas, A. M. Shah, and E. A. Ramaswamy, pp. 1–18. Delhi: Oxford University Press.

Stacey, Judith. 1988. "Can There Be a Feminist Ethnography?" *Women's Studies International Forum* 11, no. 1: 21–27.

Staiger, Annegret Daniela. 2006. *Learning Difference: Race and Schooling in the Multiracial Metropolis*. Sanford, CA: Stanford University Press.

Stephens, Gregory. 1991. "Rap Music's Double-Voiced Discourse: A Crossroads for Interracial Communication." *Journal of Communication Inquiry* 15, no. 2: 70–91.

Stocking Jr., George W. 1990. "Malinowski's Diary and a Humanistic Anthropology." *Anthropology and Humanism Quarterly* 15, no. 4: 110.

Stokes, Martin. 1994. "Introduction." In *Ethnicity, Identity and Music: The Musical Construction of Place*, ed. Martin Stokes, pp. 1–28. Oxford: Berg Publishers.

Strachota, Dan. 2006. "Outer Bongolia: Black Fiction's Trippy Tunes Take Listeners to Unusual Places." *SF Weekly*, August 23. Available online at http://www.sf weekly.com/2006-08-23/music/outer-bongolia/.

Straight, Bilinda. 2002. "Introduction: Conflict at the Center of Ethnography." *Anthropology and Humanism* 27, no. 1: 3–9.

Strathern, Marilyn. 1987. "An Awkward Relationship: The Case of Feminism and Anthropology." *Signs* 12, no. 2: 276–291.

Strauss, Neil. 1999. "The Hip Hop Nation: Whose Is It? A Land with Rhythm and Beats for All." *The New York Times*, August 22, Section 2, 1, 28–29.

Straw, Will. 1991. "Systems of Articulation, Logics of Change: Communities and Scenes in Popular Music." *Cultural Studies* 5, no. 3: 368–388.

———. 1997. "Sizing Up Record Collections: Gender and Connoisseurship in Rock Music Culture." In *Sexing the Groove: Popular Music and Gender*, ed. Sheila Whiteley, pp. 3–16. London: Routledge.

Sue, Jennie. 2002. "Itching to Scratch." *AsianWeek.com*, July 12–18. Available online at http://www.asianweek.com/2002_07_12/arts_dmc.html.

Szwed, John F. 1999. "The Real Old School." In *The Vibe History of Hip Hop*, ed. Alan Light, pp. 3–11. New York: Three Rivers Press.

Tafoya, Sonya A. 2002. "Mixed Race and Ethnicity in California." In *The New Race Question: How the Census Counts Multiracial Individuals*, ed. Joel Perlmann and Mary C. Waters, pp. 102–115. New York: Russell Sage Foundation.

Tai, James. 1998. "Living Legends (the Next Hundred)." *URB* 58 (March/April): 56.

Tannenbaum, Rob. 1990. "Sucker MC." *Village Voice*, December 4, 69.

Tanz, Jason. 2007. *Other People's Property: A Shadow History of Hip Hop in White America*. New York: Bloomsbury.

Tate, Greg. 2003. "Introduction: Nigs R Us, or How Black folk Became Fetish Objects." In *Everything But the Burden: What White People Are Taking from Black Culture*, pp. 1–14. New York: Broadway Books.

Taylor, Paul C. 2005. "Does Hip Hop Belong to Me? The Philosophy of Race and Culture." In *Hip Hop and Philosophy: Rhyme 2 Reason*, ed. Derrick Darby and Tommie Shelby, pp. 79–91. Chicago: Open Court.

Tempelman, Sasja. 1999. "Constructions of Cultural Identity: Multiculturalism and Exclusion." *Political Studies* 47: 17–31.

Thompson, Robert Farris. 1996. "Hip Hop 101." In *Droppin' Science: Critical Essays on Rap Music and Hip Hop Culture*, ed. William Eric Perkins, pp. 211–219. Philadelphia: Temple University Press.

Thornton, Sarah. 1995. *Club Cultures: Music, Media and Subcultural Capital*. Cambridge: Polity.

Tiongson Jr., Antonio T. 2006. "Introduction: Critical Considerations." In *Positively No Filipinos Allowed: Building Communities and Discourse*, ed. Antonio T. Tiongson, Jr., Edgardo V. Gutierrez, and Richardo V. Gutierrez, pp. 1–25. Philadelphia: Temple University Press.

Tiongson Jr., Antonio T, Edgardo V. Gutierrez, and Richardo V. Gutierrez. 2006. *Positively No Filipinos Allowed: Building Communities and Discourse*. Philadelphia: Temple University Press.

Titon, Jeff Todd. 1997. "Knowing Fieldwork." In *Shadows in the Field: New Perspectives for Fieldwork in Ethnomusicology*, ed. Gregory F. Barz and Timothy J. Cooley, p. 87–100. New York: Oxford University Press.

Toop, David. 1984. *Rap Attack: African Jive to New York Hip Hop*. London: Pluto Press.

———. 2000. *Rap Attack #3: African Rap to Global Hip Hop*. London: Serpent's Tail.

Touré. 1999. "Hip Hop Nation: Whose Is It? In the End, Black Men Must Lead." *The New York Times*, August 22, Section 2, 1, 28.

Trepagnier, Barbara. 2006. *Silent Racism: How Well Meaning White People Perpetuate the Racial Divide*. Boulder, CO: Paradigm Publishers.

Tsuda, Takeyuki. 1998. "Ethnicity and the Anthropologist: Negotiating Identities in the Field." *Anthropological Quarterly* 71, no. 3: 107–124.

Tuchman, Barbara. 1962. *The Guns of August*. New York: The Macmillan Company.

Turner, Edith. 2007. "Introduction to the Art of Ethnography." *Anthropology and Humanism* 32, no. 2: 108–116.

U.S. Census Bureau. 2001. "Census 2000 Brief: Overview of Race and Hispanic Origin" *United States Census 2000*. Available online at http://www.census.gov/population/www/cen2000/briefs/index.html.

———. 2002. "Race and Hispanic or Latino Origin by Age and Sex for the United States: 2000 (PHC-T-8)." *United States Census 2000*. Available online at http://www.census.gov/population/www/cen2000/briefs/phc-t8/index.html.

———. 2008. "Percentage of the Projected Population by Race and Hispanic Origin for the United States: 2010 to 2050." *Population Division, U.S. Census Bureau*. Available online at http://www.census.gov/population/www/projections/2008projections.html.

Verán, Christina. 1999. "Breaking It All Down: The Rise and Fall and Rise of the B-Boy Kingdom." In *The Vibe History of Hip Hop*, ed. Alan Light, pp. 53–59. New York: Three Rivers Press.

Vergara Jr., Benito M. 2008. *Pinoy Capital: The Filipino Nation in Daly City*. Philadelphia: Temple University Press.

Waller, James. 2000. *Prejudice Across America*. Jackson: University Press of Mississippi.

Wang, Oliver. 2000. "Getting Digi With It: Anticon—Hip-Hop Straight Outta Cyberspace." *San Francisco Bay Guardian*, May 31, 63–64.

———. 2004. "Spinning Identities: A Social History of Filipino American DJs in the San Francisco Bay Area (1975–1995)." PhD. diss., University of California, Berkeley.

———. 2007. "Rapping and Repping Asian: Race, Authenticity, and the Asian American MC." In *Alien Encounters: Popular Culture and Asian America*, ed. Mimi Thi Nguyen and Thuy Linh Nguyen Tu, pp. 35–68. Durham, NC: Duke University Press.

———. "n.d. As the Tables Turn." *Hardboiled* 2.2. Available online at http://www.hardboiled.org/2-2/dj1.html.

Warren, Jonathan W. and Francis Winddance Twine. 1997. "White Americans, the New Minority? Non-blacks and the Ever-Expanding Boundaries of Whiteness." *Journal of Black Studies* 28, no. 2: 200–218.

Waters, Mary C. 1990. "Choosing an Ancestry." In *The Social Construction of Race and Ethnicity in the United States*, ed. Joan Ferrante and Prince Browne Jr., pp. 235–238. New York: Longman.

Watkins, Mel. 1999. *On the Real Side: A History of African American Comedy*. Chicago: Lawrence Hill Books.

Watkins, S. Craig. 2005. *Hip Hop Matters: Politics, Pop Culture, and the Struggle for the Soul of a Movement*. Boston: Beacon Press.

Watts, Eric K. 2004. "An Exploration of Spectacular Consumption: Gangsta Rap as Cultural Commodity." In *That's the Joint: The Hip-Hop Studies Reader*, ed. Murray Forman and Mark Anthony Neal, pp. 593–609. New York: Routledge.

Way, P. 2000. *From All Angles* (CD liner notes). San Francisco, CA: Soul Note Records, Lifelines Publishing.

White, Armond. 1996. "Who Wants To See Ten Niggers Play Basketball?" In *Droppin' Science: Critical Essays on Rap Music and Hip Hop Culture*, ed. William Eric Perkins, pp. 192–208. Philadelphia: Temple University Press.

Whitehead, Tony Larry and Mary Ellen Conway (eds.). 1986. *Self, Sex, and Gender in Cross-Cultural Fieldwork*. Urbana: University of Illinois Press.

Whitmer, Peter. 1996. *The Inner Elvis: A Psychological Biography of Elvis Aaron Presley*. New York: Hyperion.

Williams, Kim M. 2006. *Mark One or More: Civil Rights in Multiracial America*. Ann Arbor: University of Michigan Press.

Williams, Kissah. 2004. "Hip Hop's Unlikely Voice." *The Washington Post*, January 12, A1. Available online at http://www.washingtonpost.com/ac2/wp-dyn/A8747-2004Jan11.

Willis, Paul. 1978. *Profane Culture*. London: Routledge and Kegan Paul.

Wimsatt, William. 1993. "We Use Words Like 'Mackadocious' (and Other Progress from the Front Lines of the White Struggled." *Source*, (May): 64–66.

———. 1994. *Bomb the Suburbs*. Chicago: The Subway and Elevated Press Co.

Wolf, Diane. 1996. "Situating Feminist Dilemmas in Fieldwork." In *Feminist Dilemmas in Fieldwork*, ed. Diane Wolf, pp. 1–55. Boulder, CO: Westview Press.

Wolf, Margery. 1992. *A Thrice Told Tale: Feminism, Postmodernism and Ethnographic Responsibility*. Stanford, CA: Stanford University Press.

Wood, Joe. 1998. "The Yellow Negro." *Transition* 73: 40–63.

Yasin, Jon A. 1999. "Rap in the African-American Music Tradition: Cultural Assertion and Continuity." In *Race and Ideology: Language, Symbolism, and Popular Culture*, ed. Arthur K. Spears, pp. 197–223. Detroit, MI: Wayne State University Press.

Index

Anthony Kwame Harrison holds a Ph.D. in anthropology from the Maxwell School of Citizenship and Public Affairs at Syracuse University. He is assistant professor in the Department of Sociology/Program in Africana Studies at Virginia Polytechnic Institute and State University. He is an associate editor for *The Journal of Popular Music Studies*.